PRAISE FOR DON GEORGE

"These stories made me fall in love with the world again."

—Isabel Allende, author of *The House of the Spirits,*
Eva Luna, and *Maya's Notebook*

"Don George is a legendary travel writer and editor."

—National Geographic's Intelligent Travel

"What shines with crystal clarity through all of these wise and wonderful essays is Don George's irrepressible generosity of spirit. He loves the world he finds, and the world loves him back in equal measure. Those of us lucky enough to know him have long recognized Don as a seriously life-enhancing kind of fellow: this marvelous collection serves amply to reinforce the notion. And no: no favors were sought or offered for this message. Not a one."

—Simon Winchester, author of *Pacific,*
The Map That Changed the World, and *Krakatoa*

"If you meet Don George on the page or in the flesh, you quickly see that he's always tilted toward the sun, as a perpetual singer of yes to life, to fun, to innocence, to vulnerability, and to surrender. All his writing, and much of his being, seems to be about rendering oneself open, daring to listen, and putting forward one's best and most hopeful side, in the conviction that it will be answered in kind."

—Pico Iyer, author of *The Lady and the Monk,*
Video Night in Kathmandu, and *The Art of Stillness*

"Don George, the acclaimed and award-winning editor of ten anthologies of travel stories, has finally produced a collection of his own and it's everything you'd expect from a Don George project: passionate, insightful, and humorous. What can I say? The brilliant editor is a brilliant writer."

—Tim Cahill, author of *Jaguars Ripped My Flesh,*
Pass the Butterworms, and *Hold the Enlightenment*

"Don George is an inveterate adventurer and master storyteller, with the biggest, most generous heart on the open road."

—Andrew McCarthy, actor, director, and author of *The Longest Way Home*

"Don George describes himself as a 'travel evangelist' but he is much more than that. Yes, he loves to talk about the life-changing possibilities of travel, but he is also a bestselling author, regarded by many as the preeminent travel writer of his generation."

—Christopher Elliott, consumer advocate, journalist, and author of *Scammed*

Travelers' Tales Books

Country and Regional Guides
30 Days in Italy, 30 Days in the South Pacific, America, Antarctica, Australia, Brazil, Central America, China, Cuba, France, Greece, India, Ireland, Italy, Japan, Mexico, Nepal, Spain, Thailand, Tibet, Turkey; Alaska, American Southwest, Grand Canyon, Hawai'i, Hong Kong, Middle East, Paris, Prague, Provence, San Francisco, South Pacific, Tuscany

Women's Travel
100 Places Every Woman Should Go, 100 Places in France Every Woman Should Go, 100 Places in Greece Every Woman Should Go, 100 Places in Italy Every Woman Should Go, 100 Places in the USA Every Woman Should Go, 50 Places in Rome, Florence, & Venice Every Woman Should Go, Best Women's Travel Writing, Family Travel, Gutsy Mamas, Gutsy Women, Mother's World, Safety and Security for Women Who Travel, Wild with Child, Woman's Asia, Woman's Europe, Woman's Passion for Travel, Woman's Path, Woman's World, Woman's World Again, Women in the Wild

Body & Soul
Adventure of Food, Food, How to Eat Around the World, Love & Romance, Mile in Her Boots, Pilgrimage, Road Within, Spiritual Gifts of Travel, Stories to Live By, Ultimate Journey

Special Interest
365 Travel, Adventures in Wine, Danger!, Fearless Shopper, Gift of Birds, Gift of Rivers, Gift of Travel, Guidebook Experiment, How to Shit Around the World, Hyenas Laughed at Me, It's a Dog's World, Leave the Lipstick, Take the Iguana, Make Your Travel Dollars Worth a Fortune, More Sand in My Bra, Mousejunkies!, Not So Funny When It Happened, Penny Pincher's Passport to Luxury Travel, Sand in My Bra, Soul of Place, Testosterone Planet, There's No Toilet Paper on the Road Less Traveled, Thong Also Rises, What Color is your Jockstrap?, Whose Panties Are These?, World is a Kitchen, Writing Away

Travel Literature
The Best Travel Writing, Deer Hunting in Paris, Ghost Dance in Berlin, Shopping for Buddhas, Kin to the Wind, Coast to Coast, Fire Never Dies, Kite Strings of the Southern Cross, Last Trout in Venice, One Year Off, Rivers Ran East, Royal Road to Romance, A Sense of Place, Storm, Sword of Heaven, Take Me With You, Trader Horn, Way of the Wanderer, Unbeaten Tracks in Japan

THE WAY OF WANDERLUST

THE BEST TRAVEL WRITING OF DON GEORGE

DON GEORGE

TRAVELERS' TALES,
AN IMPRINT OF SOLAS HOUSE, INC.
PALO ALTO

Travelers' Tales and Solas House are trademarks of Solas House, Inc.
2320 Bowdoin Street, Palo Alto, California 94306.
www.travelerstales.com

Credits are given starting on page 271.

Art Direction: Kimberly Nelson Coombs
Cover and Interior Illustrations: Candace Rose Rardon
Page Layout: Howie Severson, using the fonts Centaur and
    California Titling
Author Photograph: Jennifer Nunn Tarbutton
Production Director: Susan Brady

Library of Congress Cataloging-in-Publication Data

George, Donald W.
  The way of wanderlust : the best travel writing of Don George / by
Don George. -- First edition.
     pages cm
  ISBN 978-1-60952-105-9 (pbk.)
  1. Travel--Anecdotes. 2. George, Donald W.--Travel. I. Title.
  G151.G47 2015
  910.4--dc23
                                        2015022620

First Edition
10 9 8 7 6 5 4 3 2
Printed in the United States of America

For Mom and Dad,
Kuniko, Jenny, and Jeremy,
and all the pilgrims who have enriched
and enlightened my journey

Table of Contents

Foreword:
Saying Yes to the World

Pico Iyer

THE LAST TIME I RAN INTO DON GEORGE, it was one of those piercing, radiant early autumn days in Japan that leave you exultant and strangely wistful all at once. The sky was a richer, deeper blue than you'd see in California; the sun was so warm, even shirtsleeves seemed too much; most of Kyoto was spilling out into the leafy lanes, to enjoy yuzu-flavored "soft creams" and aloe-and-white grape juice cordials and the exhilarating buoyancy of a "second summer" Sunday afternoon scented with what smelled like daphne. Don and I sat out by a stream, the blaze of the sun beating down on us, and spoke of some of the wandering heroes—Peter Matthiessen, Jan Morris, Donald Richie—who had sent us out into the world to be transformed.

Both of us, in our twenties, had chosen Japan as our secret home; both had married women from western Japan and raised kids on Doraemon, the 22nd-century blue robotic cat from Japan who has a *"doko-demo"* (or "anywhere you want") door in his stomach. Both had found in Japan a way of making gentleness, courtesy, affirmation, and robust public cheerfulness seem not the stuff of childishness, but something seasoned and mature. But Don spoke perfect Japanese, as I could never dream of doing;

Don had taught English here and appeared as a talk show host on Japanese TV. Don could open the door of any Japanese person we met along the streets, with his idiomatic, unaggressive, always smiling manner; it wasn't hard to imagine that he had taken the optimism and openness of his longtime home in California and somehow wed it to a natural sweetness and unintrusive sympathy I associate deeply with my home near Kyoto.

As we sat in the sun, drinking tea made from maple leaves (seasoned with apple and apricot), as we meandered through the 19th-century European park that leads toward the tiny lane on which our favorite tatami tea house is hidden—Don had come here ten months earlier to collect himself after his Japanese father-in-law died—I thought how distinctive Don's relaxed and responsive spirit can be. I'd walked these same streets with other friends for twenty-seven years now, many of them celebrated travelers; they'd fired questions at me, shot out theories, spun this notion about Japan and that judgment.

Don, by comparison, hung back. He seemed eager to take in as much as he possibly could. He didn't have agenda or preoccupation, and in that regard appeared to rejoice in the rare traveler's gift of allowing the day and the place to take him where they wanted him to go.

He recalled for me the dorm advisers at Princeton who had opened the door to Asia for him, forty years before; the way he'd read *This Side of Paradise* before going to university, and still remembered his first reading of *Tender is the Night*. He reminded me of his early travels to Paris and Greece and then to an M.A. writing program in the hills of Virginia; by the time he was barely thirty, he had a lovely Japanese wife, a new perch in San Francisco, and a job that allowed him to call up writers as established as Jan Morris and invite them to write for his newspaper on the places that had changed their lives.

"How's your mother?" I asked him, as we walked along the narrow, willow-lined lane of Kiyamachi, in central Kyoto, side-stepping girls in pinkly flowering kimono sipping at Starbucks's seasonal frappuccinos.

"She's ninety-eight!" he said with an astonished laugh. "But she doesn't complain about a thing. She has this way of greeting everything that happens to her, and not getting sidetracked by what she's lost."

"So that's where you got it from," I said, and he laughed again. "*Hidamari.*" The Japanese, not surprisingly, have a word for the strip of light the sun makes on otherwise chilly days, akin to the one where we had been sitting, by the stream.

As a boy, traveling between California and England, I'd come to think, in my simplistic way, that the cultures of the Old World were the cultures of "No" (or, at best, "Maybe"), and those of the New World the ones of "Yes." That's much too reductive, of course, but if you meet Don on the page or in the flesh, you quickly see that he's always tilted toward the sun, as a perpetual singer of yes to life, to fun, to innocence, to vulnerability, and to surrender. All his writing, and much of his being, seems to be about rendering oneself open, daring to listen, and putting forward one's best and most hopeful side, in the conviction that it will be answered in kind.

This is in any context a kind of balm, but never more so than in the realm of travel, which is one of life's most charged leaps of faith (writing, of course, is another). Every time you set out from home and throw yourself into somewhere as alien as Tokyo or the Peloponnese, you're trusting in the universe, you're counting on the capacity of friendliness to inspire friendliness in return, and you're assuming you don't have all the answers and don't even need them.

There are many travelers, from Old World and New—Paul Bowles, V.S. Naipaul, Paul Theroux—who revel in the shadows, and in unsettledness and dislocation; all of them give us wonders with their readiness to look unflinchingly at the dark. Don gives us something else, healthy and cheerful and forward-looking, that tells us that, if you leave yourself at home and are eager to let the world remake you as it sees fit, you can be at home almost everywhere you go. Home is the condition, the state of unencumbered ease, you export to everyone you visit.

—Nara, Japan
October 2014

Introduction

I TOOK MY FIRST SERENDIPITOUS STEP on the path to becoming a travel writer the summer after I graduated from Princeton. While all my friends were preparing for graduate school, law school, business school, or medical school, or starting jobs with banks, I arranged to go to Europe for a year, first to spend the summer in Paris on a Summer Work Abroad internship and then to teach in Greece on an Athens College Teaching Fellowship.

When I set off for Europe, I was thinking that year would be a brief interlude between undergraduate and graduate schools, but then, one sun-dappled June morning in Paris, the course of my life changed. As I had every morning for the previous two weeks, I took the rickety old filigreed elevator from my apartment—right on the rue de Rivoli, looking onto the Tuileries—and stepped into the street: into a sea of French. Everyone around me was speaking French, wearing French, looking French, acting French. Shrugging their shoulders and twirling their scarves and drinking their *cafés crèmes*, calling out "*Bonjour, monsieur-dame*," and paying for *Le Monde* or *Le Nouvel Observateur* with francs and stepping importantly around me and staring straight into my eyes and subtly smiling in a way that only the French do.

Until that time I had spent most of my life in classrooms, and I was planning after that European detour to spend most of the rest of my life in classrooms. Suddenly it struck me: This was the classroom. Not the musty, shadowed, ivy-draped buildings in which I had spent the previous four years. This world of wide boulevards and centuries-old buildings and six-table sawdust restaurants and glasses of *vin ordinaire* and fire-eaters on street corners and poetry readings in cramped second-floor bookshops and mysterious women who smiled at me so that my heart leaped and I walked for hours restless under the plane trees by the Seine. This was the classroom.

Hungry in a way I'd never been before, I gorged on Paris. I marveled at Molière at the Comédie Française and the Ballet Béjart in the park; I idled among the secondhand shelves at Shakespeare and Company, eavesdropping on poets and *poseurs;* I immersed myself in Manet and Monet in the Musée d'Orsay; got lost in the ancient alleys of Montmartre and the Marais; savored the open-air theater from a sidewalk seat on the Champs-Élysées; and conjured Hemingway on rue Descartes and in Les Deux Magots café.

At the end of that summer, I rode the Orient Express to Greece and settled on the campus of Athens College. As it turned out, my fellowship duties were to teach five hours of literature and writing classes a week, write occasional speeches for the college president, and write and edit articles for the school's quarterly alumni magazine. This left me uncharted expanses of free time, which I exuberantly filled reading Plato by the Parthenon, sipping ouzo on bouzouki-bright nights in the Plaka, communing with muses among the red poppies and white columns of Corinth, and exploring the beaches of Rhodes and the ruins of Crete. Winter and spring vacations afforded the time to venture even farther, and I wandered footloose through Italy, Turkey, and Egypt, intoxicated with the newness and possibility of this unfurling world.

My wanderlust bloomed. Every moment seemed unbearably precious, every outing an exhilarating lesson in a new culture, place, and people—full of thrilling sights and smells, tastes and textures, creations and traditions, encounters and connections: a whole new world!

That year changed my life. And as the end of the school year approached and the question of what to do with my life loomed again, I found the courage to relinquish the student's hand-me-down desire to become a tweedy professor and choose instead the uncharted path of becoming a writer. I had no idea where that path would lead; I just knew that I wanted to walk it, wild and wide-eyed, daring to dream.

I entered an intensive one-year Master's program in creative writing at a small school in Virginia called Hollins College. I lived in a log cabin on a lake and wrote a collection of poems, a few desultory chapters of a novel, and a description of an impromptu expedition I and a traveling companion had made up Mount Kilimanjaro the summer after my stay in Greece. I learned much about the rigors and rewards of being a professional writer that year, but no clear career path emerged. And so, as winter thawed into spring and the question-filled future arose once more, I followed my wanderlust and applied for a two-year Princeton-in-Asia Fellowship. Miraculously, I won and was awarded a position teaching at International Christian University in Tokyo.

Before leaving for Japan, through some polite and persistent letter-writing, I was able to meet with a few magazine editors in New York, and I brought my Kilimanjaro story with me as a writing sample. To my astonishment, when I arrived in Tokyo in September, a telegram was waiting for me from one of these, the Travel Editor at *Mademoiselle* magazine. It read: "A hole opened up in our November issue and we put your Kilimanjaro story in it. Hope you don't mind."

That was my first published travel article.

Over the ensuing two years, I continued to write poetry, but I also began keeping copious journals, writing long letters, and absorbing as much travel information and experience as I could. I wrote two articles for the Japan Airlines inflight magazine and a couple more for other Asia-based publications, and then I was given an assignment by *Travel & Leisure*. At the same time, I ventured throughout Japan and on to Singapore, Malaysia, Indonesia, Hong Kong, Thailand, Nepal, India, Sri Lanka, and the Maldives. And perhaps most important, I began to explore and frame the world with a travel writer's mind.

When that fellowship ended and the future stretched directionless once more, I felt drawn by the enlightened, cosmopolitan atmosphere of San Francisco, and moved there without home or plan. A few months later, through an extraordinary series of serendipities, I was hired as a Travel Writer by the *San Francisco Examiner* to replace the Travel Editor while she took a one-year leave of absence.

That was my first real job, and travel writing has been my profession ever since. Through the decades I've broadened from newspaper to online and book publishing, and I've incorporated editing, teaching, speaking, consulting, tour leading, and being a spokesperson into my professional portfolio, but travel writing has always remained at the core of what I do and who I am.

In the thirty-eight years since that first Kilimanjaro piece was published, I have written more than 700 articles for some two dozen print and online publications. I've also edited ten anthologies of literary travel writing, and written a guide to becoming a travel writer. But I've never published a collection of my own travel pieces.

So I was thrilled and honored when the wonderful folks at Travelers' Tales approached me about compiling a selection of my writing. At first the task seemed daunting, but as I read through those hundreds of articles, a few stood out as having a particularly powerful sense of personal engagement, and of focusing on the inner as well as the outer journey.

Aided by the editorial acumen and invigorating energy of Candace Rose Rardon, the talented writer and artist who created the enchanting cover illustrations, maps, and icons that grace this book, I winnowed these finalists down to the stories that compose the final collection.

These pieces cover a broad spectrum. Chronologically, they range from that first story about Kilimanjaro, which was published in 1977, to an article that appeared in 2015. Geographically, they roam from my childhood home in Connecticut, through my temporary homelands in France, Greece, and Japan, to my current home in California, stopping in twenty countries on six continents en route. The world of publishing is widely represented as well, with fourteen print and online outlets included.

Once we'd selected these stories, we still had to decide how to organize them. After contemplating a number of methods—by decade, publication, publishing medium, geographical setting, narrative message—we realized that the pieces seemed to fall organically into three themed sections: Pilgrimages, Encounters, and Illuminations. (To our astonishment and delight, these were the same three words I had chosen to highlight on the cover of my website a year earlier.) As we grouped the stories into these categories, we found that eleven pieces seemed to fit snugly within each. We decided to present the stories within each section chronologically, according to their date of publication, so that readers could follow the evolution of my writing. We also decided that to enhance the continuity of the reading experience, it would be helpful to include a short introductory note before each story, to set the context and background for the piece and to trace a skeletal biographical outline throughout the book.

On further reflection, we decided to add two more stories. One seemed to summarize the prevailing themes of all the pieces, and we made that the Prologue. And one addressed the larger art and heart of travel writing, and seemed the perfect Epilogue to the entire collection.

And that's the book you hold in your hands.

In the process of reading these tales afresh, I realized that they were all the fruits of the wanderlust that had been seeded in Paris four decades before. And so "The Way of Wanderlust" seemed the perfect title for the book. The phrase has a fluid movement, an internal flow. It suggests both a journey (the path followed, the map traced/filled in) and a philosophy/life practice (as in "the way of tea"). And it captures both the adventurer/explorer and the philosopher/evangelist sides of my life and work; it has a bit of the map-maker and a bit of the pilgrim. Finally, it has a pleasing cadence and alliteration, adding a little touch of the poet who has been a part of me from the beginning.

Now, with the finished text before me, I feel humbled, exhilarated, and blessed beyond measure. It is a dream come true for me to have this collection in print. It gives a substance, a weight, a palpability to my career as a writer that those 700 articles dispersed across the vast plains of publishing never had.

I also feel suffused with wonder and gratitude at two mind-spinning, soul-plucking truths this collection has crystallized: The first is that somehow I have been able to make a living pursuing and practicing the two things I love most, traveling and writing, for my entire professional life; the second is that this journey would simply not have been possible without the many extraordinary people—family, friends, fellow writers and editors, mentors, students, readers—who have guided, supported, and inspired me in innumerable small and large, life-changing ways. I cannot adequately express my thankfulness for these riches.

At some point during the course of my journey, I came to think of myself as a travel evangelist, and compiling this collection has reinforced that notion. I was profoundly influenced by a Protestant pastor who eloquently preached the gospel of love when I was a youth, and by the precepts and practices of Buddhism that I first encountered when I lived in Japan, but in many ways, travel is my religion.

As I have learned over and over, travel teaches us about the vast and varied differences that enrich the global mosaic, in landscape, creation, custom, and belief, and about the importance of each and every piece in that mosaic. Travel teaches us to embrace our vulnerability and to have faith that whatever energy we put into the world will come back to us a hundredfold. Travel teaches us to approach unfamiliar cultures and peoples with curiosity and respect, and to realize that the great majority of people around the world, whatever their differences in background and belief, care for their fellow human beings. And in all these ways, travel paves the pathway to global understanding, evolution, and peace.

Ultimately, I have come to think, travel teaches us about love. It teaches us that the very best we can do with our lives is to embrace the peoples, places, and cultures we meet with all our mind, heart, and soul, to live as fully as possible in every moment, every day. And it teaches us that this embrace is simultaneously a way of becoming whole and letting go.

That's the way of my wanderlust. And now, with the same mixture of apprehension and exhilaration that I feel at the beginning of every journey, I let go of these tales and send them out into the world, on their own adventures. Thank you for taking them into your hands, heart, and home. I hope you find pieces that connect with your own life's puzzle, and that confer meaning and inspiration on your wanderlust way.

Prologue:
Every Journey Is a Pilgrimage

When an editor with whom I had worked at Salon moved to Yoga Journal, *she asked me if I would like to write an essay about my philosophy of travel, what travel had taught me through the years. This essay, written in early 2004, was the first piece where I succinctly expressed two ideas that had been germinating for decades and that have become the very foundation of my philosophy now: Travel is a way to collect pieces of the vast global puzzle so that we can understand that puzzle better, and travel is an act of pilgrimage that sanctifies the world, wherever and whatever the path we walk. In retrospect, I believe this all happened exactly as it should: It took a journal devoted to yoga, shining its light on me at a particular moment in my own journey, to ripen these seeds to full fruition.*

ONE OF THE MOST REWARDING TRIPS OF MY LIFE was a five-day solo odyssey I made a few summers ago around the Japanese island of Shikoku. Shikoku has been a place of pilgrimage since the 9th century, when the beloved scholar and monk Kobo Daishi established a path of eighty-eight Buddhist temples that circle the island. Completing this circuit is supposed to give you great wisdom, purity, and peace, but I was on a pilgrimage of another kind. My wife grew up on this island, and I had first visited it with her some twenty years before. Now I had returned to see if the singular beauty, serenity, and slow pace of the place I remembered—and the country kindness of its residents—had survived.

A few hours into my journey, I stopped a wizened woman, clad in the pilgrim's traditional white garb and cone-shaped straw hat, scuffling along a leaf-paved path. She was on her second temple circuit, she told me. "The thing about the pilgrimage," she said, "is that it makes your heart lighter; it energizes you. It refreshes your sense of the meaning of life." Then her eyes locked into mine, deep and shining as a cloudless sky.

During my five days on Shikoku, I ate fresh-from-the-sea sashimi with fishermen, philosophized in steaming public baths with farmers, spun bowls with fifth-generation potters, and talked baseball and benevolence with Buddhist monks. I lay down in rice paddies, lost myself in ancient forests, stared at the sun-spangled sea, and listened—with the help of an eighty-year-old "translator" I had met as she was mending a fishing net on a pier—to the whispers of ghosts in the trees. By the end of my odyssey, I too felt lighter, refreshed, and energized, but not because of the sanctified sites. The island itself had become one big temple for me.

That trip confirmed a truth I had sensed during two decades of wandering: You don't have to travel to Jerusalem, Mecca, Santiago de Compostela, or any other explicitly holy site to be a pilgrim. If you travel with reverence and wonder, with a lively sense of the potential and preciousness of every moment and every encounter, then wherever you go, you walk the pilgrim's path.

I began to learn this after I graduated from college and moved to Athens, Greece, to teach for a year. By the end of that year, the wonders of the world had ensnared me. I would sit for hours on the Acropolis, staring at the bone-white Parthenon, trying to absorb the perspective of the ancients. I consulted the crimson poppies and fluted marble fragments at Delphi. I meditated on Minoan marvels—bull dancers, mosaic makers—among the tangerine-colored columns of Knossos on Crete. I drank ouzo with fellow teachers and excavated the hidden truths of Aristotle and Kazantzakis on a sun-spattered terrace overlooking the Aegean. I danced with wild-haired women under bouzouki-serenaded stars. I fell in love with the world.

In his seminal essay, "Why We Travel," Pico Iyer writes, "All good trips are, like love, about being carried out of yourself and deposited in the midst of terror and wonder." Travel stretches us so that our mental clothes don't fit anymore; it reminds us over and over that the anchoring assumptions of our youth lose their hold in the global sea. Travel to strange places can make us strangers to ourselves, but it can also introduce us to all the exhilarating possibilities of a new self in a new world.

Inspired by my experience in Greece, I applied for a two-year fellowship to teach in a place that was far more foreign to me than anywhere I'd been before: Japan. I knew nothing of Japan's customs, history, or language, but something was pulling me there. Trusting and terrified, I won the fellowship and took the plunge.

It was while I was living in Tokyo that the first great lesson of travel revealed itself to me: The more you offer yourself to the world, the more the world offers itself to you.

This revelation began with my getting lost. I have an uncanny ability to become lost in even the most obvious circumstances, and in Japan, this predisposition was heightened by my inability to read Japanese. Because I was always losing my way, I had to learn to rely on people. And they came through: Time after time, Japanese students, housewives, and businessmen would walk or drive fifteen or even twenty minutes out of their way to deliver me to the proper train platform, bus stop, or neighborhood. Sometimes they would even press little wrapped red-bean sweets or packets of tissues into my hands when they said goodbye.

Buoyed by these kindnesses, I traveled to Singapore, Malaysia, and Indonesia for the summer. Once again, I knew no one and couldn't speak the language; I was at the mercy of the road. But I was beginning to trust. And as it turned out, everywhere I went, the more I opened myself up to people and relied on them, the more warmly and deeply they embraced and aided me: A family at an open-air restaurant in Kuala Lumpur noticed me smiling at their birthday celebration and invited me to join the feast; two boys in Bali pedaled me to a secret temple set among glistening rice paddies.

Looking back, I realize that I was refining my practice of vulner-ability, a practice as rigorous and soul-scouring as any contempla-tive art. Becoming vulnerable requires concentration, devotion, and a leap of faith—the ability to abandon yourself to a forbid-dingly foreign place and say, in effect, "Here I am; do with me what you will." It's the first step on the pilgrim's path.

The second step is absorbing a lesson that grows from the first: The more you humble yourself, the greater you become. I have felt this in Notre-Dame Cathedral in Paris, imagining the ceaseless processions of worshippers who had come before me and would come after. I have felt it in the main train station in Calcutta, adrift in a sweaty, sharp-elbowed, eternally jostling, cardamom-scented sea of humanity. I have felt it walking alone on the Karakoram Highway in Pakistan, between towering peaks so ancient and enormous that I felt smaller than the tiniest grain of sand. Travel teaches us how small we are—and when we truly understand this, the world expands infinitely. In that moment, we become part of the larger whole; we lose ourselves to the Parisian stone, the Indian crowd, the Himalayan crags.

This truth has led me over the years to a third illumina-tion: Every journey takes us inward as well as outward. As we move through new places, encountering new people and food and artistic creations, new languages and customs and histories, a corresponding journey winds within as we discover new morals, meanings, and imaginings. The real journey is the ongoing and ever-changing interaction of the inner life and the outer.

When we travel, we connect the external world with the one inside. On the best trips, these connections can become so complete that a kind of larger union is achieved: We transcend not just the barriers of language, custom, geography, and age but the very barriers of self, those illusory isolations of body and mind.

These moments do not last. We exit Notre-Dame, buy our ticket in Calcutta, climb back into our minivan in the Himalayas. But we come back from those moments—like the Japanese pilgrim I met—lighter and energized, with a refreshed sense of the meaning of life.

What I relearned on my circuit of Shikoku is that every journey is a pilgrimage. Every sojourn offers the chance to connect with a sacred secret: that we are all precious pieces of a vast and interconnected puzzle, and that every trip we take, every connection we make, helps complete that puzzle—and ourselves.

Thinking of this now, I realize that the goal of all of my life's journeys has been to connect as many pieces—as many places, as many people—as possible, so that at some point, I could complete that picture puzzle within myself.

This completion hasn't happened yet—but what rewards I am finding along the way! Travel has taught me to see beyond barriers. It has taught me to abandon myself to a sashimi celebration in Japan and the spine-tingling hush of Notre-Dame, to the gift of two bicyclists on Bali and the soul-plucking Hellenic stars. I may not know what I will encounter, endure, experience, or explore on my next journey, but I know that it will enrich and enlarge me, and illuminate a little more of the whole.

CONNECTICUT

STINSON
BEACH

HALF DOME

GALÁPAGOS

MACHU
PICCHU

PART ONE:
Pilgrimages

Climbing Kilimanjaro

"Climbing Kilimanjaro" was my first travel story, published in November 1977. I had climbed the mountain on a summer trip to East Africa between Greece and creative writing graduate school in the U.S., and I wrote this story as an assignment in a non-fiction writing workshop. Perhaps because I wasn't a travel writer and didn't really have any idea what travel writing was or was supposed to be, I wrote this more as a short story-meets-essay, with substantial doses of both dialogue and personal reflection. And perhaps that's why it stood out for the Mademoiselle *Travel Editor. Thirty-eight years later, I'm still astounded—and grateful—that my first attempt at a travel story, written as a workshop assignment and handed to an editor as a writing sample, would become my first published article in a national magazine, and just a few months after I wrote it. This was a very encouraging beginning to my travel writing career!*

THREE GREEKS AND TWO AMERICANS DRAG five army-green duffle bags from a glaring white Range Rover into equatorial noon, hoist bags onto cotton workshirts already soaked with sweat, and trudge along a dirt path, up eight rock steps to a polished log cabin titled in teak—Kilimanjaro Climbers' Registration Office.

Outside, between the registration office and the Kilimanjaro National Park store, trickles finger-numbing water that has plunged from the ice cap we cannot even see at 19,340-feet: Uhuru—Swahili for "freedom"—the highest point in Africa. Ahead, the mountain base soars bright with clay and banana leaves.

We decided to climb Kilimanjaro only ten days ago, while touring Amboseli National Park in southeast Kenya. Suddenly the clouds had cleared, and in front of us surged a mountain unlike any I had seen before: dark pines rising and falling to a bleached strand of grassland that bordered a black, cragged crater foaming with snow.

Three of us—George, Nicos, and Takis, Greek brothers whose family is temporarily living in Tanzania—had never climbed before, and John and I had never climbed above 12,000 feet.

"Should we try it?"

"I'm willing if you are."

"It would be incredible, to climb Kilimanjaro."

"It takes five days to go up and come back," Takis said. "A friend of Dad's did it. You stay at huts along the way."

"Well..."

"Yeah. Yeah, let's do it. We may never come this way again."

That night we radioed the Marangu Hotel, renowned to adventurers throughout the world (according to its brochure in the Amboseli Tourist Office) for the Kilimanjaro expeditions it has organized since 1948, and booked hut reservations and local assistants.

Three days later we arrived at the Marangu, where soft mattresses and continental meals stretched two nights into three.

This morning, the fourth day, we stored our suitcases in a square room after brunch and drove to the park gates.

Godfriye, our guide, who had left earlier in the morning to gather the food and bedding for the climb, appears now in a red parka, patched pants and sandals, followed by his assistant guide and five porters. He is a short, sinewy man with darting eyes and a quick, high-pitched laugh.

We all shake hands. Godfriye is in his twentieth year of climbing Kilimanjaro, twice a month, eight months a year, and he looks at us and laughs. "It is good?" That seems to exhaust his English, but fortunately the brothers speak Swahili.

The other porters stamp out their cigarettes, walk toward Godfriye, and squat. He lifts the duffle bags, each weighed this morning on the veranda of the Marangu at precisely forty pounds, onto each head. They rise slowly, wobble a few steps balancing the bags, then start off with short, easy, choppy strides.

Day I

For the first twenty minutes we walk up a tarred road, past a plaque commemorating Dr. Hans Meyer, the man who first reached Kilimanjaro's summit in 1889. The tarmac gives way to a dirt road that could easily accommodate jeeps and trucks. We wind along this road for about an hour, surrounded by thick, lime-green bush and thorny vine and huge camphor and podo trees interspersed with pines.

Soon the path gets rougher and narrower, but still with room for two to walk side by side. The road ascends gently, the trees provide shade, and flowers, birds, and insects divert sense and thought: We might be taking a Sunday constitutional, not scaling the highest peak in Africa.

After two hours we enter a rain forest. The air is dank and gloomy, lightened infrequently by a flutter of sunlight on the leaves high overhead. It is a world of enchantment, completed by the burble of a stream that parallels the path, and recalls childhood fantasies of knights, castles, and dragons. Now the castle has become Kilimanjaro, the knight a writer, the dragons his own muscles and lungs.

I trail behind, busy with camera and notebook, and when I look ahead, the four climbers and the six porters, bags atop their heads, seem a late-night TV movie scene.

The rain forest ends in a burst of blue sky and blinding light. We come out into a field of waving wheat-colored grass. On the left, hills studded with cedar and pine roll toward the peak; on the right, Tanzania unfolds a patchwork of green and brown.

We arrive at Mandara Hut at 16:10 and sign the camp register. I feel fine except for a pulled muscle at the top of my left leg that has nagged me from the beginning, unaccountably intensifying then fading away. The climb has not been strenuous...has indeed been invigorating and unexpectedly beautiful.

The huts of Mandara are small, to retain heat, but still comfortable: three mattresses set like three sides of a six-foot square in wood frames on the floor, and another mattress above the middle on a shelf. We each choose a mattress and I stretch out in the musty smell.

When we had been arranging porters and provisions, the manager at the Marangu had offered a choice between their fully equipped climb and the "hard way." Going the "hard way," the climber is responsible for his own food and equipment, and obtains guides, porters, and hut bookings through the hotel.

For about twice the price, 820 shillings ($100) per person, the fully equipped climb provides everything. Traveling on a backpack budget, we had decided that our wants didn't warrant the extra money, and over dinner that night, while the cold and hunger and hurt implicit in the name lingered in our minds, we had vowed to climb Kilimanjaro the "hard way."

Now I sit back and revel while Godfriye and his assistant pour tea and spoon steaming plates of peas, beans, and corned beef.

We eat alone. As we are mopping up the beans with bread, the other climbers of the day troop in for dinner, rubbing their arms, blowing into their hands, and milling around. When they are all seated, a caterer's army of porters and guides sweeps in with lanterns, tablecloths, dishes, silverware, and glasses, subsequently graced with soup, salad, bread with jam, meat and vegetables, and cake or fruit, with a choice of water, coffee, or tea.

"So that's the luxury climb," John says. "Glad we avoided that. Chrissake, we would have had to dress for dinner."

Sunlight dims to lantern light. One of the guides starts a fire in the fireplace, everyone eats and talks and laughs, and finally cigars and cigarettes and pipes are brought out, and all prior sense of disjunction diffuses into smoke-filled air. The ascent assumes that strange logic, the appropriateness, of dream.

Day 2

Godfriye wakes us at 7:00, a rap and a yellow smile sliding past the door. *"Jambo!"*

The morning is cold and clear, as such mornings should be, and offers a spectacular view of the clouds shadowing Tanzania. We suck in the air, each breath a tingling reminder of nostrils and lungs, and survey trees and rocks and huts as they complete in the morning rays. I have forgotten this crisp demarcation of self and of thing that climbing confers.

We breakfast, then pack our bags, clothes, and equipment and set off at 8:00. At 10,500 feet the last pines give way to rock and scrub brush, dotted with purple lilies, miniature sunflowers, and snowflake anemones. At about 11,000 feet the bird sounds stop. Thereafter, the slopes are starkly silent except for a wind that sweeps like a scythe through the brush.

We sign in at Homboro at 13:30. The walk has made us hungry, and we gather immediately for lunch. Afterward, I lie on the hill above our hut, letting the sun massage my back and legs. To this point the ascent has seemed nothing more than a pleasant stroll.

The greatest challenge has been to establish a walking rhythm slow enough that I still advance steadily. I have never walked with such concentration before, and in so doing I have discovered three different rhythms, or "gears," in which my body moves fluently. Accordingly, I proceed in a strangely exhilarating continuum of body control, restraining myself on the hills and shifting into a quicker coordination on the plains.

We're at 12,335 feet. The air has cooled but the sun remains strong at this altitude, and we sit silently enjoying the combination of chill and warmth. Ahead, Uhuru turns from white to orange to crimson to a hyacinth blue.

Later that night, in the hut, I sit by the fireplace, writing and observing my fellow climbers. Germans, Austrians, French, Dutch, Belgians, and Italians...we could almost convene a mountainside meeting of NATO.

Most of us, about twenty-five in all, have been climbing together these two days, but a handful have descended from the top this afternoon, and it is to them we direct, whether consciously or unconsciously, our hopes and fears. How odd—and yet as always, how appropriate—to hear so many accents of English in this insular air:

"Und how vas it at tsee tope?"

"Ees eet zo vehry deefeecult az zay say?"

"Ant ze breating, eez it tso vehry hart?"

"Whaut is thear too see waunce you hauve reached the taup?"

It is 21:30. Everyone has gone to bed. I walk onto the terrace of the main hall. The air is icy, redolent with burnt wood and wet flower and fern. The stars cover the sky like a quilt laid over the mountain. No other noise. I try to imagine a car honking, a plane. Silence. Enjoy this silence, unlike any other, silence of rock and bush and star deep in the sky.

Day 3

We leave Homboro at 8:00. Today it is clear and we can see the tin roof of Kibo Hut gleaming on the other side and far above the near rim of the summit crater.

As we begin the trek across the desolate, rock-strewn sands, I think we must look like the astronauts picking up their feet in slow motion over the surface of the moon. Despite frequent halts along the way, George and Nicos have developed headaches and stomach cramps. We have outdistanced the other climbers and we are absolutely alone: ahead the peak of Uhuru massed with clouds, behind the burnt-red sand.

George says he can't go on, his stomach hurts so much he can't move. John and I take him by the arms and hold him up until his legs strengthen and hold. Arm in arm we shuffle along, thoughts fixed on the reflection ahead.

We reach the camp at 14:30. Unfortunately, Kibo's air-tight A-frames are still being constructed, and we huddle bodies and belongings in the most sturdy looking of three twenty-year-old tin shacks.

We are at 15,520 feet, and the wind howls and whistles through the hut, clanging a stray strip along the roof and shoving tea bags and socks to the floor. The temperature outside is about 10°F. The sun blazes almost directly overhead.

We wad arms and legs and spare clothing into our sleeping bags and pass the hours trying to extract warmth. Throughout the afternoon, climbers straggle into camp, numb with cold and pain, a babble of groans and complaints.

George and Nicos are miserable, Takis and John woozy, and I feel giddily strong and decide to inspect the surroundings. The wind almost pushes me over.

Clouds charge across the saddle, engulfing Uhuru and Mawenzi and Kibo Hut in the same wet, blind gray that seems to stick to clothes and walls. It is 16:30, but it could be dusk. Through the window of their shack I watch Godfriye and the porters scrunch in a corner around a fire of cardboard, can labels, wood scraps, and grass.

Could money alone make a man do this twice a month, eight months a year? Maybe him. Not me, that's for sure. And yet he hasn't shown any love of mountains or climbing. He has been courteously attentive and prompt, and has organized the porters flawlessly. But love? It's probably money, I think, and go back to my sleeping bag.

Eventually John and I manage a meager dinner of bread and jam while the others sip biscuits dissolved in tea. Nearly all the climbers have complained of stomach pain or headaches, and dinner time passes in self-pitying silence. I feel all too well, however, and containing myself no longer, begin to sing.

Before long the others pluck up their spirits and join in, and we serenade the slopes of Kilimanjaro for a half hour as guides and porters appear, retreat, and appear again in ever-greater numbers at hut windows and doors.

Before I fall asleep that night my head begins to pound like the old Anacin commercial that showed a diagrammed head with a sledgehammer inside, and cold steals up from benumbed toes to ankles and calves. All of us toss and turn, none wanting to disrupt the silence, although each seeks the reassurance of shared distress.

Day 4

At 1:15 Godfriye pounds on the door. I have been living with that sound inside my head for fifteen minutes, tired and sick, focusing all my energy on getting out of bed and ready to begin walking before I can feel or reflect.

I react instantaneously, jump out of bed, and tie one boot before my fingers freeze. I sit on my hands for five minutes and tie the other boot, sloppily. The cold clings to clothes and skin.

All of us are up except George, who rolls over, groans. "Go on. I'm not going anywhere but to sleep."

I put on another sweater, a windbreaker, gloves, and goggles. We stumble into blackness that burns our faces and freezes in our lungs.

The scree, romanticized by the half-moon, rises at a slope of about fifty-five degrees...loose gravel that swallows eleven inches of every twelve taken. We zigzag after Godfriye's lantern. It is 2:05 when I look at my watch.

I slump on my walking stick, nauseated, gasping to get air into constricted lungs. Suddenly heat surges from my feet to my head, followed by a blast of cold, then nothing but my heart thumping; my arms collapse, my knees bend, and for the first time in my life I "see stars."

Nicos decides to turn back and descends with the assistant guide. We— Takis, John, and I—continue.

Gradually I find a new rhythm, slow, heavy, careful. "Everything we've done has been for this," I think, and "for this" rings in my head as seconds pass and minutes pass and foot slides past foot. 2:35. We stop. I sit on the pricking broken rocks and the sweat in my gloves and socks freezes. Thin clouds sail by like dreams, like sleep, like waking at the Marangu Hotel past the moon.

4:15. We lie inside a boulder hollowed by the wind into a cave, halfway to the top. I am too tired to talk, too tired to move, too tired to do anything but close my eyes.

Takis, who vomited before we started, has climbed with the least difficulty so far. John has already been sick twice and has just crawled back into the cave.

Walking slowly and breathing deeply has become instinctive, for when I walk too rapidly or fail to breathe deeply enough my stomach bubbles, my throat tightens, and I have to stop.

At 4:25 Godfriye leaps up. Takis has been standing for five minutes; now he walks over to us and says, "Come on! We've got to go now or we won't get to the top for the sunrise."

Oh jeezus...I don't want to move. I just want to stay here and my feet and my legs and my arms and my head just lie here and sleep....

We plod on, feet skidding forward, trapped in an interminable idea: climbing Kilimanjaro. Always there are lights in front, always lights behind; more to do, more we have done.

Eventually the pain stabilizes and the mind stops inspecting and only records.

At one point we pass the Germans, the first to get off this morning, slumped in silence on the side of the trail.

We arrive at Gillman's Point—18,635 feet—as the first light of day scales the rim of the Earth. While we watch, the light leads others: Yellow, green, orange, red, blue, purple climb the sky, and the tip of the sun flares into sight. For a moment Earth and sun hang suspended in a web of light.

Alone, we lie back exhausted and content. This sunrise is ours, I think, as arms and legs go limp, something no one else has ever experienced or ever will experience.

People watch it around the world every day, and yet nothing like this—these colors, this feeling, like watching it from another world, our own world, where somewhere underneath the clouds people are doing what they do every day—I'll never have that again.

I roll over. My God, I hurt everywhere.

"Godfriye wants to go back now," Takis reports, shaking my shoulder. John and I have been asleep for an hour.

"Back? Back where?" John sits up. "We've got to go to Uhuru."

I wince to my knees, jab my walking stick into a cleft in the rocks, and push up.

Godfriye is arguing with Takis.

"He says it's impossible, there's not enough time." He wants to get back to Homboro before sunset.

"What the—? We didn't bust our butts passing everybody on the slope for nothing. We're going on to Uhuru, whether he wants to lead us or not."

Godfriye listens immobile to Takis's translation, then spurts off without a word at a pace double that of before. We follow him along the rim of the crater past three-story ice blocks and ice caves gleaming with stalagmites and stalactites twice my height. I stop every ten minutes.

I reach the summit with John after an hour and a half. We collapse by the plaque that marks the highest point on the continent.

I have never felt so terrible in my life. My head, my lungs, my stomach; thudding, straining, tightening. Everything hurts.

Sky, ice cap, and crater surround us. Unearthly clarity: the taut blue sky striped with white clouds, the black crater crags edged, distinct, demarcating the peak, the brilliant ice white, chiseled into the air, tumbling and rolling and flowing away beyond my own sense of space and time.

Forget pain, forget worry, forget food and sleep; forget question, forget blood, forget breath.

After twenty minutes, Godfriye will say we have to leave to reach the middle hut by sundown. The next afternoon, when we reach the park gates, Godfriye will lead the three of us to the park warden, who will present us with certificates featuring sketches of Kilimanjaro and a baobab in green, black, and white, and signed by Godfriye, the park warden, and the director of Tanzania's National Parks: "This is to certify that Mr. Donald W. George has successfully climbed Kilimanjaro 7th July 1976."

A Night with the Ghosts of Greece

This article was written for Signature *magazine in 1981. I'd visited Delos at the beginning of my fellowship year in Athens, and that trip had been one of my most moving experiences in Greece. Happily, I'd written about it at length in my journal and in letters home, so when an editor at* Signature *expressed interest in the piece four years later, I had freshly recorded details from the trip still at hand.* Signature *was a hospitable place for this piece; the editors liked articles that told a story, and gave their authors considerable literary freedom. Of all the pieces I wrote for the magazine—about Tokyo neighborhoods and Kyoto temples and little-visited islands in the Caribbean—this was my favorite, partly because spending the night on a forbidden island was such an unexpected and tantalizing subject, and partly because the circular nature of the piece, which arose organically from my experience there, really appealed to me. Beginning with this story, the notion of creating this kind of circle became a goal in my writing. When the end circles back to the beginning, I discovered, the reader sees the end/beginning in two ways: On the surface the scene looks exactly the same, and yet it is layered with all that has been lived and learned along the way.*

THERE ARE NO TAVERNAS, NO DISCOTHEQUES, no pleasure boats at anchor; nor are there churches, windmills, or goatherds. Delos, three miles long and less than one mile wide, is a parched, rocky island of ruins, only fourteen miles from Mykonos, Aegean playground of the international vagabonderie. Once the center of the Panhellenic world, Delos has been uninhabited since the 1st century A.D., fulfilling a proclamation of the Delphic oracle that "no man or woman shall give birth, fall sick, or meet death on the sacred island."

I chanced on Delos during my first visit to Greece. After three harrowing days of seeing Athens by foot, bus, and taxi, my traveling companion and I were ready for open seas and uncrowded beaches. We selected Mykonos on the recommendation of a friend, who suggested that when we tired of the Beautiful People, we should take a side trip to Delos.

On arriving in Mykonos, we learned that for less than three dollars we could catch a fishing trawler to Delos (where the harbor is too shallow for cruise ships) any morning at 8:00 A.M. and return to Mykonos at 1:00 P.M. the same afternoon. On the morning of our fourth day, we braved choppy seas and ominous clouds to board a rusty, peeling boat that reeked of fish. With a dozen other tourists, we packed ourselves into the ship's tiny cabin, already crowded with anchors, ropes, and wooden crates bearing unknown cargo.

At some point during the forty-five-minute voyage, the toss and turn of the waves became too much for a few of the passengers, and I moved outside into the stinging, salty spray. As we made our way past Rhenea, the callus-like volcanic island that forms part of the natural breakwater with Delos, the clouds cleared and the fishermen who had docked their *caiques* at the Delos jetty greeted us in bright sunlight.

At the end of the dock a white-whiskered man in a navy blue beret and a faded black suit hailed each one of us as we walked by: "Tour of Delos! Informative guide to the ruins." A few yards beyond him a young boy ran up to us, all elbows and knees, and confided in hard breaths, "I give you better tour. Cheaper too."

I had read the Delphic oracle's proclamation the night before and wondered what these people were doing on the island. I asked the boy, and he pointed to a cluster of houses on a knoll about a thousand yards away. "I live here. Family."

At first glance, Delos seemed the quintessential ruin: broken bits of statues, stubby pillars, cracking archways, and isolated walls. Nothing moved but the sunlight, glinting off the fragments like fish scales scattered over a two-acre basin.

Other movements had once animated the alleys and temples before us. Legend has it that Delos was originally a roving island when Leto, mistress of Zeus, landed there racked with birth pains. Poseidon anchored the island in its present position while Leto brought forth Artemis and Apollo, the Greek sun god and protector of light and art. Apollo eventually became the most revered of the Greek gods, and religious devotion, coupled with the island's central, protected situation, established Delos as the thriving center of the Mediterranean world, religious and commercial leader of an empire that stretched from Italy to the coast of Asia Minor.

Wandering the ruins of this once-boisterous center, we found temples both plain and elegant, Greek and foreign; massive marketplaces studded with pedestals where statues once stood, now paved with poppies; a theater quarter with vivid mosaics depicting actors and symbolic animals and fish; a dry lake ringed with palm trees; a stadium and a gymnasium; storehouses and quays along the waterfront; and an ancient suburb where merchants and ship captains once lived: the haunting skeleton of a Hellenistic metropolis.

At 12:45 the captain of the trawler appeared at the end of the dock and whistled once, twice, three times, then waved his arms. He repeated this signal at 12:50 and 12:55. My friend left, but something about those deserted ruins held me, and I decided to spend the night on the island. I watched from the top of Mount Cynthus, the lone hill, as the boat moved away toward the mountains of Mykonos on the northeast horizon. Looking around, I felt at the center of the Cyclades: to the north, Tinos, to the northwest, Andros, then Syros, Siphnos, Paros, and Naxos, and beyond them Melos and Ios—all spokes in the sacred chariot of the sun god.

Below me the ruins were absolutely desolate, shimmering silently in the midday sun. A lizard slithered over my boot. The boat crawled father away. The wind sighed. Droplets of sweat seemed to steam from my forehead.

I walked down the hill to the shade of the tourist pavilion, the one concession to tourism (besides a three-room museum) on the island. I walked inside and asked the owner, a large, jolly man with a Zorba mustache, what he was offering for lunch. He looked surprised to see me. "You miss the *caique?*"

"No, I wanted to spend the night here."

"Ah." He looked beyond me into the glaring, baked ruins. "We have rice, meat, vegetables."

"Do you have any fish?"

"Fish? Yes." He directed me to a case in the back room, opened it, and took out five different fish, each caked with ice. "Which do you want?" I pointed to one. "Drink?"

"A beer, please."

He nodded, pointed out the door to a terrace with tables and chairs scattered at random like dancers at a Mykonos discotheque, and said, "Sit, please," motioning me into a chair.

The heat hung in the air, folding like a curtain over the pillars and pedestals, smothering the palms and reeds. Occasionally a dusty-brown lizard would scuttle from one shadow into another. The owner moved from kitchen to terrace like a man who has never waited, never worried about time, wiping off the table, bringing a glass of cold beer, then fish, fried potatoes, and a tomato salad.

Eventually, two old men dressed in the same uniform as the man who had greeted us that morning walked up carrying two pails filled with water. One went inside and began to talk animatedly with the owner. The other sat down on the edge of the terrace, dipped his callused hands, and pulled out a white and black octopus. He rolled the octopus in a milky white liquid from the other pail, twisting and slapping its tentacles against the cement until he was satisfied it was clean. Then he laid it aside, and dipped in again, pulling out another slippery creature. He cleaned five octopuses in all, leaving them oozing in the sun, their tentacles writhing and their suction cups puckering.

At 4:00 P.M. a cock crowed. What is he doing here? I wondered. And, more important, why is he crowing at 4:00 P.M.? The sound broke the silence with an eerie premonition. I looked at the bottles, chairs, tables, heard the reassuring murmur of voices inside. Beyond the terrace, in the light and heat, seemed another world.

An hour later I walked into the ruins, following the wide central avenue (the "Sacred Way") toward the waterfront, the theater district, and the hillside temples. On my way I passed columns carved with line after line of intricate symbols with no breaks between the words; sacrificial altars; huge cisterns for storing rainwater and oil; and vast foundations outlining meeting halls and marketplaces by the wharves. I explored the remains of private houses, passing from room to room, trying to imagine where their inhabitants had cooked, eaten, and slept, awakened from my reverie only by an occasional spider web or lizard trail. As I walked on and the setting sun cast the halls and walls in an orange-pink light, the ruins seemed to take on a strange life all their own.

What had been eerie desolation became an intense timelessness, a sense of communion with other peoples and other eras. My boots crossed rocks other sandals had crossed; my hands touched marble other hands had touched. When I reached the mosaics, they seemed a living thing, green-eyed tigers and blue dolphins, flowers of every shape and color, the same to me as they were to the countless merchants and artisans who had admired them centuries before. I continued up the hill to the temples of the Syrian and Egyptian—as well as Greek—gods, and reflected how many different cultures had met in that silent hollow below.

While I was sitting in the temple to the Egyptian gods, a figure appeared walking up the hill toward me. It was not the owner of the pavilion, nor any of the fishermen I had seen previously. This was a man in shorts and a Western shirt with a satchel and a walking stick. We exchanged waves and wary glances until he came up and sat next to me. "You are English?"

"American."

"Ah, good." He stuck out his hand.

He was a physicist from Hungary on leave from a national research project for two weeks. "I have been saving my passes for this trip," he said. "Isn't this wonderful? Yesterday I examined all the ruins from there"—he waved a finger toward the stadium at the distant end of the basin—"to here. Today I have walked the circuit of the island." He paused to catch his breath, his cheeks as grainy as the rocks on which we sat. "There really isn't that much else to see."

The mountains were turning purple over the poppy-red water. The ruins were fading into shade. I wanted to explore further before darkness set in, so we agreed to meet for dinner.

When I entered the tourist pavilion, the owner greeted me like a long-lost friend and brought out three glasses and a bottle of ouzo. "We drink." The Hungarian appeared through another doorway that, I learned later, led to the pavilion's four "guest rooms," distinguished by the presence of a mattress and wash basin. We finished one bottle and began another, talking in Greek, Italian, French, German, and English about everything and soon thereafter about nothing. When one language failed, we tried another, until we were all speaking in the universal tongue of Loquacious Libation.

In another hour or two the owner fixed us a feast of fish, lamb, fried potatoes, rice, tomatoes, and cucumbers, with baklava and rice pudding for dessert. While we ate, the physicist and I talked. I learned that the cluster of houses I had seen earlier had been built by the French School of Classical Studies when it was digging on Delos in the 1950s and '60s. When the last archaeologists left, the curator of the museum moved in with his family. It was his son I had met that morning. The old man who had hailed our arrival was a fisherman from a local island who turned to guiding when the fishing was slow.

After finishing our second bottle—compliments of the owner—of sweet, resiny retsina, we drank a good night toast of thick Greek coffee. Then the physicist retired to his room, preceded by the owner's wife, who had drawn a pitcher of cold water for his use in the morning. I was traveling on a backpack budget, however, and when the owner offered me the use of his roof for twenty drachmas (less than a dollar), half the cost of the guest rooms, I gladly accepted.

I walked up two flights of cement stairs to a cement roof enclosed like a medieval fortress with a four-foot-high wall. The stars glinted like a nighttime mirror of the marble ruins. I unrolled my sleeping bag in a protected corner, thankful that the lizards could not reach me at that height, and rummaged in my backpack for soap, toothpaste, and a toothbrush.

"Could you use this?" The physicist held out his flashlight. "I've come to ask you to hurry in preparing your toilet. The owner wants to turn off the electricity."

After I had washed and brushed and stumbled back up the stairs to my sleeping bag, I heard a scuffling of footsteps; voices thundered back and forth through the blackness, and the lights went out.

The footsteps returned, a door squeaked and banged shut, chairs scraped. Then everything was silent. No machine sounds, no human sounds, no animal sounds. Absolute silence. I lay in my sleeping bag, and the ruins encroached on my dreams—the swish of the lizards scrambling over the rocks, the moist coolness of the marble at sunset, the languid perfume of the poppies dabbed among the fluted white fragments.

Streaming sunlight awakened me. I turned to look at my watch and disturbed a black kitten that had bundled itself at my feet. In so doing, I also disturbed the ouzo and retsina that had bundled itself in my head, and I crawled as close as I could to the shadow of the wall—6:45. I pulled my towel over my head and tried to imagine the windy dark, but to no avail. The kitten mewed its way under my towel, where it set to lapping at my cheek as if it had discovered a bowl of milk.

I stumbled down the stairs and soaked my head in tepid tap water until at last I felt stable enough to survey the surroundings. Behind the pavilion a clothesline ran to the rusting generator. Chickens strutted inside a coop at the curator's house. Rhenea stirred in the rising mist.

Again I wandered through the ruins, different ruins now, bright with day and the reality of returns: The tourists would return to Delos, and I would return to Mykonos. I ate a solemn breakfast on the terrace with the physicist, then walked past the sacred lake and the marketplace to the Terrace of the Lions. Standing among the five lions of Delos, erected in the 7th century B.C. to defend the island from invaders, I looked over the crumbling walls and stunted pillars to the temples on the hill. Like priests they presided over the procession of tourists who would surge onto the island, bearing their oblation in cameras and guidebooks. As the trawler approached, a bent figure in a navy blue beret hurried to the dock, and a boy in shorts raced out of the curator's house past the physicist, past me, and into the ruins.

Ryoanji Reflections

I became Travel Editor at the San Francisco Examiner *in 1987, and began writing a Page Two column for the Sunday Travel Section shortly thereafter. I was an innocent and exhilarated editor—I wanted to transform the Travel Section into the* New Yorker *of newspaper travel sections—and one of my fervent goals was to publish deep, personal travel writing that vividly recreated an author's experience but also probed into the heart and meaning of that experience. This essay, published in the fall of 1987, was one of my first fledgling attempts to do this in my weekly column. I wanted to speak directly to the reader, and I wanted to talk about a place and experience that had deeply moved me, taught me, changed me. This, I thought, was the potential of great travel writing, to create experiential bridges between reader and writer. This column was published as part of a special section on the theme of sacred places, a context that allowed me to plumb a seemingly simple place that had resonated to my core. To my surprise and delight, this article was chosen from among thousands of international entrants as the Best Travel Article of the Year in the Pacific Asia Travel Association's annual Gold Awards competition. That award hugely buoyed my determination to continue writing in this style.*

WHEN I THINK OF THE SACRED PLACES I have encountered in my own travels, I recall the Temple of Poseidon on the cliff of Cape Sounion in Greece, where I spent a wild night huddled in my sleeping bag among the moonlit columns, surrounded by tearing wind, the crashing of waves, and ghostly, godly dreams.

I think too of Bali, of the lush, lovingly sculpted land and the gentle people, more profoundly imbued with a sense of sanctity—of life as a holy gift to be celebrated—than any other I have met.

But most vividly of all I think of a simple plot of sand and rocks and moss in Kyoto—the rock garden at Ryoanji Temple.

The guidebooks will tell you that the rock garden was built in the 15th century, probably by a renowned, Zen-influenced artist named Soami, and that it is considered a masterpiece of the *karesansui* ("dry landscape") garden style. It consists of fifteen irregularly shaped rocks of varying sizes, some surrounded by moss, arranged in a bed of white sand that is raked every day. A low earthen wall surrounds the garden on three sides, overhung by a narrow, beamed wooden roof; on the fourth side, wooden steps lead to a wide wooden platform and the main building of the temple itself. Beyond the wall are cedar, pine, and cherry trees.

Such a description gives a sense of the history and look of the place, but to understand its power, its pure *presence*, you have to go there. The first time I visited Ryoanji I was overwhelmed— first by the spareness of the site and second by loudspeakers that every fifteen minutes squawked out a recorded message about the history and spirit of the garden to the busloads of obedient schoolchildren and tourists who filed through.

But something held me there. Morning passed to afternoon, and still I sat on the well-worn platform, staring. Kids in black caps, tiny book-filled backpacks, and black-and-white school uniforms passed by, studying me while I studied the garden, and adults in shiny cameras and kimonos clicked and clucked and walked on.

Clouds came and went, and the branches beyond the garden bent, straightened, bent again. I saw how the pebbly sand had been meticulously raked in circles around the rocks, and in straight lines in the open areas, and how those lines stopped without a misplaced pebble when they touched the circular patterns, and then resumed unchanged beyond them. I saw how pockets of moss had filled the pocks in the stones, and how the sand echoed the sky, the moss echoed the trees, the wall and roof balanced the platform, and the rocks seemed to emanate a web of intricate, tranquil tension within the whole.

It was an exquisite enigma, telling me something I couldn't put words to, and so it has remained.

I have seen Ryoanji in spring, when the cherry trees bloomed, and in fall, when their branches were bare; in winter, when snow covered the moss, and in summer, when the cicadas buzzed beyond the wall. I have been there among giggling teenagers and gaping farmers, bemused Westerners and beatific monks. By now it has become a part of me—and still it eludes me.

I love the place partly because it is so emphatically not a ten-minute tourist stop. Its dimensions defy the camera—I have never seen a true picture of the place—and its subtle simplicity defies quick assimilation. It makes you sit and study, slow down and stare until you really see it— in its particularity and in its whole, simultaneously.

And yet—and here the enigma expands—you cannot see all of Ryoanji at one time: The rocks are so arranged that you can see only fourteen of the stones wherever you stand. You have to visualize, imagine, the final one.

How wonderful! It is in this sense that Ryoanji is, for me, the essential sacred place: It is complete in itself, but for you to completely perceive it, you have to transcend the boundary between inner and outer—to travel inward as well as outward, to find and finish it in your mind.

And the gigglers, the camera-clickers, and the squawking loudspeakers are all, in their exasperating reality, part of this completion. Beyond a great irony of modern Japan—loudspeakers instructing you to appreciate the silence—they embody a much larger meaning: You must embrace them all—the monks and the moss and the trees, the schoolkids and the stones—to really be there, to be whole.

Connections:
A Moment at Notre-Dame

After I became Travel Editor at the Examiner, *my first trip was a pilgrimage to Paris. That was a glorious re-immersion in and celebration of poignant places from my past, and the most poignant of all was Notre-Dame Cathedral. Notre-Dame is one of the planet's touchstone places for me, and this essay was, in a sense, an attempt to stop time: to focus on a remembered moment in a place, and to dive archaeologically into the imaginative and emotional layers of that moment. I was intensely surprised and stirred by the layers that excavation revealed.*

NOTRE-DAME FROM THE OUTSIDE IS MAGNIFICENT, monumental, solidly of the earth and yet soaringly not. But for all its monumental permanence, its context is clearly the present: Visitors pose, focus, click; portable stalls sell sandwiches and postcards; tourist groups shuffle by in ragtag formation.

Walk through those massive, humbling doors, though, and suddenly you breathe the air of antiquity. Let your mind and eyes adjust to the inner light, and you begin to realize that there is much more to Paris than the life of its streets, and a small sense of its magnificent and moving past comes back to you.

When I entered Notre-Dame on my most recent trip, I was overwhelmed by the solid, soaring arches and columns I had forgotten, by the depth and texture of the stained-glass windows with their luminous blues and reds and greens. I thought of how many people had worked to build this magnificence, and of how many people since then had stood, perhaps on the very same stones as I, and marveled at it. I thought of all the faith and hope and sacrifice it manifests.

I walked through the fervent space, awed by the art and the hush that seemed to resonate with the whispers of centuries, and just when I was beginning to feel too small and insignificant and was getting ready to leave, I saw a simple sign over a tiny stone basin of water, on a column near the doors.

The sign said, "In the name of the father and the son and the Holy Spirit" in seven languages, with pictures that showed a hand dipping into the water, then touching a forehead.

I touched my hand to the cool, still water, then brought it to my head, and as I did so, chills ran through my body and tears streamed into my eyes.

Somehow that simple act had forged a palpable contact with ages past, had put everything into startling focus: the ceaseless flow of pilgrims to this special place, the ceaseless procession of hands to water and fingers to forehead, all sharing this basin, this gesture.

I felt a new sense of the history that flows with us and around us and beyond us all—of the plodding, tireless path of human-kind and of the sluggish, often violent spread of Christianity through Europe and the rest of the world—and a new sense of the flow of my own history, too: my Protestant upbringing, a pas-tor whose notions of Christian love have had a deep and abiding influence on my life, the old and still inconceivable idea of God.

For a few moments I lost all sense of place and time—then a door opened and a tourist group entered, looking up and around in wonder, and I walked into the world of sunlight and spire again.

I stopped, blinked at the sandwich stalls and postcard ven-dors, then turned back toward that stony symmetry and thought: Sometimes you feel so small and insignificant in the crush of his-tory that you lose all sense of purpose and self. Then something will happen to make you realize that every act and every encoun-ter has its own precious meaning and lesson, and that history is simply the sum of all these.

Sometimes it comes together, as it did for me that moment in Notre-Dame; sometimes the world is reduced to a simple sign, a stone basin, the touch of water to head—and the vast pageant of the past and the living parade of the present take on a new, and renewing, symmetry and sense.

Conquering Half Dome

In the mid-1990s, I left the Examiner and joined Salon, a feisty, bright, and ambitious web magazine that had been started by friends and colleagues from the Examiner. The founders' goal was to produce a site distinguished by intelligent commentary, excellent writing, and groundbreaking journalism, and within that context, they asked me to create the travel section of my dreams. I christened the section Wanderlust, and we launched in 1997, with the passionate mandate of publishing unvarnished dispatches and soul-stretching narratives. "Conquering Half Dome," published in 1999, was my own attempt to write a soul-stretching narrative about an adventure not far from my Northern California backyard, in Yosemite National Park, but threaded with far-ranging themes of frailty, family, and overcoming our fears. When I read this now, I can't help but compare the narrator of this piece with the heedless young man who ascended Kilimanjaro on a whim.... And I think: Our mountains also evolve over time.

SOMETIMES WE KNOW A JOURNEY WILL BE a grand adventure—the three-week expedition I made along Pakistan's avalanche-laden Karakoram Highway to enchanted Hunza comes to mind. Other times we know it will be a little one—on a recent quick business trip to Paris I was content with stumbling upon a wonderful ancient restaurant and a precious new park I'd never known about.

But sometimes our trips surprise us.

In the summer of 1999, my family made a five-day excursion to Yosemite. It was supposed to be a little camping lark, but it turned out to be a much grander—and much more terrifying—adventure than I'd ever imagined.

The trip seemed innocent enough: Our plan was to drive to Yosemite on a Saturday, spend the next three days camping and hiking to the top of Half Dome, then hike back to our car and drive home on the fifth day. This would require three days of four to six hours of hiking. The only moderately troublesome part would be the final ascent of Half Dome, that iconic granite thumb that juts almost 9,000 feet over the meadows and waterfalls and lesser crags of California's Yosemite Valley. But I had seen pictures of the cable-framed walkway that leads to the top of the mountain, and it didn't look too difficult. My wife and I felt confident that our eight-year-old son and twelve-year-old daughter could handle it.

So off we went. We made the winding drive from the San Francisco Bay Area to Yosemite National Park in about four hours. It was a splendid day, all cotton-candy clouds against a county-fair sky. Eating carrots and apple slices in the car, we sped through the suburbs and into parched golden hills, and before we knew it we were off the main highway and passing hand-painted signs advertising red onions, fresh-picked tomatoes, almonds, peaches, and nectarines. Our eyes lingered on the weather-beaten stands, where we could see shiny red mounds of tomatoes and green mountains of watermelons, but we pressed on.

We reached Yosemite as the sun was setting, picked up our trail permit, pitched our tent, cooked a quick camp supper, and went to bed.

Our plan was to get up early, hike more than halfway up—to the highest source of water on the Half Dome trail—and camp, thereby minimizing the distance we would have to cover the next day before making our assault on the peak. If you're young and strong, or old and foolhardy, you can hike from Yosemite Valley to the top of Half Dome and back in a day. In previous trips to Yosemite we had met people who had done just that; they would leave at daybreak and plan to get back around dusk. But we wanted to take it easy on ourselves. We also had built in an extra day so that if for any reason we couldn't make Half Dome the first time, we would have a second chance, so we weren't in any hurry.

The next day took longer than we had planned—as it invariably does. By the time we had gotten the kids rousted and had packed up our tents and ground covers and cooking gear, it was about 10:00 A.M. and the sun was high and hot in the sky.

We set off along the John Muir Trail, winding into the rocks and pines. The first section of this trail is still a little like Disneyland, and you pass people in flip-flops and even occasionally high heels, sweating and puffing and swigging fresh-off-the-supermarket-shelf bottles of spring water.

After about a half hour's stroll you reach a picturesque bridge with a fantastic foaming view of the Merced River cascading over the rocks—and a neat wooden bathroom and a water fountain that is the last source of water that doesn't have to be filtered. The flip-flops and high heels turn back with a grateful sigh at this point, and the few people you do pass hereafter on the trail exchange friendly nods and greetings and the smug satisfaction of getting into the real Yosemite.

Then you walk and you walk and you walk, stepping heavily over rocks, kicking up clouds of dirt that settle on your legs and socks and boots. Occasionally you'll be cooled by a shower of water trickling from high rocks right onto the trail, or by a breeze blowing unexpectedly when you turn a corner. But for the most part you step and mop your brow and swat at mosquitoes in the patches of shade and take swigs of water, careful to roll the water in your mouth as your long-ago football coach taught you, until you're surprised by a dazzling quilt of purple flowers or a tumbling far-off torrent shining white and silver and blue in the sun, and you stop and munch slowly on granola bars and dried apples and nectarines and notice how the sunlight waterfalls through the branches of the trees.

After four hours we reached the halfway point at Little Yosemite Valley. It's a popular camping spot with loosely demarcated camping areas—framed by fallen tree trunks, with rock-outlined fire circles and tree stumps for tables and stools—plus a resident ranger, an outhouse, and easily accessible water in the form of the Merced River fast-flowing by. We hadn't really prepared for the trip physically, and were already grimy and sweaty and exhausted. On top of that, we had received conflicting information about where exactly the last source of water on the trail would be, so rather than press farther up, we decided to stop there for the night. Tomorrow we would rise early and climb Half Dome.

We had planned to get up at 6:00 and be on the trail by 8:00. Again, reality intruded, and we got up at 8:00 and set out for Half Dome around 9:30. This was not wise. We had never hiked this trail before and didn't know how long it would take or what obstacles it would present; besides that, we'd been told that the best time to climb Half Dome is the morning, since clouds tend to come in by the afternoon. Weather changes quickly in the mountains, and you don't want to be anywhere near the summit when the clouds come in, rangers had said. The mountain is a magnet for lightning. All Half Dome hikers are explicitly told that if they see rain clouds on the horizon, they shouldn't attempt the ascent. Lightning strikes the dome at least once every month—and at least a few careless people every year. Even the cables that run up the final 800 feet of the slope are lightning magnets.

So we wound up through the trees as fast as we could. We passed through deep-shadowed, pine-needled stretches of forest path like places in a fairy tale, and we emerged onto sun-blasted stretches of rock that offered amazing views of the surrounding peaks—and of Half Dome towering precipitously into the sky.

We reached the base of Half Dome, after a final, extremely arduous half-hour zigzag trek up a series of massive steps cut out of the stone, at about 1:00 P.M. Clouds were massing to the east and to the west, but we pressed on. A motley pile of gloves left by previous climbers lay at the spot where the cable walkway began. We chose gloves we liked, grabbed hold of the cables, and began to haul ourselves up.

This is when our little lark turned into a grand adventure.

In the pictures we had seen before the trip, the cable route didn't look all that daunting. Basically, they showed a gang-plank-like walkway with thick steel cables running along either side that stretched up the slope of the mountain. In the pictures, hikers with daypacks strode confidently up the slope as if they were out for a Sunday stroll.

Somehow the pictures hadn't prepared me for the reality. The cables are set about four feet off the ground and are about three feet apart. As a further aid to climbers, wooden planks connected to the posts that support the cables are set across the moun-tain-path at an interval of about every four to five feet. This is not as comforting as it sounds.

I'd read before the trip that the path slopes up at an angle of about sixty degrees. In my mind I had pictured that angle and had mentally traced a line along the living room wall. That doesn't seem too steep, I had said to myself.

Beware estimates made in the comfort of your living room. From the plushness of my couch, with a soothing cup of steaming tea in my hand, sixty degrees hadn't seemed too steep—but in the sheer, slippery, life-on-the-line wildness of Yosemite, it seemed real steep. I looked at the cables, and I looked at the sloping pate of the mountain—and I thought, This is a really stupid way to die.

Why, I continued, am I consciously choosing to risk my life like this? What's the point? All it would take would be one slip, a hand loosened from the cables.

I could already see myself sliding down the face of Half Dome, grabbing frantically at the smooth surface, thudding-scraping-bumping along the rock until, if I was really lucky, I managed to grab a bloody finger-stub handhold on the rock face or, if I wasn't really lucky, I just slipped off the face of the rock, with all the assembled climbers gasping and screaming and my wife and kids yelling not knowing what to do, how to prevent my fall, and then it would be a brief free-fall flight before bone-crushing oblivion. Hopefully, I thought, I will pass out before contact and die relatively peacefully.

All this flashed through my mind as I stood at the base of the cables.

"What are we waiting for?" my daughter asked impatiently.

"We're waiting until we grow wings," I wanted to say.

But she was ready—ah, youth, that hath no fear—and began to scramble up the slope. And then my wife went. And then my son started—a little apprehensively, being eight years old and all. But he was on his way. None of them seemed to understand that what we were doing was inherently suicidal!

Still, they were gone, and there really was nothing to do but grab hold of the cables and start to pull myself up this suddenly stupid and hateful mountain.

The whole thing seemed so absurd. Hadn't I evolved beyond this kind of macho risk-taking decades ago?

Somehow the fact that all kinds of people, from base-ball-capped teens to silver-haired seniors, had scrambled up that day and were now headed down the very walkway I was staring up, and that numerous others were perched on the face of the mountain in mid-ascent a dozen yards above me, scrambling up even as I quaked—somehow this was of no comfort.

I was scared. I wasn't exactly convinced I was going to die—I thought I probably had a chance of making it alive—but I felt I was consciously subjecting myself to an experience that could really kill me.

But so we started. My first few steps were leaden. My hiking boots kept slipping; my arms, which hadn't done anything all day, suddenly felt dead-tired and couldn't haul up the dead weight of my body. In a classic case of self-fulfilling prophecy, I kept slipping and sliding, just as I thought I would. I was utterly miserable.

One thing you should never do—or at least one thing I should never do—when climbing Half Dome is look around at the view. The view is what can kill you. You stop and brush your brow with your sleeve and your eyes steal a look to the left and—whoa!—it's a long, long way down. Your view drops right off the side of the cliff to green trees the size of matchsticks and postage-stamp meadows. You don't want to see this and you definitely don't want to think about it. I swayed and held onto the cables and stayed frozen, letting other climbers brush by me, until the dizziness and the wave-swells in my stomach stopped. My mouth was drier than I could ever remember it being. My arms ached.

After about fifteen wooden planks, my son and I paused. My wife Kuniko looked down from a perch a few posts ahead. "How are you feeling, Jeremy? Do you want to keep going, or do you want to stop?"

Say you want to stop, Jeremy, I prayed. For the love of God, tell her you want to stop!

He was undecided. I was probably green in the face. "How are you doing, honey?" Kuniko asked, concern creasing her face.

"I don't know," I said.

We looked around and saw bulbous black clouds blowing swiftly in.

"Maybe we should head down," Kuniko said.

Yes! Yes! a little voice inside me said.

"I want to keep going!" Jenny said.

"No, I think we should head down," Kuniko said.

"I think so, too," I said, whining with as much authority as I could muster. "I don't like the look of those clouds."

So, much to Jenny's loud disappointment, we slid down— which was almost as terrifying as hauling up, except that now your body was helping gravity pull you to your death.

At one point I really did completely slip—my feet just went out from under me, I landed with a sacroiliac-smacking thud and before I knew what was happening I began to slide down the face of the mountain. Luckily I managed to stomp the sole of one boot squarely against the iron post that supported the cable, thus stopping my fall. Mortality had never seemed nearer.

I lay on the side of the mountain for a few minutes, trying to slow my heart, waiting for my arms to stop shaking.

"Are you all right?" people asked as they stepped gingerly by me.

Then I said to myself, Just go down slowly, one by one, and I did. And suddenly I was at the bottom, stepping off the last plank onto level rock, and I was sitting down and sluggishly taking off my gloves and Jenny was asking, "Dad, are you OK?"

The hike back to camp seemed about ten times longer than the morning's walk. My head was black-clouded with doubts and fears about attempting the climb again the next day. What a stupid way to die, I kept thinking.

But at the same time I felt that I had to do it. The kids were going to do it, everyone was doing it—I couldn't say, "Gee, I think I'll just stay down here and watch."

So even though I knew I was putting my life unnecessarily at risk, I also knew I had to make the climb.

I tossed and turned for hours that night, thinking about that blasted slippery-slope cable walkway. I knew it was virtually all mental, that I was psyching myself into failure. It didn't matter. I couldn't magically find the switch in my mind.

After a fractured sleep we woke up and retraced our path of the previous day. I wish I could say that everything had changed, that I had come to peace with the idea of climbing Half Dome and had found a deep pool of confidence in myself, but I hadn't. I had made up my mind to climb Half Dome, but I was fundamentally unsettled about it all.

Still, everything seemed a little more propitious this time. We got an earlier start and so we were passed by only a handful of day-hikers, which felt good. The sky was a broad expanse of blue, with only a few puffs of white here and there. I was hiking strongly, and we covered the same territory in about an hour less than the previous day. We reached the arduous rock-steps at about 10:30 and were at the glove-heaped base of Half Dome by 11:00. We paused to take some deep swigs of water and eat an energy bar, and then we were ready.

Jeremy and Jenny set off first, fearlessly. Kuniko and I had decided that I would go up next, so that if I slipped, she might be able to help me. I swapped the thick leather gloves I had used the day before for lighter cloth gloves that permitted more feeling in my fingers. That seemed to help some.

I knew it was all mental, but that knowledge wasn't helping much. It was still terrifying. But this time I thought: If you just focus on each step, you'll be OK. Don't think about the slope to the left or the right. Don't think about what's beneath you or how much more you still have to go. Just focus on each step, step by step.

I took my first step and pulled myself up by the cables. Took another step and did the same. Took another step and I was at the first wooden plank.

I repeated the process, planting my foot slowly, making sure it was secure on the rock face before using my arms, then pulling myself up to make the next step. Three steps and I had reached plank No. 2.

It seemed easier than yesterday.

Gradually my body relaxed. The tension left my arms and they didn't ache. The fear left my legs and they were more flexible; I was finding secure sole-holds in the rock. I didn't slip, and I was learning to focus my breathing and energy in discrete spurts of arm-pulling.

The trick, I thought, is to restrict the world to the small plot of rock in front of me and the cables on either side, to extend my arm about ten inches up the cable, like this, grab tight hold of it, secure my grip, like this, say "OK, now!" and pull—ugh! and up!—and then pause a while to catch my breath and coil my energy, and then repeat the process, hauling myself up, step by step.

I reached the point where we had stopped the day before and dimly recorded that it had been much easier so far. If I could just focus on each rung.

I kept pulling myself up, foothold then handhold, plank by plank. At one point, with a quick glance up, I realized that

Jenny and Jeremy, who seemed to have sprinted up the slope, had disappeared. They were already running freely around the broad summit. Somewhere inside me, I registered the fact that I was going to make it, too.

There were still a few tricky places—places where a two-foot fissure appeared between the part of the slope-trail I was on and the slope where the trail continued. Here I had to simultaneously pull myself over the displacement and up the slope, a doubly difficult and slippery task.

But by focusing precisely on what I was doing—plant the foot there, make sure it's secure, OK, now pull yourself up on the cable, move your other foot forward, pull yourself up again—I was able to make it without slipping.

There was one particularly steep step where I felt my arms begin to falter and in mid-stride I felt my body begin to sway backward, as if my arms weren't going to be able to pull my body up. Death flickered in my brain and in a millisecond I thought, *You've GOT to pull yourself up*, and the adrenaline zapped through my arms like lightning and I forced myself—brain and arms pulling together—to the next rung. The prospect of death had glimmered, but it hadn't paralyzed me as the day before.

After about twenty-five minutes I reached the point where the summit begins to taper off and the angle eases. Another ten wooden planks and the end of the ascent was in sight.

I almost ran the last few steps, so exhilarated to have made it to the top. Jenny and Jeremy saw me from their post at the peak and came jumping over the summit. We gave each other big bear hugs.

"You made it, Dad!" they said.

In another few minutes Kuniko came to the top, grinning widely.

We explored the summit, took in the extraordinary 360-degree panorama of snow-capped peaks, piney slopes, glistening water-falls, and green meadows far below.

And we felt on top of the world.

We shared a celebratory chocolate bar I had stuffed in my pocket, and after a half hour snapping photos and walking to the extreme compass points of the peak, we heard thunder to the east and saw black clouds massing, moving with deceptive speed our way.

We shared a huge family hug and set off.

Jenny and Jeremy fairly skipped down the slope—or at least that's the way it seemed to me. I slipped and slid—three times I slowly let myself down on the seat of my pants from one rung to another—but never lost control and within about a half hour I was standing again on level rock, tossing my gloves into the heap, my heart pounding wildly and my head splitting-spinning with the triumph.

I had done it! I had overcome all those fear-boulders that we throw up in front of ourselves, that keep us from doing the things we are capable of doing.

We had climbed Half Dome, and from now on, whenever we looked at that stunning granite jut from afar, we would have the joyful and astounding knowledge that we had once stood on that very peak, looking down on the whole world around us. We had conquered the slippery slope of Half Dome, and we would have much to celebrate that night.

It seemed symbolic of so many things in life, and I was just beginning to enjoy the light-footed walk back to camp and to feel the success suffuse my body from the top of my head to the tips of my fingers and toes, when Jeremy turned to me and said, "Dad, can we do this again next year?"

Impression: Sunrise at Uluru

At the beginning of 2001, I left Salon to become Global Travel Editor at Lonely Planet, thrilled to be working with founders Tony and Maureen Wheeler, longtime heroes of mine who had also become close friends. My duties at LP were marvelously multifaceted: editing one literary anthology a year; representing the company to the media and the public as spokesperson; and writing a weekly column for the website. In synch with the company ethos of mindful exploration of the wide-ranging world, I was encouraged to write about anything I wanted and to be as personal as I wanted to be. Soon after joining the company, I was called to the Melbourne headquarters for planning meetings, and I was able to tack on time afterwards to realize one of my longtime dreams: to visit Uluru, the red rock monolith in the Outback, sacred to the Aboriginals. I thought Uluru would be a powerful place, but I had no idea it would affect me as profoundly as it did. When I set out to write about this experience, the account poured out of me in the second person rather than the first person, "you" instead of "I." This was unusual for me, but looking back, I think that I somehow subconsciously sensed that writing in the second person would allow me to make an intensely personal experience more universal; I wanted to break down the barrier between me and the reader, precisely because my encounter with Uluru had been so deeply subjective, and sacred.

THE FIRST TIME YOU APPROACH ULURU, the world is still dark. You are rolling through the pre-dawn desert in a minivan when the big black monolith looms suddenly through the side window. It is difficult to judge how far away it is, or how close you are, because the whole world is monotone and flat. Yet you feel the power.

You have been wary of your preconceptions about the place—the accumulation of iconography and clichés, photographs seen and descriptions read. You don't want to feel exactly what you know you are *supposed* to feel. You want a raw connection with the thing. You want to wipe your brain clean, approach the rock like the first human ever to take it in, stumbling incredulously toward it like some red sun-trick on the horizon that doesn't disappear, but only grows larger and larger until finally all you can do is fall on your knees before it.

And then you see it, and suddenly your wariness falls away. You are drawn to the dark immensity purely, simply, irresistibly, and with a power that comes from the thing itself and not, as far as you can tell, from your own desire to feel the power. Because it catches you by surprise and because it is such a strong, pit-of-the-stomach pull, you trust it.

As you get closer, you creak and crane your neck to see as much of it as you can, until you notice—because you'd been so obsessed with seeing the rock, you'd missed this—that you are passing other minivans and buses and dozens upon dozens of people. They wear jeans and warm jackets and hold steaming cups of coffee in their hands; some stamp their feet, others set up their cameras. They have come to see exactly what you have come to see, and you realize there is no point in trying to feel better than them or different from them. You have to share Uluru with them.

Your minivan parks and you emerge, brushing off the cobwebs of some conversation about kangaroos and dingos. All you want to do is concentrate on the rock itself: Uluru.

You position yourself at one of the barriers beyond which visitors are not allowed to step, less than a kilometer from the rock, and you look. The rock is a smooth, sloping burnt-orange rise against a deep gray-blue sky. Before it are dark waves of vegetation, which surprise you; somehow you imagined the rock standing solitary in a vast flatland extending red and cracked-dry to the horizon.

For the next half hour, as the Earth slowly tilts toward the sun at your back, you watch.

The rock gradually grows more orange, more bright, and you begin to see the fissures and pocks in its side, shadowy sluices where rainfall must flow, deep gouges sculpted by wind and water and time.

The sky lightens from dark blue to a pastel peach-pink, the bushes and trees in the foreground take a silver-green shape, the rock's orange brightens, and pocks darken like caves in its side.

The sky grows lighter and lighter, the rock face brighter and brighter; more veins and pits emerge in relief.

And then, in what seems one miraculous moment, birdsong bursts from the bushes and trees and the sun fires up the face of Uluru and it is as if the rock is glowing from within, pulsing, breathing, one huge burning ember. And then it is like nothing you've seen before and you simply don't have the words to describe it. It is alive with some kind of earth energy of its own. It pulses. It gathers everything into itself. It beats with a luminous orange energy that courses through the world around it. It is the heart of the soil and the rocks and the roots beneath the soil, coming to life.

You think of the elaborate sun temples that ancient civilizations had constructed, of Stonehenge, Teotihuacan, Machu Picchu, Sounion. And for a moment you think that this could be nature's sun temple, a construct manifesting a connection so far beyond comprehension that the only possible response is awe.

And then the moment ends. The people pack up their cameras and pile into their buses. Within minutes, they are gone.

But you remain, listening to the birdsong, looking at the rock.

You've had enough mysticism for one morning, so you drop to your knees and pick up a handful of soil. You want to ground yourself.

But as you let the soil sift through your hands, slowly, softly, you feel it: some kind of electrical connection. The particles passing through your fingers are the same as the particles that molded to form the rock. And you consider: Are those particles really so different from the particles that molded into the big blue and green rock on which you now kneel?

Sift, sift. The grains tilt through your dusty hands, bursting into sun-lit life.

Castaway in the Galápagos

In 2002 I was exhilarated when the editor of Islands *magazine asked me to take my family to the Galápagos and write a piece about our adventures on the islands. My two children were twelve and sixteen, perfect ages for the Galápagos, and for years I'd wanted to visit this seemingly enchanted and enchanting archipelago. Could it really be as magical as everyone said? Off we went. The ensuing journey was life-changing in ways we never could have imagined. And the writing journey was equally stretching and broadening. Over the years I'd become used to writing about my own journey, inward as well as outward, but in this case I had to re-create a family odyssey, apprehending and evoking the lessons we'd all learned, inner and outer, individually and together. The story forced me to experience, recall, and shape the trip in a new way, and this ended up adding one more layer to the islands' imagination-stretching legacy.*

I WAS SITTING IN THE HOLLOW OF A ROCK carved over thousands of years by the incessant pulse of wind, rain, and wave. The sounds rushed in: *Swissshhh-schwooosh. Tcha-tcha-tcha-tcah. Arerr, arerr, arrer. Chikoo-chikoo.*

It was midmorning; a few hours before, my expedition group had ridden Zodiacs onto the beach at horseshoe-shaped Darwin Bay on Isla Genovesa, one of the northernmost islands in the Galápagos chain. The others in my group had moved on to snorkel off the far tip of the island, but I stayed behind to see how it felt to be the lone soul in that singular place.

Well, the lone *human* soul anyway, since I had lots of other company. To my left, dozens of charcoal-brown juvenile red-footed boobies perched among saltbush branches; their parents whirled around the sky. Two black-and-white Nazca boobies waddled past me. Soft-needled cacti sprouted from a cleft in the rock beside me; with no animals to eat them, they've evolved without their protective hard spines. To my right lay a sand-crusted driftwood tree trunk borne from who knows where.

The ancestors of some of the wildlife around me had probably arrived on just such a trunk, clinging perilously to the surface of the storm-tossed wood or embedded snugly inside, like passengers on an accidental ark. The volcanic rock around me—pocked with air holes and studded with brown and red stones—had been tossed from the earth's fiery crust through a hotspot that sent molten lava spewing onto the seabed in such quantity that it piled up and eventually broke the surface, forming Isla Genovesa, the other almost sixty islands in the chain, and even the hollow in which I sat.

Suddenly, from a thick stand of mangroves I heard a choked squawking, a male red-footed booby trying to attract a mate. Then, straight ahead, oblivious to the human playing castaway among them, three Nazca boobies screeched and squabbled in fierce beak-to-beak combat. Two were ganging up on one, and when the victim rose to confront her tormentors, I saw a light blue egg glistening beneath her. She occupied prime real estate, and the newlyweds wanted it.

A juvenile booby practiced landing to my left, its body wavering to and fro as it fluttered onto a branch. A male frigatebird flew overhead, flashing the red pouch that he puffs into a bright balloon at mating time. Black-and-white swallow-tailed gulls, their eyes outlined in brilliant red, fluttered onto a rocky perch.

At the waterline, black marine iguanas padded across black lava rocks, also dotted with red-and-white Sally Lightfoot crabs. A couple of sea lions fenced with their snouts, bellowing at each other while a whiskery pup flopped along after the bigger one, trying to nurse even while its mother barked at the intruder. Sea lion yelps and roars filled the air and the salt-scented Pacific swashed blue and white.

I swigged water and considered Charles Darwin. Certainly during his seminal visit to the Galápagos aboard the HMS *Beagle* in 1835, the father of evolutionary theory had sailed into the bay now named for him and set foot on this island. But, I thought, it was quite possible that no other human had ever sat precisely where I was. All islands are to some extent worlds apart, but few, as Darwin noted in *The Voyage of the Beagle,* are quite so profoundly separate as the Galápagos. "The natural history of this archipelago is very remarkable," he wrote. "It seems to be a little world within itself; the greater number of its inhabitants, both vegetable and animal, being found nowhere else."

Sitting in my little corner of that world 600 miles off the coast of Ecuador, I couldn't imagine wanting to be anywhere else. And to think that just a week before I'd been having doubts about this trip.

Darwin's voyage from England took four years and was plagued by seasickness; the worst we faced on our two-day trip from San

Francisco were airplane meals and in-flight movies. But I contended with one foe that Darwin didn't: long-distance déjà vu. Long before we departed, a film of the Galápagos reeled through my mind. I had already seen countless times—complete with James Earl Jones narration—boobies, iguanas, frigatebirds, sea lions, giant tortoises, and the rest of the islands' famously fearless birds and beasts. How could reality compete with the digitally enhanced version playing in my head?

Also, I am not really a wildlife person. Generally speaking, in my travels I've sought people, art, culture, and cuisine. But with my daughter turning seventeen and my son soon to be thirteen, my wife, Kuniko, and I thought this seemed the chance to put together one final grand family fling before Jenny went off to college and Jeremy eschewed all travel with the folks. And what could be more climactic than the Galápagos? Given all that, I feared that not even Darwin had dragged so much baggage onto the islands.

Our voyage began late on a Saturday afternoon. After settling into cabins aboard the MS *Polaris*, meeting our guides, and hearing the first of our daily natural-history lectures, seventy of us passengers and six naturalists piled into *pangas* (motorized Zodiacs) and headed for our first excursion on Isla Santa Cruz.

As we cut through the waves, the warm wind scrubbed away my jet lag and the salt water on my lips awakened my senses. As Jeremy took in his surroundings and spotted a great black frigatebird soaring over us, he wondered aloud at its wingspan.

"Up to seven feet," answered naturalist Paul McFarling.

"Wow!" said my son, reaching for his camera.

"You know what it's looking for?" Paul asked.

Jeremy shook his head.

"A booby," Paul continued. "Frigatebirds are the pirates of the skies. They snatch food from other birds, especially boobies.

I've even seen them reach down the neck of a baby booby and take out the fish a mom or dad just fed it."

Jeremy swallowed hard.

"Look!" Jenny cried, pointing to eight bright yellow leaves the size of platters under the water, their edges gently flapping in the current. When the leaves began to swim, I thought my eyes were playing tricks.

"Ah, golden rays," Paul explained. They soared along with exhilarating ease, undulating in formation like oceanic Blue Angels. Jenny grabbed her camera. *Click, click, click.*

In two hours we motored past a spectacular succession of wildlife: pelicans up there, sea turtles over there, sea lions and sharks, two kinds of iguanas, three kinds of mangroves, hundreds of Sally Lightfoot crabs. Overwhelmed, all we could say was "Look! Look! Look!" as if the world were being reinvented before our eyes.

The next morning, after an overnight passage to Isla Espanola, we boarded *pangas* bound for Punta Suarez. As we pulled up to shore, sea lions slid through the waves beside us and bellowed and flopped onto the beach, oblivious to our arrival. Hopping onto black volcanic rock, we realized with a start that all around us were marine iguanas as black as the rock. They sprawled over every available surface, and where no rock was available, they sprawled over each other, sunning themselves, motionless.

Momentarily disoriented by the sheer abundance of life on the beach, I failed to see an iguana that was literally underfoot.

"Dad, look out!" Jenny shouted.

I froze, stopping my boot two inches above the creature's head. It didn't even blink.

As I recovered from my near-misstep, Paula Tagle, our naturalist guide for the day, reviewed the rules. "One, don't touch the animals." (Jenny shot me a grin.) "Two, don't take anything—*anything.*" (A glance toward the L.L.Bean-clad septuagenarian holding a seashell.) "Three, don't bring any food onto the islands. And four, stay with your group; don't stray off the trails or beyond the marked areas, and don't wander around on your own."

Jeremy whispered to me, "Do we really have to stay with the group? Can't we just explore on our own?" There was only one answer: When in the Galápagos, you go with the group. So we walked with everyone else, our straggling line rising over boulders and slithering past sere silver-green scrub until we came to a bleak, wind-blasted depression.

"We're approaching a prime blue-footed booby nesting spot," Paula said. A moment later we turned a corner and there they were. At first glance—at least to my untrained eyes—they looked like any other gray-and-white birds. But then I spotted my first pair of blue feet. Superb, magnificent, like Dr. Seuss creatures come to life. Blue feet to the left of me, blue feet to the right of me, blue feet in the sky above me and nearly under my feet: "Honey!" my wife, Kuniko, called as I narrowly missed placing a big brown boot on two webbed blue beauties, whose owner looked up at me with curious brown eyes.

"Excuse me, your boobiness," I said with an elaborate bow.

Just then, a booby landed to our left with a feathery flourish, splaying its feet out, like Fred Flintstone braking his prehistoric car.

"See that display?" Paula asked. "That's the male's way of attracting a mate."

"Guys," Jenny sighed.

Around another bend we witnessed another mating ritual, which I came to think of as the blue-footed booby stomp. Two birds face each other, and one lifts its left foot high in the air, holds it there, and then sets it ceremoniously down. It does the same with its right foot, like a blue-soled sumo wrestler limbering up before a match. Watching them, I realized that there was no comparison between seeing this on the small screen in my living room and actually being here.

It only got better, especially for Jenny and me. Having lagged a little behind the others, we were strolling along when, on the path right in front of us, a female lifted herself to reveal a bright white egg.

"Dad!" Jenny cried, gripping my arm and pointing. Right then, the shell cracked and a new, wet chick appeared. We watched, stunned, as it struggled into the world and its mother plopped protectively over it.

"I've never seen anything like that," Jenny said.

Me neither, I thought. Me neither.

I hadn't really associated the Galápagos with underwater life, but as we plunged beneath the waves off Isla La Tortuga, I realized I had omitted an important part of the equation. Black-white-and-yellow Moorish idols with thin arcing top fins, blue-eyed damselfish, and banded butterflyfish swam lazily below us. A pair of sea turtles stroked gracefully by. I finned ahead through a school of brilliant gold-and-blue surgeonfish, which parted to pass me. For a few glorious moments their fins were close enough to tickle my cheeks.

I had been hoping for some bonding family moments, and as we poured out our day's stories over dinner that night aboard the ship, I realized that there was something about encountering these extraordinary creatures in their own wild world that cleansed the mind and tugged at the soul.

In the old days, Paula told us, sailors thought the islands were enchanted because they seemed to drift; they were never quite where mariners' maps said they would be. The islands were also working some kind of magic on us, but still, there was the occasional minor mutiny, like when Jenny announced over dessert the next night, "I'm not going to the lecture tonight."

"Why not?" Kuniko and I asked simultaneously. Not go to the lecture? It was unthinkable.

"I'm suffering from an advanced case of I.O.," Jenny said.

"Ai-yo?" I asked, imagining some sort of exotic malady.

"I.O.—Information Overload," she said, and then wandered off to stargaze on deck.

Over the next few days, I too began to experience symptoms of I.O. On every excursion, we had a naturalist assigned to our group, who was invariably a walking encyclopedia, proffering a staggering array of information about whatever serendipity sent our way.

Our morning walk on Isla Genovesa began with the unusual discovery of a frigatebird skull near the path. Picking it up, Paul said, "See the little channels that run down the beak here? They're unique to the frigatebird. It desalinates water through its eyes and the salt runs out down these channels in its beak. Very efficient.

"Oh look!" he continued, pointing to a speck in the sky. "There's a lava gull, the rarest gull in the world. There are only about 800 of them; they're endemic to the Galápagos. Completely gray and they have a very funny laugh. They're little scavengers; I've seen them pick up booby eggs and smash them to get at the food inside."

I was filled with guilt, wonder, and longing. Who knew the world was so rich with facts—but who could possibly retain them all? Wouldn't it be nice to take a morning off and just sit on the deck in the sun, sipping something cool? But who knew what I'd miss? That would be the day everyone would come back exclaiming about the once-in-a-lifetime (fill in the blank) they'd seen.

I tuned back in to Paul's narration. "Ah! Now here we have the large ground finch. You've heard about Darwin's finches and how they were the key to his theory of evolution? On each island the finches developed different characteristics in order to survive. Well, the large ground finch has developed a beak that enables it to crack open and eat enormous seeds—look at that beak! It could probably crack open a Brazil nut. But the thing is, to have a beak that big and a body so small is very disproportionate, so when it jumps around, it always seems to be pitching forward. Its small body seems to be trying to catch up with its big bill."

It was dazzling and dizzying. In fact, the naturalists provided four checklists for guests—one each for plants, birds, and fish, and another that combines mammals and reptiles—to keep track of what they see. One afternoon Jenny and Jeremy kept count and identified thirty-two entries on the mammals-and-reptiles list, sixty-six birds, sixty-seven plants, and seventy-eight fish.

At the Charles Darwin Research Station in the main town of Puerto Ayora, on Isla Santa Cruz, researchers are doing vital work, trying to redress some of the biggest problems man has introduced to the islands, such as the goats that eat the vegetation indigenous creatures need to survive. The Ecuadorian government has been performing a delicate juggling act since it declared much of the islands a national park in 1959. That same year the Charles Darwin Foundation was established, and five years later the research station opened. The station works closely with the Galápagos National Park Service to monitor the wildlife on the islands and the interaction between the species, including humans. In this setting, we are the threat—that's why we're guarded by naturalists and confined to narrow paths while the animals and birds roam free.

The researchers and naturalists have won small but significant victories, such as raising 2,500 tortoises and repatriating them on their native islands, where they had been nearly wiped out by human predation and goats.

We encountered several of those Santa Cruz tortoises one afternoon in the island's lush highlands. There, in a world of spindly evergreens, moss-draped cat's-claw brush, and lush, broccoli-like *scalesia* trees, we came upon a field of tall, dripping grasses where a group of giant tortoises had paused on their laborious migratory journey to the ocean. With their thick-ringed carapaces, scaly bent-in legs, long leathery necks, and squat, wrinkled heads, the tortoises seemed survivors of another age.

"Paula says fossils show that tortoises—or at least mammals a lot like tortoises—were alive when dinosaurs lived," Jenny told me.

Ah, I thought, not even I.O. can keep the good stuff from sinking in.

I squatted down in front of one tortoise and tried to imagine the weight of the shell on my back, the slow, plodding journey over mud and rock and sand. "I wonder what it's thinking?" I said aloud, lost in my reverie.

"Not much," Jeremy said, walking by. "Paul said their brains are about as big as a walnut."

In ensuing days, we witnessed a bloody head-butting battle between land iguanas, walked over ropy flows of *pahoehoe* lava, followed a zigzagging school of leaping dolphins, spied vermilion flycatchers and Galápagos penguins, explored moonscapes of rust-colored volcanic spatter cones, and contemplated repeatedly the sheer miracle that life had ever taken root on these distant, bleak, and barren islands. While snorkeling, Jeremy encountered a shark that was bigger than him, and on another day, a couple of frisky sea lions seemed to single Jenny out as their playmate. Kuniko had gone from amazement at not having to use a zoom lens to becoming emotional at the idea of so many different species living together in raucous harmony on these isles. And I had my castaway hour.

If we are lucky, we take a few journeys in life that send roots deep inside us, that live and grow with us. If we are extraordinarily lucky, we get to share such a journey with others we love, and it becomes a bridge between us.

Our Galápagos odyssey was just such a bridge. Our dinner conversations are still enlivened by sharks and sea lions, birds and iguanas. And as I recall the beating sun and the screeching birds, it occurs to me that maybe we are unwitting accomplices in a greater evolution than even Darwin knew, one designed to bring back seeds of peace and wonder to plant in the hard rock of our larger world.

Machu Picchu Magic

*After six extraordinarily fulfilling years at Lonely Planet, in early
2007 I decided to spread my writing and editing wings and become
a freelancer. So I was unfettered in early 2010 when a high-spirited
travel website named Gadling asked if I would become their features
editor, commissioning and editing high-quality literary articles and
writing my own stories regularly as well. I leapt at the chance, and a
few months later, I was able to assign myself a trip to a place I'd been
wanting to visit for decades: Machu Picchu. As with Uluru and the
Galápagos, this longtime longing freighted the journey with anticipation and apprehension from the beginning. Could the site possibly meet
my expectations? As it turned out, as so often happens with travel,
that quest for one particular experience led me to multiple, unexpected
lessons and riches, and I ended up writing a five-part series about my
explorations throughout the Sacred Valley. But my two days in those
airy, isolated Inca ruins, described in this excerpt, were the highlight of
the trip, where a connection occurred that I will never forget.*

FOR DECADES, MACHU PICCHU HAD BEEN at the top of my Places to Go list, but somehow, in twenty years as a travel writer visiting more than seventy countries, I still hadn't gotten there. In the spring of 2010, I was beginning to despair that I ever would. Then, through a combination of serendipities, I was invited to take an eight-day trip to the Sacred Valley, culminating in a visit to Machu Picchu.

I spent my first days in the Sacred Valley exploring cultured, cosmopolitan Cusco and the ancient sites of Moray, Pisaq, and Ollantaytambo. Then, on my third day, I awoke at 5:40 to bird trills, wood smoke-scented air, and barely containable excitement. Today was a day I'd been waiting for most of my traveling life: We were going to Machu Picchu!

My guide, Manuel, and I hit the highway at 6:00 A.M., passing sheep, pigs, and cows being herded into pens and villagers in brightly woven capes and great hats walking along the side of the road. After twenty-five minutes we arrived in Ollantaytambo, where porters in bright red ponchos waited for Inca trail trekkers; too pressed for time to make the four-day trek, we were taking the quick route: a storybook blue train to Aguas Calientes, the town nearest Machu Picchu, where a bus would wend to the base of the site.

On the twenty-minute train ride, Manuel pointed out where bridges had been washed out or railroad tracks twisted and tossed into the river by the floods that had raged a half year before: stark reminders of nature's raw power. This train, he said, had restarted operations only three months earlier. I thought of the Inca temples we'd seen and of Manuel's words at the beginning of our trip: "The Spaniards called them idolators and maybe they were—but I think they did very well; they had a big respect for nature."

Then we reached booming, ragtag, pizzeria-and-hostel Aguas Calientes, where we walked through a market maze and boarded the bus for the twenty-minute back-and-forth bounce up the dusty road to the ruins.

Here's the thing about Machu Picchu: No matter how many photographs you've seen, stories you've read, or posters you've absorbed, nothing can prepare you for the surreal whoosh of actually being there. From the spot where the bus drops you, you walk up some narrow stairs and some winding paths, the sun beating on you, the sweat starting to trickle down your back, and then you reach a level area and take a few more steps and—whoosh!—suddenly there it is, spreading out before you, the gray granite walls and poky roof remains and green open lawns and jungly green rock-thrusts just beyond. Suddenly it hits you: Machu Picchu—I've arrived!

For a while you just stand and stare, absorbing it, letting it seep into you. Then eventually you become aware of the other travelers, some as stunned as you, and you decide it's time to head into the ruins. And then time suspends, and you spend two, three, four—you don't know how many—hours wandering, letting your hands trail along the rock, smelling the grass and the granite baking in the high-altitude sun. You visit the agricultural sector and the industrial zone, the Temple of the Three Windows and the Temple of the Condor, the Sacred Square and the priests' chamber, the House of the Virgins of the Sun, the Watchman's Hut, the cemetery, the Temple of the Sun and the sundial. But what you are really doing is walking through time.

You're imagining what it was like 500 years ago when a thousand people lived here—their woven clothes, the potatoes and maize they grew, the grain they stored, the granite they dragged laboriously from the quarry and the gold and silver and chisels, the wood and water, they used to break down and shape the stone. You imagine the runners arriving from Cusco, the robed priests, the weavers and warriors, the singers and teachers and pottery-makers.

And then you're imagining what it was like ninety-nine years ago, when a twelve-year-old boy brought a discouraged Hiram Bingham to this rocky revelation. What must it have felt like to gaze on this tumble-jumble of intricately wrought walls and plazas, trees and vines? You imagine the crescendo of emotion and astonishment, the arc of enlightenment, as Bingham gradually realized what he'd found, what he called the Lost City of the Incas.

And then you think about what this discovery set off, a succession of events every bit as tangled and dramatic as those ruins: A foreigner recognizes the significance of this remote site, clears and plunders it, and in so doing creates a global icon that is responsible for sustaining as much as 80 percent of the local economy today, and that has literally put Peru on the international tourist map. This eventually encourages the Peruvian government to reallocate significant resources to study and preserve other ancient sites and artifacts in the area. The ever-swelling procession of Machu Picchu pilgrims, even as it underpins and integrates the local economy, threatens to undermine and disintegrate the site itself.

You recall what Manuel said on the train, how the torrential rain and floods of earlier this year dramatically demonstrated just how economically fragile the economy of the Sacred Valley is, how much it depends on this one site: From February to April, when floods took out those tracks from Ollantaytambo to Aguas Calientes, 78 percent of visitors to the region canceled their trips.

So visiting Machu Picchu is, like the site itself, multi-layered: There's the historical backstory, the cultural backstory, and the economic backstory. And then there's the pure human experience of being present at Machu Picchu. All of this roiled inside me as we roamed the ruins. I felt a pulsing presence there, but something wasn't quite connecting, somehow it wasn't getting through to me. Before the thought formed in my head, I knew it in my heart: I had to come back at dawn.

The next morning I awoke as the sun was just starting to tint the sky, and made my way in the crisp Andean air through the warren of just-opening stalls selling booklets, blankets, and bug repellent, to the Aguas Calientes bus stop. With about two dozen Peruvian guides and Western and Japanese tourists, I piled into the bus for the weaving 1,500-foot ascent to the ruins. As the bus jounced and switchbacked through the lightening dawn, a feeling I'd had for years, a yearning, an expectation—that something was waiting for me at Machu Picchu, that something would be revealed to me there—weighed undeniably in my stomach and my mind.

As the sky brightened, I worried that I was too late. But I had forgotten that Machu Picchu, despite its high altitude, is still a bowl surrounded by towering peaks. I raced up to the site and saw with relief that while the peaks to the west were tipped with bright sunlight, the ruins were still in shade. I made my way directly to the sundial, known as Intihuatana or "hitching post of the sun," which sits atop a pyramid-like construct of terrace and wall in the site's northwest quadrant.

I positioned myself at the sundial and waited, absorbing the stony stillness and the fresh scent of grass, the texture of tree. I watched the sun's rays light the peaks behind and around me, slowly getting higher and higher, closer and closer.

Minutes passed. The molecules in the air ever so slightly brightened. Then, in a suspended moment, light flared over the top of the mountain directly in front and touched the sundial.

I was looking through the lens of my camcorder when it happened, and at the moment the sun appeared, rays shot out in six searing streaks at forty-five-degree angles. I felt like one streak was searing through me as well. I felt transfixed, transformed. For a suspended moment I felt drawn into the sun, enwrapped by the sun, plucked into some profound energy-stream of sun worship that coursed through the ground where I stood. This flowing energy seemed to stitch through me and through the world around me—the sundial, the rock plazas, doorways, and walls, the temples and the terraces. For a moment I felt a thoughtless understanding, a pure, empty-headed universe-connection, a solar spear-tip that pierced my heart and soul.

Then it was gone. A group of gossiping students clambered over the rocks, guides replayed their learned lectures, camera-wielding couples postured and posed. But somehow, everything had been transformed.

In retrospect, all I can say is that some deep energy radiates from that place. It's a combination of the altitude, the pristine quality of the ruins themselves, the purity of the air and the sky and the sun—and something else too, a kind of spiritual energy that courses like water-springs through the site. I had felt it on the Sacred Plaza and by the Temple of the Sun, but I felt it especially at Intihuatana at dawn: the hitching post of the sun.

At mid-morning, Manuel joined me and we took a walk along the Inca Trail. Most trekkers take the trail from Ollantaytambo or from an intermediate stop called Kilometer 104 along the rail line to Aguas Calientes, but Manuel and I met at the Watchman's Hut and walked up the trail in the opposite direction, away from the ruins and toward the Sun Gate, or Intipunku, where trekkers first see Machu Picchu. We shared the paved path with orchids and llamas and workers who were trying to repair one section of the trail that had been weakened during the rains. Looking into the jungle to the right of the trail we could see more Inca walls in the thick shade. Manuel said there were probably Inca walls scattered throughout the mountains. The dense slopes seemed alive with them, echoing with the spirit of the people who tilled, ate, and slept, planted, played, and prayed here 500 years before.

We reached Intipunku and then continued along the Inca Trail away from the site. We descended into a world of luxurious blossoms and thick cloud forest shadows. I remarked to Manuel that I was amazed by how well the path was paved, and he told me that at its height, the Inca empire had been laced by a network of 19,000 miles of trails, virtually all paved. I stopped and touched my hand to the rough stone and tried to conjure the imagination and organization, technology and toil, required to complete such a feat. I tried to picture the worker who had placed the very stone on which I stood, whose fingers had touched the very pocks and ridges my fingertips traced. What did he eat? Where did he sleep? What did he dream?

We walked for a half hour to a point where we could see another ruin on a mountain slope: Winay Wayna, a cleared site most trekkers detour to explore. I thought of the deep-shaded walls we'd passed before—who knew what secret cities these vast jungles still held?

The trails wound on and on, I realized, some into the cloud forest fastnesses, some into the secret cities of the soul. Then I thought back to that dawn moment when some inexplicable energy had stitched the sun to all—and on that lonely, well-trod mountain trail, I finally felt whole.

⌒

A Pilgrim at Stinson Beach

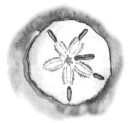

Stinson Beach, in Northern California's Marin County, is the natural equivalent of Ryoanji or Notre-Dame for me. I first discovered it in the late 1980s during my ramblings as the Examiner's Travel Editor. *Something about the place touched me deeply and immediately, and it quickly became a place where I would go at the beginning of each year for a kind of gathering and grounding of myself. Over the years, these journeys expanded to other seasons as well, and this piece describes a pilgrimage in the summer of 2011, when much had changed in my life from those first visits two decades before. I wrote this essay for Gadling. As with so many of the stories in this book, writing for an understanding editor—that is, me—allowed me to write exactly the way I wanted, infusing these reflections and questions, this attempt to make sense of things, with what I hope is a poignant poetry.*

JULY 20, 2011; 11:30 A.M.—I'm sitting at the southern tip of Stinson Beach, a glorious mile-long stretch of sand that borders the unincorporated, population 650 hamlet of the same name in Marin County, Northern California.

Stinson Beach is a ragged, flip-flops, bikinis, and board shorts kind of town, and whether you're a Bay Area visitor or resident, it's a terrific place to stop. A couple of inviting restaurants face each other across the sole street—famed Highway 1—that runs through town; both have sun-umbrella'd patios that are intimations of heaven on a balmy, blue-sky day like today. There are arts and crafts galleries, a quintessential little-bit-of-everything market, B&Bs, and a beguiling bookstore with a compact, ecumenical, and eminently Marin mix of books ranging from Zen treatises and Native American history and culture to mainstream mysteries and fiction, and a proud selection of work by local authors.

I love these riches, but they're not why I come here. Stinson Beach is about an hour's winding drive from my house, so it's not exactly an on-a-whim destination for me; rather it's a touchstone place where I come to gather myself. And today I need gathering.

So here I am, ensconced on a rock beyond an outcrop of massive boulders that separates this thin slice of sand from the main beach, where a couple hundred people are blissfully surfing, strolling, and sunbathing.

I've been in this spot for twenty minutes and I haven't seen anyone—except a teenaged couple who appeared holding hands literally just as I wrote "I haven't seen anyone" and jumped when they saw me and now have abruptly turned back—and I like it that way.

In the 1980s and '90s, when I was the Travel Editor at the San Francisco newspaper, I used to make a pilgrimage here every spring to write a column. This was the place where I gathered my thoughts, looked back on the triumphs and failures of the year past and ahead to the new year's goals and dreams.

It's still a good place to take stock of things. The simplicity of the scene strips away the veneers of life, reduces the distracting complexities. Sea. Rocks. Sand. Sun. That's it. The spareness helps me—makes me—slow down and pay attention.

The roar and swash of the waves echo in my ears, the salty sea-smell fills my nose, the sun warms like a hot compress on my shoulders, my toes wiggle into the wet cool sand. The water white-froths in, spreads into rippling fans over the sand, then rushes back. Again. And again.

A seagull web-walks through the waves, leaps onto a rock, scans the water for food. It prances with oddly brittle legs along the sand, flaps to the top of a rock, and imperiously surveys the waves.

A slick six-foot seaweed pod washes onto the beach. A tiny insect scurries over my keyboard, a neon-green bug lands briefly on my screen.

I let the sea wash over me, let the waves fill my head and lungs, lose myself to this inconceivably old and ageless place.

I think: This is the same scene I witnessed two decades ago, quite possibly even the same rock I sat on then, scribbling in my journal as I tap into my laptop now. And if I come back in twenty years, it will almost certainly be the same still.

But of course, much has changed in those two decades. My children have grown up and moved on. My dad and other loved ones have passed away. New jobs, new places, new books, old dreams.

And suddenly these words flow into my brain: Where does it all come together? What does it mean?

The sea swashing ceaselessly scrubs the mind clean.

I palm the rough, sandy surface of the boulder to my left, warmed by the sun, cradling sand in its pocks and green ridges of moss in its cracks, etched by wind, wave, and rain.

Wisps like smoke from a seaborne fire drift around me, and on the horizon a bank of gray-blue fog gathers, curling at the top so that it looks like a frozen tidal wave. I think of the tsunami in Sendai, where my daughter traveled recently and saw the destruction with her own eyes, where the local man who was guiding her broke down and cried. All those uprooted lives....

Where does it come together? What does it mean?

The waves push glinting pebbles onto the shore, fan, recede. The seagull flaps away, unsatisfied, searching. Life is precarious, uncertain, brief. There is a precious precariousness at the heart of all things.

The sea swashing ceaselessly scrubs the mind clean.

The waves roar-splash in, getting a little closer now. The tide is coming in; the blue pebble we inhabit is turning in the celestial sea.

Where does it come together? What does it mean?

Focus. Enjoy the moment while you have it. Enjoy your loved ones while you have them. Recognize the gifts the world gives you: Inhale the sea, sink your toes into the sand, let the ocean-roar silence your mind.

Then take this simple scene home with you: Sun. Sand. Rocks. Sea.

The sea swashing ceaselessly scrubs the mind clean.

What it all comes down to, I think, is the relationships you forge, the experiences you embrace, the lessons you bestow, the bridges you make, the ideals you seed, the love you live and leave.

Dedicate yourself to creating something of value with your days. Something that will last.

The sea swashing ceaselessly scrubs the mind clean.

Where does it come together? What does it mean?

Sun. Sand. Rocks. Sea. A Stinson Beach clarity.

Japan's Past Perfect

Almost immediately after I left Lonely Planet in 2007, Keith Bellows, then the Editor in Chief of National Geographic Traveler *magazine, asked me to become a Contributing Editor, writing a monthly column about new books with a distinctive sense of place, as well as essays and feature stories. "Japan's Past Perfect" resulted from a conversation we had in his office about my favorite place in Japan, my wife's home island of Shikoku, and why it was special for me, from its pristine nature to its kind and welcoming character as a traditional place of pilgrimage. My challenge with this story was to find a way to write "publicly" about the spirit and charms of a place that had such a deeply personal connection for me. As it turned out, my wife's family provided the perfect compass for my explorations to find the heart of Shikoku.*

⌒

I'M SITTING ON THE POLISHED WOODEN STEPS of a 300-year-old farmhouse in Japan's Iya Valley, looking out on a succession of mountain folds densely covered in deep green cedars. Skeins of morning mist rise from the valley floor, hang in wispy balls in the air, and tangle in the surrounding slopes. No other houses are visible. The only sound is the drip of predawn rain from nearby branches and from the farmhouse's roof of thick thatch. The faint scent of charcoal from last night's hearth rides on the air. I feel as if I'm in the hermit's hut in a 17th-century ink-and-brush painting.

"Extraordinary, isn't it?" says Paul Cato, the expatriate manager of this farmhouse, inn, and living-history classroom. "There are mornings when I wake up here and wonder what century I'm in."

We're at Chiiori, the project of an American author named Alex Kerr, who fell in love with this part of Japan when he was a student in Tokyo in the 1970s and bought this farmhouse as a way to preserve the traditions he treasured.

The Iya Valley is set deep in the mountainous interior of Shikoku, the smallest of Japan's four principal islands, cradled between Kyushu to the west and the main island of Honshu, with the Inland Sea to the north and the Pacific Ocean to the south.

I fell in love with Shikoku in the 1970s too, on a visit with my then girlfriend, Kuniko, who brought me to her family home here from the university in Tokyo, where we were both living. On that trip I discovered a Japan I hadn't known existed: a place of farms and fishing villages, mountainside shrines and seaside temples, rugged seacoasts and forested hills, time-honored traditions and country kindness. Thirty-two years later, in the summer of 2010, I've come back with Kuniko to celebrate our twenty-eighth anniversary and to see if I can rediscover that special place. While Kuniko relishes time at home with her family, I'm on a solo sojourn tracing pilgrims' trails and winding one-lane roads in search of this lost Japan.

Kuniko's hometown, Johen, is a tranquil place of about 9,000 people in the southwestern corner of Shikoku. Although it is a main island, Shikoku is what most Japanese consider *tooi inaka,* the deep countryside. Though there are a handful of famous sights—the 17th-century castles of Matsuyama and Kochi, Ritsurin Koen garden in Takamatsu, and the hot spring spa of Dogo Onsen in Matsuyama—and though three bridges now link the island to Honshu (the first opened in 1988), Shikoku remains a mystery to the average Japanese. It's even more mysterious to foreigners, who rarely venture this far off the beaten path.

On my first visit here, I literally fell off the beaten path. Everything was going beautifully until Kuniko and I reached her family's house, which was located on a lane that seemed narrower than our rental car, with a ditch on one side and a stream on the other. When I tried to turn the corner, a rear wheel slipped into the ditch. And that's how I met my future parents-in-law, asking if they could help me lift my car from the trench. Kuniko's mother, Obaachan, recalls this moment thirty-two years later, as the entire family gathers outside their home to bow me off on a sunny September day. "Don-san, stay away from the ditches!" she calls in Japanese as I pull away.

I'm bound for Cape Ashizuri, the island's southernmost tip. Last night, over sushi, beers, and a shiny new Shikoku map, I had asked Kuniko's parents and two brothers to tell me where to go to find the heart of Shikoku. Kuniko's older brother, Nobuhisa, had nominated Cape Ashizuri, the same place he took us on my first visit. "Be sure to take this road," he said, tracing a squiggle with his chopstick. "For me, that's the best way to see what we call *aoi kuni Shikoku:* 'blue country Shikoku.' Blue sky, blue mountains, blue rice paddies, blue sea." Blue rice paddies? He noted my quizzical look. "In old Japanese, *aoi* means both blue and green."

A half hour out of Johen, I'm already immersed in classic *aoi* scenery: a deep blue sky over evergreen-cloaked mountains, sloping down to emerald rice paddies with a silver-glinting river ribboning through. There are hints of human presence: handmade scarecrows in straw hats placed among the paddies, wooden farmhouses darkened by age, and a diminutive Shinto shrine, with its stout *torii* gateway and sacred rope, set at the foot of one slope.

After a couple of hours driving through a thousand shades of green, I stop in a one-street hamlet of about two dozen wooden homes. The main street curves along the seafront, past a placid row of shops: vegetable market, hardware store, hair salon, bakery. Behind one house, three men in wide-brimmed straw hats tend a fire of backyard vegetation, the smoke stinging the air. At the end of the street, a bent old woman in a sunbonnet pushes a three-wheeled walker. She smiles and bows as I pass. Three kids pedal by on bikes. In the half-moon harbor, fishing boats gently rock. A thickly forested hillside rises steeply behind the houses, and gray cemetery obelisks zigzag in patches of cleared land up the slope. The summer air is still.

"Wah!" the grandmotherly woman behind the counter at the bakery says when I walk in. "A foreign guest!" She is about five feet tall and is dressed in the region's traditional blue and white dyed *kasuri* pants and a floppy floral shirt. Her wrinkled, tanned face crinkles into a bright smile.

I ask if she grew up in this village.

"Oh, yes, I was born here and have lived here all my life." She counts on her fingers. "Seven decades."

Has she ever thought about living anywhere else?

"Oh no!" she quickly responds. "Why would I want to live anywhere else?"

How about the young people, I ask, do they stay here, too?

"Ah, well, the young people," she sighs, "they don't think there's much to do here, so they all go to Nagoya or Kobe. They prefer the city. But I like it here; it's peaceful and close to nature. For me, there's no reason to leave."

When I pass her some coins to pay for my canned ice coffee, she waves them away. "I'm honored to have a foreign guest," she says. "Thank you for visiting Shikoku. Have a safe journey!"

Threading my way through fish-pungent villages, I eventually reach the tip of Cape Ashizuri and stand on the lookout point where Kuniko, Nobuhisa, and I stood thirty-two years before. I gaze at the gleaming white lighthouse, the craggy coast, the cedar-covered mountains sliding into the sea. This is a picture I carried in my head and heart all those years—pristine, peaceful, offering a wideness of sight and soul that you never find in urban Japan. I call Kuniko and describe the scene.

"Yes," she says, as if she's known this all the time, "that's why I was able to marry you. Shikoku opens up your mind and your heart like no other place in Japan can."

That night I stay in a nearby inn with a sweeping view of rice fields, mountains, and one of the longest white-sand beaches in Japan—and an owner whose own mind and heart seem as expansive as the view.

"Welcome to Kaiyu Inn!" Mitsu Ohkada booms in English when I walk into the open-to-the-breezes lobby. He started the inn after years working at an international hotel chain in Bali, he tells me. "I love the slow pace and the tranquility here—and of course the nature. Do you know *aoi kuni Shikoku*?"

I do.

The next day, I'm white-knuckling along one-lane roads through the green, steeply sloping mountains of the Iya Valley. Villages are carved into occasional clearings on the mountainsides, and I pass farmers hoeing and digging, with occasional bushels of barley standing on hardscrabble plots. It's late afternoon when I reach Chiiori, the renovated farmhouse-cum-inn where Kuniko's younger brother, Fumiyaki, had urged me to stay.

Chiiori is a vision straight out of a Japanese storybook: a long, low wooden farmhouse crowned by a shaggy roof of two-foot-thick thatch.

"*Irasshaimase!* Welcome!" calls Paul Cato, the American resident manager, as he slides open the inn's wooden doors. The interior of the house is exquisitely empty, one open room about forty feet long by twenty feet wide, all gleaming wooden floorboards, thick exposed wooden beams, rice paper lanterns, and rice paper screens. Stepping over the threshold is like stepping back in time.

"That's actually true," Cato says when I mention this feeling. "Chiiori is an actual 300-year-old farmhouse. Author Alex Kerr had fallen in love with traditional Japanese architecture and aesthetics, and his dream was to restore this place so that it resembled as closely as possible a typical Iya farmhouse of three centuries ago.

"It's not just about the architecture; it's the way of life, too. Look up," Cato says. Instead of a ceiling, I can see all the way to the roof's blackened rafters. "In the old days," he explains, "tobacco was a primary crop. Because of the wet climate, the farmers would hang the leaves from the rafters to dry inside, over the smoking hearths. That's why there's no ceiling. They were ingenious in other ways, too." He lifts a broad wooden floorboard to reveal a pile of stored potatoes. "Alex loved the farming customs and old-fashioned peace he found in Iya, and he wanted to preserve them. Volunteers have come from throughout Japan and around the world to live here, work the crops, and maintain the farmhouse, and local farmers teach the traditional techniques. So this truly is a piece of old Japan."

One modern feature of Chiiori is excellent Wi-Fi, and I get an email from Kuniko. "We're following your route," she writes. "How is Iya and Chiiori? Fumiyaki says it's the most peaceful place on Shikoku."

As dusk shrouds the mountains, Cato and I slice and dice radishes, onions, cucumbers, carrots, potatoes, and pumpkins from Chiiori's garden for a rich stew that we eat around the charcoal-fired hearth. Then I snuggle into thick futons under 300-year-old wooden beams and 25-year-old thatch. I tap out a sleepy email: "Please thank Fumiyaki for his great advice: Staying here is an immersion course in the relation between nature and man."

The following afternoon, I arrive at Okuiya Niju Kazurabashi, or "double vine bridge." Except for a lone ticket taker, the site is absolutely deserted. I descend a hundred steps into a primeval scene of thick foliage and floating clumps of mist. Two "wedded" bridges appear spectrally—each a set of intertwining vines stretched across a rushing river. The higher and longer bridge is traditionally known as the male; the lower, shorter one the female. Fog rises from the river and obscures the surrounding hills.

Of all the sights in Iya Valley—the mountains and temples and hot springs—this is the one other place Fumiyaki told me I had to go. "The bridge was said to be built by the Heike clan in the 12th century, when they fled from Kyoto after losing a civil war with the Genji clan," he told me. "The Heike settled deep in the mountains of Iya, and they built these vine bridges for protection, because they could easily destroy them if the Genji ever approached. Only two vine bridge sites remain. The other one is touristy, but you can get a sense of old Shikoku at this one."

A sudden wind sways the vine bridge, slick with the day's rain. Tentatively I set a sandaled foot on the first vine-entwined wooden plank, wishing I'd brought better footwear. I shift my weight, take a deep breath, and set my other foot on the second plank. Swoop!

My sandal slips, and suddenly I'm sprawled on my rump and my foot is wedged between wooden planks. I try to wiggle it out, and the vines claw and cling, lodging it deeper. The woods, the mist, the ghosts of the Heike warriors, all close in on me.

"The people of Iya still believe that gods live in the mountains," Fumiyaki had said, and now I understand why. I can hear them laughing in the trees.

Finally I find a way to detach my foot from my sandal, scratch and scrape my foot through the planks, and extricate my sandal from the bridge. But I can't leave—how could I face Kuniko's family? With the vines dancing and the wind creaking the boughs, I carefully place my re-sandaled foot and clutch the vine-looped handrails with both hands. Focus, focus. Slowly I step from plank to plank, the bridge bouncing and creaking. After a heart-pounding ten minutes, I jump triumphantly onto the other side. I think of Fumiyaki and raise a silent prayer to the mountain gods.

In the main hall at the Zentsuji temple complex, incense spirals into the air and monks intone a solemn chant while a half dozen elderly visitors bow and pray; outside, another young monk assiduously sweeps the dirt ground with a broom made of twigs. At one end of the complex, Japanese tourists led by a flag-wielding guide admire a soaring five-story pagoda; nearby, a quartet of meticulously coiffed women *ooh* and *aah* before a stupendous camphor tree that looks to be older than the temple itself.

Zentsuji is the birthplace of the beloved Buddhist scholar and high priest Kobo Daishi, who built the temple in the early 9th century. This is the place Kuniko's father, Ojiichan, had said I should see. "To understand Shikoku," Ojiichan said, "you have to understand the pilgrimage, which follows in the footsteps of Kobo Daishi. There are eighty-eight temples all around Shikoku in the circuit, and pilgrims—*o-henro-san*—walk from temple to temple to gain wisdom and purity. I remember when I was a little boy the pilgrims would approach our door—you could hear the *ting-ting* of the bells they carried—and my mother would tell me to bring them rice and oranges. That's why we welcome strangers on Shikoku."

A shop displaying books, beads, walking sticks, and other pilgrimage accoutrements entices me, and I lose all sense of time perusing a children's picture book showing the life and legends of Kobo Daishi. When I emerge, pilgrims are everywhere, clad in identical conical bamboo hats and loose, immaculate white jackets and pants, all carrying straight, sturdy staffs. I approach one couple who look to be a father and daughter. Youthful energy radiates from the father's time-lined face. When I ask them about the pilgrimage, the daughter reaches into a shoulder pouch and carefully lifts out a book with a cover of gold and red silk. "At every temple, the priest writes the name of the temple on a page and then stamps it with the temple's stamp," the father says. They turn the pages for me. "Every time I make the pilgrimage, my steps become lighter and my vision becomes clearer. I feel like I can do anything after I've finished the journey," he says.

"Of course," the daughter says, "this is only our 4th circuit. That *o-henro-san* there"—and she points to a wizened man draped in colorful sashes and dressed all in black—"is doing the route for the 333rd time!"

As I watch the pilgrims pray and pose for pictures, I realize that they are a benedictory presence on Shikoku. In their fervent, plodding path, they remind us to slow down and keep a higher spiritual purpose in mind. And I realize too the deep truth of Ojiichan's words, that the tradition of hospitality, kindness, and openness on the island must trace its roots to the pilgrim's own openhearted quest.

I tour the island for two more days, stopping to feel the texture of old straw-and-clay farmhouses, idling in serene fishing villages, bowing to pilgrims I pass. At a hot spring spa, a half dozen middle-aged women befriend me and insist on paying for my dinner. When I'm lost at a coastal intersection, a truck driver goes a half hour out of his way to deliver me to the right highway. At a roadside snack stand, the proprietress asks me if I'm doing the pilgrimage and when I tell her no, that I'm looking for the heart of Shikoku, she exclaims, "Then you're a pilgrim, too!" and presents me with a strawberry shaved ice.

On the fifth day, I arrive back at Johen just as dusk is falling. The family is waiting for me with a feast of fresh-from-the-harbor *katsuo* sashimi and grilled *aji*, and fresh-from-the-garden mushrooms, tomatoes, and cucumbers.

As we sit on tatami mats around a low table, Obaachan fastens me with her bright eyes. "Well," she says, "did you find the heart of Shikoku?"

"I did," I say, and they all look at me expectantly. "But it's not one particular place. I found it in farmers' fields and fishermen's villages, and in the pilgrims who give a sense of the sacred to daily life. And I found it over and over in everyday people who greeted me with a wide spirit and heartfelt hospitality."

For a second I'm not sure if anyone has understood my mangled Japanese. Then they all nod and smile.

Ojiichan ceremoniously pours beer for everyone and raises his glass. "Don-san, it's good to have you home. *Kanpai!*"

We all drain our glasses, then Obaachan raises hers again. "And I'm glad you missed the ditch this time!"

⌒

Home for the Holidays: A Thanksgiving Pilgrimage to Connecticut

I have been going to my childhood home in Connecticut to spend Thanksgiving with my parents since the mid-2000s, when travel across country became too difficult for them. Before then, my family had visited Connecticut for a number of summer and Christmas vacations, and I had written numerous essays about these trips and the meaning of Connecticut for me. But this particular essay was especially poignant: I wrote it for a series on AOL Travel that was focused on the theme of going home for the holidays, and so it propelled me to assess and celebrate the meaning of my Connecticut pilgrimages within the larger context of home. Where was home for me now? What did "home" mean? Writing often helps me make sense of life, and sometimes it produces something even greater. In the process of writing this piece, I embraced family and friends, present and past, near and far, landscape, emotion, and memory, in a new and deeper way, and the interweaving threads of Connecticut, Thanksgiving, and home took on a completing clarity.

IN MY FAMILY, AS IN MANY FAMILIES around the U.S., Thanksgiving has always been a day to gather with loved ones and celebrate family and home. So when I moved from Connecticut and began to raise a family in California three decades ago, my parents would often cross the country to celebrate the holiday with us. Eight years ago, when this trip became too difficult for them, I reversed the route to celebrate with them in Connecticut.

My dad passed away two weeks before Thanksgiving in 2007, and since then, this journey has become an even more precious rite. One trip in particular, in 2011, crystallized the meaning of this pilgrimage for me.

That Thanksgiving was special for a couple of reasons. My daughter, Jenny, had been studying in graduate school on Long Island and had been able to join my mom and me for the previous two holidays. But she would be graduating in June and moving back to California, so this would be her last East Coast Thanksgiving, at least for a while. In addition, my best friend from childhood, Philip Porter, had invited us all to join his family's celebration.

Jenny picked me up at the airport in New York the day before Thanksgiving, and as we drove into the rolling hills of west-central Connecticut, I felt like a puzzle piece clicking naturally into place. I marveled at how deeply the landscape—forests and ponds and round town greens, high-steepled churches and white clapboard houses with manicured lawns and sheltering trees—had become a part of me.

I had grown up in just such a setting in Middlebury, and when we moved my mom and dad to an assisted-living facility in 2007, we found a similarly situated place in neighboring Southbury. That afternoon, as Mom and Jenny admired the woods and pond outside her new home, I discovered a passage I'd written in my journal twenty Thanksgivings before:

This is not the tourist's New England of blazing fall foliage. It's the native's New England of stark brown branches tinged with the barest tips of red against a pewter sky. A cold, dry wind slices through the trees. The grass emanates a shaggy, melancholy gray-green. The sun casts a threadbare shawl over the bony branches in the last light of day, and the sky streaks at sunset with icy rose and purple tatters like some wind-torn medieval banner. Darkness falls at 4:00 P.M.

And yet somehow it exhilarates me. Mom and Dad and I take long walks through these winter-tinged afternoons, and the longer we look, the more we find a profoundly moving beauty in that stark bareness, an amazing range of colors in those grays and browns.

Jenny and my mom began to relive summer visits to Middlebury. Jenny remembered how Grandma and Grandpa would toss Frisbees around our basketball court-sized backyard for her and her brother, Jeremy, to run after. Mom recalled the picnics they'd impetuously concoct on the weathered picnic table under the massive oak tree—plopping fresh-shucked corn into boiling water as Jenny and Jeremy raced down to the bee-buzzing raspberry bushes, returning breathless with overflowing baskets just as the tuna salad sandwiches, corn, and lemonade appeared. I remembered how Dad would pretend to chase his giggling grandkids and how his eyes would glitter as he watched them fly.

Mom laughingly reminded me of how, when I was young, we were all supposed to help with Thanksgiving dinner, but somehow she always ended up creating and choreographing the cranberry sauce and stuffing, mashed potatoes, corn, peas, gravy, crisp-skinned turkey, and pumpkin pie while my brother and I joined the throng of neighborhood kids playing football at the Porters' house up the street.

The Porters didn't live up the street anymore, but when we arrived at Phil's house the next day, we found that his mom and dad were there, as were his brother and sister and their clans. It was a time-travel tableau and a boisterous, bustling, laugh-filled family feast just as Thanksgivings should be, with many a childhood misadventure related.

"Remember," Phil's dad guffawed at one point, "the time the boys fell through the ice into the swimming pool and thought they were going to drown?"

"Oh, yes!" my mom exclaimed, her voice skipping with delight. "When they came dripping back to our house, they dumped half your pool into our kitchen, right in the middle of our holiday party!"

Later that night, as we drove Mom home, her face was glowing. "What a perfect Thanksgiving!" she said. "I haven't laughed that much in years,"

The following day, Jenny drove us to Middlebury. Our former neighbors had recently moved and their house was for sale, so we parked in their driveway and gazed at our old house. After a while, Mom urged Jenny and me to wander into the woods while she waited in the car.

I hadn't been back there in a decade, and I wondered what tricks memory might have played. But soon we came upon the mysterious rectangular stone foundations that had seemed like ancient ruins to a child's mind. Then the rotting boards and wire mesh of a chicken coop appeared, and I told Jenny how the battered door with the fading skull and crossbones—"Look, it's still here!"—had convinced me pirates once lived there. We stepped over streams and toppled trunks, and I talked about how I used to love to watch the yellow-green buds unfolding like secret messages in spring and how I'd thrash through the crackling leaf-carpets of fall. I told her about bounding rabbits and spindly-legged deer, about the beavers we were convinced were there but never saw and about the dreams that took root in that seemingly endless expanse of rock and tree.

When we got back and told Mom about our journey, her eyes glistened. "When you were little, we used to go for walks in those woods," she said. "You'd call them adventures and you'd say, 'Can we go on an adventure now?' Sometimes we'd see foxes or deer and sometimes we'd just listen to the wind in the trees. I loved that."

We sat in stillness in the deepening dusk.

In a sense, nothing extraordinary happened that Thanksgiving. But in another sense, something deep and abiding was revealed to me. I understood the fuller meaning of home. Home is a physical structure. It is the people who lived and live in that structure. And it is the memories that were born there and that we carry with us, wherever we go. Home is the house and the woods and the touch football games, the Porters and the picnics and the treacherous pool. Home is my wife and kids and my mom and dad and all the celebrations we shared—and share still.

And I realized that this is what I'm honoring each Thanksgiving when I make my Connecticut pilgrimage: I'm giving thanks for the home that I carry in my head and in my heart, that roots me when I teeter, lifts me when I tire, connects me to all my earthly adventures past and present and to come, the home that embraces me—and the whole world I cherish—in the bare boughs of love.

BERLIN

BAJA

NICE

PERU

PART TWO:
Encounters

N

MOSTAR

DUBROVNIK

GREECE

JORDAN

PAKISTAN

Kashghar   Tashkurgan   Alam Ata

KENYA

DUBBO

In Love, in Greece, in the Springtime

As I mentioned earlier, when I was Travel Editor at the Examiner, I tried to make my Sunday column a space where I could talk very personally about people, places, and events from my life. My fervent belief was that if I wrote about these precisely and engagingly enough, they would resonate with readers and trigger connections with similar people, places, events, and lessons in their own lives. "In Love, in Greece, in the Springtime," about an enigmatic woman who became my confidante and muse when I lived in Athens and who has been a part of my interior life ever since, was one of those columns where I deeply excavated material from my own past, but in a way that I hoped would embrace and not exclude readers. It was also a chance for me to try to articulate the fundamentally life-changing effects that youthful year in Greece had on me. I hoped this piece would kindle readers' memories of similarly life-changing encounters with their muse, wherever and whoever that muse might be.

IT HAPPENS AT SOME POINT EVERY SPRING: I will be driving innocently along some rural route, and suddenly a certain slant of
sunlight will recall the way the light filtered through the pine
trees along the road that wound up the coast from Athens to
the little taverna no one seemed to know about—no one except
Gisela, the beautiful and mysterious woman with whom I had
fallen ineluctably in love that spring of 1976.

We would install ourselves in peeling white wooden chairs
around a stolid wooden table on the beach, under the pines, and
the kindly taverna owner would bring us huge chunks of hard,
delicious bread, a salad of feta cheese, tomatoes, cucumbers, and
black olives, and glasses of retsina.

We would eat and sip, but mostly we would watch the shimmering sea and listen to the sighing pines, censing the air with
their tangy perfume.

I re-create this scene, and suddenly that whole mind-opening,
life-transforming Grecian year revives in a sun-flooded succession
of images:

I recall the breath-stopping, time-skipping beauty of
just-blossomed scarlet poppies against white marble ruins
at Olympia.

I recall the Peloponnese mountain family who insisted on
sharing their meager Easter feast with my parents and me.

I recall the ethereal geometry and bony patina of the
Acropolis at dawn, before the tourists arrived, and the soul-stirring rite of reading Plato, Socrates, and Aristotle as Apollo's first
rays illumined the site.

I recall unfathomable connections on the island of Crete—
the magical frescoes and sere splendors of Knossos, and the
painter from Chania who showed me the island's harbors and
meadows, churches and town squares through his eyes.

I recall the craggy monasteries and worldly monks of sacred
Mount Athos, and the sensual abandon of the long, embracing

beach at Lindos, on Rhodes, where I communed for a week with a ragtag band of European pilgrims who were all seeking some sort of Aegean answer.

Aegean answers: Hungrily, hesitantly, I would unfold for Gisela my despairs and my dreams, but mostly I would talk about Greece: about the clarity of the rock and the light and how it was teaching me to attend to the present; about the earthy kindness I had encountered everywhere; about the sheer age of the sites and the accumulation of wisdom and sadness and celebration that seemed to hang, poignant, in the Attic air.

Summer came and I left—for Africa and then graduate school, a long, winding road. I never wrote to her, never heard from her.

Now, half of my life later, I wonder: Do we craft our memories, or do our memories craft us?

Now, half of my life later, I know: I went to Greece seeking the roots of Western civilization, and returned with a rootlessness I have never lost.

And every spring the owner shuffles toward us, bearing a laden tray. The sea shimmers. The pines cense and sigh.

The Attic sunlight gleams again in Gisela's laughing eyes.

A Day in the Life of Dubbo

A year after becoming Travel Editor at the Examiner, *I went to Australia to attend a travel conference with my wife and two-year-old daughter. This was my first trip to Australia, and while I didn't have time to undertake an ambitious journey throughout the land, I was determined to find some compact way to get outside the cities and experience rural realities. The Outback—that vast, mysterious, mostly unpeopled expanse—was magnetically alluring, its name alone seeming to promise unimaginable adventure. When I researched ways to get there, I discovered the day trip I describe in this story, and the friendly farmer who guided me indelibly into the heart of the country.*

PETER RENDALL SHIELDED HIS EYES from the midmorning sun and looked out over the green-brown wheat fields and scraggly eucalyptus trees of Dubbo. "Yeah," he said, "that's about what you get here in Dubbo: sheep, a few cattle, some fields of wheat, oats, and barley—and lots of wide-open space."

We had stopped for a "morning tea" of delicious homemade sandwiches, cake, and tea on a dirt road by a dirt field somewhere on the outskirts of Dubbo, a town of 24,000 perched precariously on the edge of Australia's vast and largely uninhabited Outback. After two and a half hours of bumping and bouncing over mostly unpaved roads and along dusty fields, I was taking some time to get used to the stillness.

Suddenly the ringing in my ears stopped—and I was stunned by the silence. The music of no sound, after the clamor of Sydney and San Francisco, was so sweet it was almost overwhelming. Then, like an orchestra tuning before a concert, isolated notes touched my ear, one by one: the trill of a far-off bird, an engine revving on a distant road, a vagrant breeze rustling the grasses, the splash of tea into a plastic cup.

"Yeah, life's a lot slower here," Rendall said, ambling over. "Up with the sun, down with the stars. Not much to do except work the fields and the flocks. Mind you, with the machines breaking down and the crops coming in, dogs messing with your sheep, the planting and the harvesting, the shearing, we're never wanting for things to do."

He looked toward the shimmering hills on the horizon and shook his head. "I couldn't live in the city. It's too busy there, all those tall buildings and the people rushing down the street. It's a different pace there, that's right, a different scale. I like it better here."

I had come to Dubbo on a day tour operated out of Sydney by a company called, dashingly enough, Jolly Swagman Tours.

The tour had begun early that morning, the sun squinting over the horizon at newspaper boys and milk delivery trucks while I squinted out a taxi window at the splendid sandstone buildings, tree-lined streets, and ornate grillwork fences on the way to the Sydney airport.

The Sydney-Dubbo flight was an education in itself. We passed over fairly dense communities for about ten minutes, then the roads and buildings began to thin out. Soon we were flying over spare, desolate, rolling brown hills, uninhabited and uninhabitable, from the look of them. After some time a farm appeared, then a scattering of houses. What seemed to be the outlines of a settlement were silhouetted on the horizon. Otherwise, all I could see from horizon to horizon were those brown, rolling hills, stuck here and there with green trees and crossed by a red road that ribboned over the crests and occasionally dipped into hidden valleys. What do people do for groceries out here? I wondered.

At about 7:20, fifty minutes into the flight and ten minutes before we were due to land, cultivated fields and scattered twelve-house communities began to appear. Then the outskirts of Dubbo became discernible, a great green and brown quilt of hills and crops, dotted with white sheep, seven-structure farmsteads, and bushy, scraggly trees that cast distorted shadows. A paved road came miraculously into sight, then the town itself—red roofs and gray metal roofs, black, multi-lane highways.

It was strangely disjunctive to see all this roof-and-road civilization, this very orderly and ordinary-looking town, in the middle of the Australian version of nowhere. We descended over grassy oblongs and semicircles that seemed to be used for sporting events, a river, a wheeling flock of birds, sheep, cows, sheep, fields, sheep—no golf courses out here, I thought—and suddenly we were bumping and skidding to a stop.

I was greeted at the airport by Rendall's Outback-open smile, hardy handshake, and "How do you do, mate." (He did not, I hasten to add, say "G'day.") Jolly Swagman's Dubbo tour can accommodate up to forty-five people, but on this day I was the sole participant, so, Rendall said, we would follow the trip's basic itinerary, but could also do essentially whatever I wanted to.

He led me to his minivan and outlined the day: touring Dubbo's downtown and outlying farms; pausing for morning tea somewhere on the road; watching a sheep-shearing; having an Aussie barbecue lunch on a farm (his own, as it turned out); taking in a sheep auction; visiting more farms and the Western Plains Zoo; and finally, if time allowed, touring Old Dubbo Gaol and the Pioneer Museum.

Downtown Dubbo is a pleasant place vaguely reminiscent of a town in the American Midwest: wide, well-swept streets lined with one-story buildings that offer a gamut of services and dis-tractions—a hardware store, a produce market, a movie theater, milk bars and restaurants, gas stations, clothing stores, sewing shops, pubs, a five-and-dime.

There were a few broken windows and vacant buildings here and there, but on the whole it looked to be a clean and contented place. The residential streets showed small, trim houses behind small, trim front lawns—nothing extravagant or ostentatious (Perhaps the Outback stunts all ambitions of extravagance, I thought), but just quiet and orderly, practical, comfortable.

"What are the benefits of living here?" Rendall asked, echoing my question. "The most important thing is there's a better family relationship; out here you tend to do things as families. Oh, I guess people aren't as close-knit as they were, not as much as they are still in the smaller towns—but everybody rallies around the schools and the like. Cities don't seem to have that same feeling."

He talked encyclopedically as he drove, telling me just about everything I could ever want to know about Dubbo, from the racial composition of the town ("There are a few Greeks and a few Chinese, but the people are mostly of English stock") to the religious affiliations ("Well now, in order I'd guess you've got the Anglican, then the Roman Catholic, the United, Baptist, Seventh Day Adventist, and so on") to the fact that, as in every rural area I've ever visited, the parents' prime worry is that the kids are leaving the country for the city.

At one point we dropped in on a neighbor farmer and talked about a machine that was being fixed, and about his getting up in the middle of the night to watch over his flock of sheep.

"Why does he have to watch over his sheep in the middle of the night?" I asked when we were on the road again.

"Because a dog's been messing with 'em," Rendall answered. "Your domestic dog, once they learn to kill, the only way to stop 'em is to give 'em a little lead." He looked straight ahead.

"Don't you have to talk with some authorities or something before you do that?" I asked, my innocence about as wide as the wheat field before us.

"Well, when a dog's been hassling your sheep, you can do three things," he said. "You can talk to the owner. If that doesn't work, you can go out like Joe there in the middle of the night, spot the dog and he doesn't come back—that takes care of the problem. Or you can talk to the local authorities and they'll take care of the problem. But once a dog has attacked a sheep, they have it in their blood; they're gone."

"Does everyone have a gun?" I asked.

"Oh, sure, you've got to have a gun out here."

I was beginning to think about frontier justice, and how in some situations people just make their own laws. I was thinking that's fine as long as everyone shares the same laws, and probably that's how life was in the old American West, when suddenly Rendall said, "Look! Over there!"

I could just make out a two-legged being, bounding, bounding, over the dusty plain. A kangaroo!

"There's more!" he shouted.

And sure enough, there were three, four, five of them bounding into a grove of eucalyptus trees.

"This is kangaroo country," he said. "Kangaroos run wild in packs all through here. The kangaroo is nocturnal, you know; it plays and breeds at night and sleeps during the day, so it's hard to see. And it blurs in with the surroundings, too. But we'll see more of 'em before the day is out."

And so we did. But first we would see sheep.

"Grab it by the base of the wool. No, no, not like that. Get your hand in there good and just grab it tight. Now start to run the clippers as close to the body as you can."

I was thinking of childhood haircuts, of squirming in the barber's smooth leather chair until I felt the inevitable cool clip of razor to skin. I felt intense empathy with the sheep.

"But I don't want to hurt it," I said.

The sheep bucked and baaed, as if in accord.

"Don't worry about hurting the sheep. The sheep hardly feels a thing, and it's forgotten about it a moment later," the master sheep-shearer said.

I gingerly ran the shears over the sheep's all-too-pink body, wincing in anticipation of a jerk and a bloody gash. As I worried, I was leaving a very fine layer of very expensive wool.

"No, no, look at what you're missing!" the master sheep-shearer shouted.

So what was I supposed to do?

"Like this," he said, wrestling the animal to the ground, grabbing an oily handful of wool and expertly skimming the shears just over the raw pink flesh.

We were watching one of the rare craftsmen of a difficult art at work, and I was gaining a whole new appreciation of sweaters. "I suppose there'll always be sheep-shearers around," Rendall had said on our way to this farm, "at least until they make a machine to do it—but there are fewer and fewer men to do it, I'll tell you. It's pretty good money, but jolly hard work."

Jolly hard indeed. Beyond the enclosed, wool-littered room where we stood, a pawing, baaing flock of about sixty penned-in sheep waited. And that was just the beginning. By the end of the day, the shearer said, he would have cropped about 150 of the farmer's sheep—about one-tenth of the total—and shoved them baaing and scrambling out another door into the suddenly cold air. And the wages for this day's work? About $175 Australian, the equivalent of $140 U.S.

He sheared sheep pretty regularly five days a week, he said, sometimes more during peak periods. And for all that he would make about $35,000 U.S. a year.

"It's not bad work, but the worst of it is the joints," he said, rubbing his fingers. "I know a mate lost the use of three of his fingers, just couldn't work 'em at all. It's the lanolin, you know; it works into your muscles and sinews until you can't move 'em anymore. Don't know who'll take my place when I go."

After the sheep-shearing we explored the enlightened and enlightening Western Plains Zoo, where representatives of the wildlife of the world roam more than 700 acres of beautifully landscaped open-range exhibit areas, separated according to continent; feasted on a hearty and delicious barbecue lunch with Rendall's family at his farm; took in a weekly sheep and cattle auction, wonderfully raucous with competing moos, baas, barks, and bids; and visited another farm, where we walked through the long fields and I bumped along for a few turns in a crop-tilling tractor.

We toured on, moving from tarred streets to dusty byroads and back again, pausing to photograph kookaburras and kangaroos, talking with farmers we met along the way.

Nothing extraordinary happened, and in many ways that was precisely the point: The tour gave me a great feeling for what happens on a day in the life of Dubbo, and in so doing offered illuminating insights into the realities of rural Australian life.

On another level, and equally important, it slowed me down to the rhythm of Dubbo, made me notice the richness of minute things I'd forgotten in the city: a wreath of wire carefully hung on a fence; the dusty, almost musty smell of turned-up soil on a hot, dry day; the pure power of the burning sun; the poignancy of a tractor hookup rusting in isolation at the edge of a field, or of a far-off plume of dust signaling another human's approach.

The day passed all too quickly, and suddenly it was time to return to the airport and Sydney. As we raced to catch my plane, slanting sunlight colored the landscape a golden orange, a light that somehow seemed to fix the permanence of each blade of grass, each sheep, each tree, each hill. I had been in Australia only three days, and already I had found a place I would never forget.

Over the ensuing week, I explored the chic surprises of Sydney and the sybaritic splendors of the Gold Coast, but in my mind I kept returning to Dubbo. And as I was packing on my last night, I thought back to my first morning in the country, when I had been given a crash course in the Land Down Under at the friendly offices of Tourism Australia.

I remembered staring at a huge map of Australia on one of the office walls, staring as if seeing the country for the first time, although in fact I had been poring over Australia maps for weeks. There was Sydney, there was Dubbo; there was the sliver of civilization that runs along the east coast from Adelaide to Cairns, and the pockets of population around Perth and Darwin. And there, inconceivably beyond them all, was the vast middle of the place, the wide-open, incredible expanse of virtually unpopulated space, the Outback.

Then I recalled Dubbo, how the people had seemed so content despite the toughness of their life, how they had seemed so much closer to the land and the weather. I remembered the astonishment of landing among those roofs and fields in the middle of nowhere, and smiling at the irony of Peter Rendall's words soon after we'd begun our tour: "We call this 'the hub of the West.' You see, the roads from Sydney to Adelaide and from Melbourne to Brisbane pass through here."

And I thought: There are geographical hubs and there are spiritual hubs, and then there are hubs in a completely different sense—places that center you, that bring you back in touch and balance with something deeply important inside yourself.

On my first encounter with all the vastness of Australia, I realized, I had already found one such hub: hot, dusty Dubbo; sweet, silent Dubbo; Dubbo of sheep and shearer, wheat and wide-open space; Dubbo on the edge of the Outback, at the center of the map in my mind.

A Passage to Pakistan

In the spring of 1990, I was feeling restive, in need of some deeply personal-envelope-pushing adventure. The Bay Area was the center of the burgeoning adventure travel industry, and I contacted a local company called InnerAsia Expeditions (now known as Geographic Expeditions, and happily, still a part of my life a quarter-century later). I had long heard rumors of a fabled place in northern Pakistan called Hunza, and InnerAsia had a three-week adventure that went to Hunza and beyond, high into the Himalaya along the equally fabled Karakoram Highway. It sounded like the stuff of dreams and I signed up eagerly. The trip turned out to be even more of an adventure than I had hoped for, and the only way I could do it justice in my articles, I felt, was to break the trip into three segments and write three long pieces for the travel section. Taken together, this is the longest article I have ever written about a trip—but in many ways, this was the most epic trip of my lifetime, and when I reread this account, even a quarter-century later, all the fear, discomfort, wonder, and exhilaration of encountering that unfamiliar world come surging back to me.

Part One: Rawalpindi, Peshawar, and the Khyber Pass

We sat around the table in the dawn-lit dining room at the Shangri-La Hotel in Chilas, Pakistan, a decidedly unparadisiacal place where a policeman had been shot during a public protest two days before, and debated what to do: It had been raining hard for at least forty-eight hours, loosening the rocks above the Karakoram Highway and increasing the possibilities of avalanche and flood. We could risk the highway and reach Islamabad by midnight, which would give us a full day to recuperate in our luxury hotel before the thirty-two-hour journey back to the United States. Or we could wait in Chilas, hoping that the rain would let up so that we could make the trip more safely the following day and drive straight to the airport.

"I don't think we should go," said Tom Cole, the trip leader from the United States.

"I think it will be all right," said Asad Esker, the leader from Pakistan.

The remaining four of us looked at each other, and the prospect of death—imminent death, actual death, death not as a benign abstraction but as a visceral reality—hung palpable in the air.

That dilemma was far in the unimaginable future, however, when I arrived in Islamabad on April 2 at 2:56 A.M.

I had left San Francisco at 11:00 A.M. on March 30 and flown a total of twenty-seven hours—via New York, Paris, and Frankfurt. Now, at last, I was in Pakistan: Hot white letters spelling "Islamabad International" blazed in the darkness, and all around them the same words danced in neon blue Arabic script.

Five of the nine total members of the tour, plus trip leader Tom Cole, had been on the same flight from New York, and we introduced ourselves, stretched sore muscles, and rubbed bleary eyes while waiting for our bags to appear. Soon they did, as did our smiling local guide, Asad Esker, and driver, Ali Muhammad, who whisked us through the dazed and humid night to our luxurious recovery rooms at the Pearl Continental Hotel in nearby Rawalpindi.

I slept fitfully for a few hours, then was awakened at 4:30 by the distant wail of a muezzin calling the Muslim faithful—who comprise 99 percent of the population of Pakistan—to prayer. Raucous crows' caws filled the air, and the rising-falling song of another muezzin braided with the first. Then sirens blared.

What's going on, I wondered. A fire somewhere? Or maybe just the impending sunrise—for we had arrived during the holy month of Ramadan, when Muslims are not supposed to eat or drink between sunrise and sunset.

The dull cacophony continued, muezzins and sirens and crows wailing and blaring and cawing until it seemed as if the whole country was speaking with one voice, and the just-waking day soared and swelled and echoed with the sound of it.

Then a solitary soul, much closer, began his plaintive call. The voice rose, held, and fell. The words were clear and strong and imbued the air with a strange and powerful fervency and mystery. I thought it was a song of supplication and hope—but who was I to say?

I knew nothing, understood nothing; everything was unfamiliar. I was a blank map, onto which Pakistan had just begun its artful scrawl.

After an orientation session in the hotel lobby, our group set out to visit downtown Rawalpindi. This first excursion introduced urban emblems that would reappear throughout the trip: dusty streets loud with horns and crammed with buses, cars, carts, and bicycles. And people! Bearded, fierce-eyed men in turbans and *shalwar kameez* (the light and loose Pakistani suit that combines a knee-length shirt with drawstring pants); little children in dusty clothes, all big eyes and quick smiles; women wrapped in gorgeous veils and scarves and *shalwar kameez*, some covered completely from head to toe, others with only their faces exposed.

Children stood behind carts piled with pyramids of figs, oranges, or grapefruit; men sat in storefront shops selling electric fans, shoes, underwear, sewing machines. Alleyways twisted past stalls displaying jewelry, bright bolts of cloth, fantastic colored mounds of spices.

As we wandered, I quickly realized that my fundamental preconception of Pakistan was wrong: I had expected a miniature version of India, but unlike the Indian cities I had visited, here there were no beggars, and none of the vaguely menacing atmosphere of poverty, decay, and hopelessness I remembered from Calcutta and New Delhi. Wherever we went, we were either ignored or greeted with hearty smiles and hellos. And even in that chaos and cacophony, there was a sense of order and purposefulness; the shops seemed well maintained, and the adults seemed markedly attentive to the cleanliness of their clothes and the neatness of their appearance.

Early the next day we flew to Peshawar, the capital of Pakistan's North West Frontier Province. Peshawar has been in the international spotlight in recent years because it is the headquarters-in-exile for the Afghanistan guerrillas who have been fighting the Soviets and the Soviet-instituted government in Kabul. Unlike Rawalpindi, Westerners were in evidence throughout the city— most, Asad said, either journalists or workers with one or another international aid organization.

The Peshawar bazaar revealed the same wonderland of colors, smells, and sounds as Rawalpindi's, but made even more complex with the addition of the people and products—the subtle but penetrating presence—of Afghanistan. In the bazaar, men occasionally tugged at our arms or pointed at themselves and said, "Afghanistan, Afghanistan," and the shops were filled with Afghan-made rugs, jewelry, and metalware.

Especially riveting were the unexpected reminders of the Afghanistan war—soldiers' caps with the red Soviet hammer and sickle, uniform buttons and insignias. When I turned one such hat in my hands, the thought came to me that a young man had once worn it, a young man probably not so different from me, with loving parents and siblings and perhaps a young wife who even now recalled with bitter tears his vow that he would return from the war alive.

Being here, near the figurative front lines, brought the news to life—or death—over and over again: Asad applied to the Tribal and Home Affairs Department for permission to go to the Khyber Pass, and was told that the day before, Afghan helicopters and planes had been flying low over the border area. They hadn't done anything, but they had unsettled the authorities enough to deny our request.

So instead we set off for Darra Adam Khel, headquarters of Pakistan's burgeoning gun-making and gun-smuggling industry.

The dusty road to Darra unfolds in memory as a series of snapshots: rough, mud-walled settlements that Asad said were Afghan refugee camps; women in flowing red and white robes balancing bright green packages on their heads; donkey carts bearing bricks; barefoot children in ragged clothes skittering through the dirt or hoisting slingshots, stopping to cry out and wave when they saw our foreign faces; eye-relieving splashes of green fields—wheat, sugar cane, and sugar beets—and stands of trees; scraggly cows and burros and sheep by the side of the road.

At some point Asad explained that we were passing into tribal territory, where Pakistani law stopped and local law took over. The tribes elect their own councils and representatives, he said, and essentially police themselves. An invisible corridor that extends forty feet on either side of the road is considered Pakistani territory; venture beyond that, and your fate is in the hands of the local tribes. "The gun is the law of this area," he added.

As we continued we passed long, dun-colored mud complexes with towering walls that looked like miniature fortresses. Asad explained that these were family dwellings. In the tribal territories, every house has its own watchtower, so that in times of tribal conflict, vigils can be kept around the clock.

And then we reached Darra. At first it looked like any other dusty town, one main street and a few side streets lined with small shops. But something heavy hung like a shroud in the air.

As we walked, we saw storefront after storefront glistening with pistols, rifles, bullets, knives. It was a little boy's fantasy world, a gun nut's dream come true—every variety of weapon you could want, right there in neat display. It was also the classic cottage industry, except that here the ultimate product was death.

"You want to try one?" A grizzled shopkeeper held out a rifle. "Shoot! Shoot!" he said, then stepped into the street outside his shop, pointed the barrel into the sky, and fired. *Boom!* I jumped.

"You want to try?"

After some prodding, I and a few other members of our group followed him to the "firing range," an area well beyond the shops with a dusty flat field that ended in a hill.

He held out a Russian-made Kalashnikov automatic rifle. The shopkeeper steadied the butt against my shoulder, then stepped away and put his fingers in his ears. I squeezed the trigger. *Pop-pop-pop-pop-pop!* The butt slammed into my shoulder, and little pings of dust traced the bullets. Weird feeling.

Again I squeezed. *Pop-pop-pop-pop-pop!* I felt awful and giddy at the same time—amazed at the pure power, the deadly power, I could unleash with a little twitch of my finger.

While others in our group were firing, another group of men bearing three rifles approached. A hawk-nosed, fiery-eyed man in an elaborate tan turban and draped in a bright blanket, separated himself from the group, crouched, aimed carefully, and fired. He tried each gun, and each try was followed by a burst of excited discussion and dispute.

I didn't know what tribe he was from, but I did know he wasn't firing those rifles so that he could write about it back home.

Later, as I walked through dusty back alleys and watched old men and young boys patiently tapping and tinkering and polishing their creations like kindly Swiss toymakers, the unreality of it all overwhelmed me. They didn't look like monsters; they were just brothers, husbands, and fathers making money to buy flour and fruit and shoes. And yet I felt that I had touched the heart of some immense evil, the vital nerve center of a sinuous and shadowy network of smuggling/oppression/conflict that operated all around the world and was vastly more powerful and pervasive—and perverse—than I had ever imagined.

On the following day we learned that we would have to alter our itinerary: We could not fly to Chitral, gateway to the pagan Kafir Kalash people of Kafiristan, because seasonal thermal updrafts—that would last about five days, Asad said—had made it impossible to land there. This was the first indication on the trip of the manifold uncertainties that come with the territory of adventure travel—obstacles that sometimes no amount of money or preparation can overcome.

After a group discussion, we decided to add one more day each to our stays in Gilgit and Hunza. I was deeply disappointed that we would not be able to see the tribes of the Kalash, who reportedly have managed to maintain their own pagan beliefs and distinct dress, speech, and other cultural practices through two millennia of passive Buddhist belief and, later, aggressive Islamic rule all around them.

Then we heard the good news: Asad had somehow secured permission for us to visit the Khyber Pass!

Martial music played and images from *Gunga Din* marched through my head as we wound due west toward the border. We passed two sprawling Afghan refugee settlements—temporary structures of mud, bamboo, and straw, stretching across the dusty flatlands—and Asad said that 35,000 people lived in one and 28,000 in another. He added that Pakistan supplies three-quarters of the cost of supporting all the camps.

Until this time, my sense of the Afghan war had been confined to television and newspaper reports viewed or read in the comfort of my living room. Now the picture had changed. "Try to imagine all the inhabitants of Burlingame, say, or Los Gatos," I wrote in my journal, "living in these patched-together structures, laced by dirt lanes on a parched plain; then try to imagine providing for all their needs in a country that is already strapped meeting the needs of its own inhabitants, and then try to imagine the sufferings of the refugees themselves—from maimed limbs to splintered families to profound psychological displacement. Imagine all these, and you begin to get some sense of the scale and depth of the problems the Afghan war has created."

As long-prowed, brightly painted trucks bearing lumber, bricks, tires, and cows honked their horns and ground their gears around us, Asad summarized the history of the region: "The road we are traveling now is a continuation of the Grand Trunk Road, which was originally built in the 14th century connecting Kabul to Delhi. It was improved on and expanded through the centuries, but most importantly by the British in the 19th and early

20th centuries. The route passes through Europe into Turkey, then Iran, Afghanistan, and Pakistan."

For a moment the "magic buses" I had seen crammed with long-haired hippies in tie-dyed T-shirts in Istanbul in the '70s came to mind, and I remembered the exotic tales of Kabul and Kathmandu. How far away that whole world seemed—and yet how near.

"So many armies have passed this way," Asad continued, "beginning with the Indo-Aryans in 1500-1200 B.C., then Alexander the Great and his troops in the 4th century B.C., and through the centuries the Tatars, Mughals, Afghans, and English....

"The mountains we are traveling into are part of the Hindu Kush. The Khyber Pass itself is thirty-three kilometers (about twenty miles) long; 98,000 people live in the area, and three different tribes control different areas of the pass.

"The main industry here, to tell you the truth, is smuggling. The tribal chiefs have huge complexes that are well guarded, and the tribespeople pass back and forth over the border at will; there are many unsupervised points where they can cross at night."

The road twisted and wound past rocky, barren bluffs with forts the same bleached color perched on their tops, etched against the cloudless blue sky. Naked children jumped and splashed in streams, and women led straggling strings of children, or balanced bulging bags, or talked in groups away from the road—their brilliant robes catching our eyes even as they hastily drew their veils around their faces to avoid our stares.

What kind of life do these people have out here? I wondered. And yet this is where they grew up, this is all they know of the world, an inner voice replied.

At one point we stopped and got out, and Asad pointed to the ribboning road we had just traveled. "If you look closely out there, you can see three roads: On the top is the road the Mughals used in the early 16th century; below that—see the dirt trail—is the path the Greeks used under Alexander; and then there is the Grand Trunk Road the British made."

At another point he motioned out the window to a grassy, depressed plain. "This was the site of a bloody ambush during the third Afghan war in 1919. The British and the Pathans fought fiercely throughout this area for more than a century."

At this Tom Cole said, "Of all the peoples the British encountered in their 300-odd years on the subcontinent, they admired the Pathans the most." And then he quoted the words the Pakistanis had chiseled in stone at the gateway to the pass, in commemoration of the end of British-Pathan conflict: "According to the British, it was here that they met their equals, who looked them straight in the face and fought against them up to the last day of their rule. But when the British quit, after a rule of 100 years, the two great peoples parted as friends."

Later we passed a honeycomb of small shops, and Asad said, "This is Ali Mastid bazaar—from the earliest days of the Silk Route, this is where the camel caravans would stop for the night. In fact, nomad caravans still do stop here."

We saw the remains of a Buddhist stupa, and tank barriers built by the British during WWII, and always the sere, steep, craggy rocks; the twisting road; the brown, baked tribal settlements set into the hills; the trucks laden with wood, metal drums of fuel, tires; pedestrians and goats and cows; buses bulging with passengers; pickup trucks bearing grizzled men with rifles slung over their shoulders; and the dust, in my mouth and on my clothes, coating everything.

As we bumped along, I realized that I had been given a great gift: In the accumulation of images and encounters, as my feet scuffed that parched ground, as I nodded at Pakistani soldiers, shook Afghan hands in the bazaar, and waved to children in the settlements, the war was becoming personalized—it was no longer their war, but my war, too. And as the sun glowered down and the earth baked as it had when Alexander's soldiers walked this way, I thought of how all wars are just people fighting people—and of how just as sun and wind inevitably shape landscape, so too do climate and countryside shape human character and culture.

We reached the last checkpoint before the border, and there we had to stop. Ahead, clearly visible less than four miles in the distance, was Afghanistan. Through binoculars we could see the row of white markers strung out along the hills that represented the border, people moving at the border crossing, and trucks, and then the sere hills stretching into the distance.

Afghanistan! It reminded me of stories I had heard of people in the days before China was open to visitors, driving to the New Territories and peering off toward the misty fields of Canton. Those far mountains were in fact no different from the very mountain on which I stood—except that at some point in the minuscule moment of human history someone had decided to lay an imaginary line between them and call it a border. What chaos that caused, I mused, and the pickup trucks with their riflemen bouncing in the back sped by, bound for—I didn't know where.

And the scrape and trudge of all the feet that had raised dust on this inhospitable path—Aryan feet, Greek feet, Mughal feet, British feet—echoed in my mind.

On the drive back to Peshawar, Asad pointed to plastic packets that were hanging along with cigarettes, oranges, and other everyday goods from just about every streetside stall. "See those packets?" he said. "They contain opium. Drug-selling is another very big business here. The tribal chiefs are very clever, and very wealthy and well protected. They sell just about everything," he added.

"Even people?" I asked.

"Oh, yes, people too," he said.

In a distant field children were flying white paper kites, and women in white robes trailed by children in red and purple *shalwar kameez* walked through waving grasses from one mud settlement to another. Eucalyptus trees and poplars—strange that I hadn't noticed them before—lined the road, sighing in the breeze.

Part Two: High Road to Hunza

April 5 dawned dark and drizzly, and we splashed through the muddy, puddling streets of Peshawar bound for the Swat Valley and the city of Saidu Sharif, ancient capital of the Kingdom of Swat. As we wound north, roadside images revealed the presence of the past in this slowly developing land: cultivated fields crisscrossed by rough-dug irrigation trenches, occasionally punctuated by walled compounds of mud and straw; children gathering branches and twigs in the rain; yoked oxen snorting through the mud; carcasses hanging in a market; men huddled around a makeshift fire in a shop.

It was not propitious weather for touring the Buddhist ruins and Alexander the Great-related sites of Swat, so instead we spent our day and a half there shopping. I dutifully but dispiritedly hefted melons, admired earrings and necklaces, and trailed fine rainbow-colored scarves through my hands—until we stopped at the village of Khwazakhela.

There, in a dark, dingy closet of a shop, maybe eight feet deep by five feet wide, we discovered a wooden and leather arrow quiver, with the arrows still inside, that both the shop owner and Asad said was at least 100 years old. Then in a grimy corner, among lanterns and coins and cooking utensils, I found a 100-year-old drum and a 350-year-old leather shield.

I twirled an arrow and felt the prick of its cool metal tip. Then I turned the drum in my hands, studying how the leather had been stretched over the beautifully worked brass, running my fingers over the creases where the leather had been stretched, smelling the dust and sweat and age of it. I beat it—dust dancing into the air—and imagined tribal palms beating that same worn spot a century ago; the dull *thonk, thonk* and *tum, tum* echoed in my ears just as—I imagined—they had echoed in tribal ears through the years.

Then I took the rough shield and imagined a Pathan warrior 300 years ago gripping those same thongs, that musty, pocked, leathery disc—about as big as a woman's floppy Sunday hat—the only thing between him and death.

The shop owner picked an old, rusted, curving sword off the wall and playfully swung it at me. I parried his thrust with my shield. His eyes were suddenly electric with mirth and inter-action—understanding that spanned cultures, connections that spanned time.

The next day mists shrouded the Himalayan peaks that Asad said loomed majestic and snowcapped in the distance, but patches of clearing revealed an entirely different Pakistan from the dusty plains of Peshawar: hillsides terraced with row upon row of lush green plots (wheat at that time of year) bright with yellow mus-tard plants and white-blossoming pear trees.

When we reached 6,300 feet, snow and pine trees unexpect-edly appeared, along with patches of pink mountain tulips. And as the countryside and climate changed, so did the inhabitants' lifestyle: Now hillside clusters of brick and rock houses with tin roofs replaced the sprawling mud and straw settlements of the lowlands; and as the slopes grew increasingly steep, tiny terraces folded down them like the ribs of an emerald fan.

At a fraying, frontier-feeling truck stop called Besham, Tom Cole announced that we were at one of the most significant points of passage on our trip. From there on, we would be traveling along the legendary Karakoram Highway, or KKH, "one of man's most magnificent and stupefying feats of engineering and endurance."

Undertaken jointly by Pakistan and China, the two-lane, 730-mile highway took twenty years to complete, with 15,000 Pakistanis and from 9,000 to 20,000 Chinese working on the project at any one time.

The KKH was dynamited and dug out of the mountains, connecting Islamabad all the way to the Chinese border and beyond to Kashgar in the wastes of Chinese Turkestan. In some places the builders followed ancient trade routes that predated even the Silk Route; in other places, because of unresolvable property disputes, they simply blasted a way through virgin territory.

The landscape through which we now wound was as wild and uncompromising as any I had ever seen. The peaks rose steep and sheer—ragged in some places, sandpapered by colossal landslides in others—from the side of the road into the clouds. In all this immensity, the highway was a filament, a puny patch of pavement that nature could reclaim at any moment through any of the elements at its command: snow or mud, rock or flood.

When we saw nomads with sheep and cows walking by the side of the Indus River far below, they looked about as big as the period at the end of this sentence. In my journal I wrote: "This is a landscape for gods, not men."

Nature's raw power was manifest in much more mundane—and mortal—ways as well: The rains of the previous days had washed many parts of the road away. Whenever we reached one of these, our driver, Ali Muhammad, would gingerly prod and caress the van over the muddy, slippery, rock-strewn stretches—air whistling beneath our windows all the way to the gray-green squiggle of the Indus.

Asad and Ali kept a constant watch on the mountainside: Tumbling streams of small rocks, Asad said, often precede huge, highway-demolishing rockslides. Whole regiments of soldiers are maintained in camps along the highway just to keep it clear, Asad said.

Eventually we passed so many mudslides and rockslides—and soldiers in bulldozers and backhoes—that I lost count and stopped scanning the mountainsides. Instead I gave myself up to the *sumi-e* serenity of peak and cloud, the occasional apparitions of umbrella-toting villagers, and the throat-tightening sight of a narrow dirt track, perhaps as old as human settlement here, ribboning along a far mountainside.

Asad and Tom Cole used this time to present some background information: From the beginning of human habitation in the region, northern Pakistan had been composed of fiercely independent valley kingdoms. The leaders of these kingdoms, who went by various titles—rajah, mir, wali—subsisted for centuries in their mountain fastnesses, raising their own food and preying on passing caravans for ceramics, silks, spices, and slaves; at the same time, they used promises of allegiance to gain bounty and maintain independence from the emperors of China and the maharajahs of Kashmir.

This political balancing act reached its climax in the Great Game of the late 19th century, when Russia and England vied through emissaries and outposts—and, finally, armies—for the favor of the local rulers and the control of these remote but strategically alluring territories.

The rulers eventually relinquished their independence, but in essence they remained semiautonomous well after Partition and the creation of Pakistan in 1947. The wali of Swat gave up rule in 1969; the mirs of Hunza and Nagar surrendered their sovereignty only in 1974. (In fact, the current mir of Hunza, who was in power at that time, is the last of the former rulers allowed to use his royal title.)

Today in many ways these areas are still hardly part of Pakistan, Asad said. They don't belong to any of the country's four full-fledged provinces, but rather to an anomalous entity called the Northern Areas. The inhabitants prefer local dialects to Urdu, the national language. And the dominant branch of religious belief is not Sunni or Shia Islam—which prevail in other parts of Pakistan—but Ismaili, a somewhat mystic and less fundamentalist, more eclectic strain.

We reached Karimabad, the "capital" of the Hunza Valley, just before sunset. Of all the exotic stops on our itinerary, it was Hunza, famed for its apricot orchards, the longevity of its inhabitants, and its fairy tale setting of a verdant valley encircled by snowcapped peaks, that had most attracted me to this tour. In the far-off United States, I had felt that something was waiting for me in Hunza, that something would be revealed to me there.

No burst of epiphanic light or even partial parting of the clouds greeted my arrival, but my first impressions were still favorable: The people were healthy-looking, with rosy cheeks and bright eyes and sturdy, colorful clothes; the cold, clear mountain air rang with the cries of children at play; and the setting was indeed spectacular, a lush bowl surrounded by peaks, some jagged and distinct against the sky, others obscured by clouds.

We spent the following day touring the highlights of Hunza, starting with Baltit Fort. Built 550 years ago and inhabited by the mirs of Hunza until the present residence was built in the 1920s, this white, high-perched palace is a stirring sight, especially when viewed from a distance against a backdrop of cloud-piercing peaks. Close up, however, it seemed a dusty, neglected, mud-plastered place. Still, looking closely and imaginatively at its massive wooden beams and intricately carved doorways and columns, we could get some sense of its former magnificence.

We were told that UNESCO has been negotiating with the mir to take over the management and restoration of the fort. If an agreement is reached, the palace will probably be sealed off, or at least partly restricted to visitors, until the restoration is completed—but it was heartening to think that this precious, poignant symbol of Hunza's history and culture might be preserved.

Altit Fort, Baltit's predecessor, was in a similar state of disrepair, but presented from its tower an enchanting tapestry of rooftop life in the surrounding hamlet: Here was a woman doing the breakfast dishes; there another doing laundry. Three women chatted and crafted masterful crochetwork almost directly below us; another group sat sorting twigs. A mother appeared with a basin under one arm and a squirming naked child under the other, and proceeded to scrub him clean, much to his displeasure. Another adjusted a wooden carrier on her back before setting out for the fields.

In all, our wanderings revealed an underlying sense of prosperity and serenity in Hunza. Solid rock houses sat beside fertile green plots irrigated by an ingenious, extensive network of canals; and everywhere thin spring willows spired into the sky, and pear, apple, and apricot trees burst into brilliant pink and white bloom. Dusty, litter-free paths interlaced the hamlets of the valley, and I noticed an aural interlacing as well: Because of the area's acoustics, a child's cry or the clanging of a cowbell at one end could be heard clearly at the other. It was as if everyone was everyone else's neighbor.

Contentment seemed to spring naturally from Hunza's idyllic and isolated setting: The valley bowl imbued the place with a stabilizing sense of community, and the peaks, even when invisible, conferred a kind of high mountain peace. How could one not be happy here? I thought.

Such romantic speculations obscured the harsh realities of the situation, however—the inhabitants' situation and, indeed, our own. We were staying at the guest house of the mir, on the grounds of the present palace, about as prestigious an address as one could hope for. But despite the name, there was intermittent electricity, little hot water, even less heat—and no mir, alas. (He was still at his winter residence in Islamabad.) Even more import-ant, the clouds that had first appeared in Swat had steadfastly followed us up the KKH, clouding the mountains and our minds. It was cold, many in our group were sniffling and coughing, the food was mediocre and the pretty pictures the tour brochure had innocently painted began to seem malevolent mockery.

At an uneasy dinner, various discomforts were brought up, and the consensus was to cut short our stay in Hunza by a day and continue up the KKH a few hours to Gulmit. Some travelers who had just come from there had spoken glowingly of a lodge with abundant hot water, blankets, heat, and good food. So we revised the itinerary once more: The following day, we would tour the Nagar Valley, across the Hunza Gorge, and then leave for Gulmit the morning after.

I decided I would forgo the excursion to Nagar and wander Hunza's dusty lanes, hoping they would reveal whatever it was I had come to see.

The next day dawned auspiciously clear, and at 5:30 Karimabad was surrounded by a spectacular panorama of peaks, each one glistening golden snow against the sky: Rakaposhi, Pari, The Throne, Ultar.

At 6:30 I walked alone down the main street, exulting at the invigorating air, the head-clearing silence, and the aloof but some-how encouraging solitude, serenity, and strength of the mountains. The entire valley seemed a soul-lightening composition of bold, basic colors: green fields, pink blossoms, white peaks, blue sky.

The day passed in a kind of counterpoint of reflective solitude and entwining encounter. Wherever I wandered, I was met with smiles and waves, but I was also left free to simply roam and reflect.

At one point a man strode up to me and said, "How do you do? I am very happy to welcome you to Hunza. Would you like to see my house?"

He gently took my arm and led me to a plot of land that had been leveled, where a cinderblock dwelling was sitting in stately half-completion. "This," he said proudly, "is my house."

He took me through it room by room, pointing out the electrical outlets, the living room's airy view, and the kitchen with its fancy new fireplace.

At another point I saw two old men sitting by the side of the road, in toothless tranquility. A young boy was standing near them, and I asked him how old they were. He asked them, and they replied, "Eh?" He asked more loudly. Same response. He walked closer and asked in an even bigger voice. Same response. Finally, he walked up so close that he was shouting almost directly into one old man's nose. "Ah," they responded, and then sang out some sentences.

"They are not sure," the boy translated. "Maybe eighty, maybe ninety." They smiled great toothless grins, and I asked if I could take their picture. I don't know what their answer was, but it sounded like, "Yes, of course, what took you so long? We have been waiting for you to ask us!"

Much later, after the others on our tour had returned from Nagar, three musicians bearing a horn and two drums arrived at the mir's palace and began to play on the lawn. Asad had arranged a dance for us, and as the primitive, pulsing music floated through the village's natural amphitheater, children began to gather from all corners; then grizzled men with canes and younger men carrying their work tools appeared as well.

First three elders in elaborate costumes presented a tale of some long-ago pilgrimage. Then two younger men with shields and swords enacted an epic battle. In the lull between performances, the children pushed and cajoled each other onto the grassy stage and danced.

Just as I was exclaiming at the wonder of witnessing this storytelling tradition that went back perhaps 2,000 years, a young man raced into the dancing area, his eyes bulging, and violently pushed away an old man who had been dancing. The children screamed and scattered.

This youth tore wildly around the grass a half-dozen times, then suddenly stopped and bent over the central drum, sweat streaming off his face, and began to call out words in a husky, disembodied voice.

"This one is a shaman," Asad said. "He has been possessed by the spirit of the fairies, and is predicting the future."

But the encounter that moved me most of all occurred earlier in the afternoon. I was returning to the mir's palace when I saw a man in his backyard crafting a beautiful wooden door. He was working slowly and carefully, and seemed so entirely absorbed that there was no separation between him and the wood he was shaping.

Suddenly he noticed me admiring his work and beckoned me to join him. I slid down a small hill to his home. He grinned. I grinned. I gestured that the door was very beautiful. He called out something, and presently a gorgeous young girl shyly walked up to me bearing a plate of apricots.

The apricots were sweet and delicious and I tried to say so. Then I pulled out some postcards of San Francisco and tried to communicate that it was where I came from. Finally I pulled out some pictures of my family and asked if I could take a picture of his family to bring home to show to my family.

His eyes lit up, and he called out something, and presently his family appeared—wife, teenage daughter, one baby, second baby, mother-in-law—peering out from inside the house. I asked if I could take their picture—not being able to take pictures of women had been one of the great frustrations of the trip—and he enthusiastically motioned me into the house.

It was too dark and I didn't have a flash, but I did have a chance to see the inside of a traditional Hunza house: We entered into the living room, which had a carpet and window at one end, a door leading into what I took to be a bedroom in another wall, a fireplace in the wall opposite the carpet and a hole in the ceiling above the fireplace, the perimeter of which had been blackened by smoke. Curtains of some rough cloth framed the window, but otherwise there was almost no ornamentation, nothing on the walls and no furniture save for one low chair.

After I had taken a photo inside, I asked if I might take their picture outside as well. They posed patiently and sweetly—the babies taking turns crying, drooling, and cooing—and when we had finished, the carpenter said something, and after a few minutes his elder daughter brought a plastic bag bulging with dried apricots and kernels.

These are for your family, he said, pointing to my pictures. I thanked him as profusely as I could, and handed him two of the San Francisco postcards I had brought. Please hang these on your wall, I said. He said thank you, then asked to have one of the pictures of my family as well. I hesitated—I didn't know what situation might arise where I would need those precious pictures—but he was so kind and friendly and I was so moved, I relented and gave him his choice.

He chose a Christmas picture of us standing in front of a brightly decorated tree and told me that he would hang it proudly on his wall between the two postcards of San Francisco. He then clasped my hand warmly and said two words that I later found out meant "family" and "brothers."

Now, half a world away, I think of that singular encounter and a whole gallery of images comes to life within me: the sword-wielding shopkeeper in Swat, the immortal mountains, the shaman's frenzied dance.

I wonder if someday my daughter will journey to Hunza and find that same carpenter's house, and our photograph still on that rough wall. And I think that time flows backward and forward, and that once in a rare while—if you are lucky and it is cloudy enough to make you see beyond your preconceptions— you stumble onto a connection that transcends it all.

Part Three: The Epic of the KKH

The adventures intensified after our Contac-quaffing, Maalox-munching, cloud-weary group left Hunza for Gulmit and the hot showers and hearty food other travelers said we would find at the Silk Route Lodge. The journey north was uneventful—skitterish rocks and precipitous drops had become commonplace by now— until we reached an avalanche about ten minutes from Gulmit.

The avalanche had buried the road long enough ago that a plow had already cut a corridor through its twenty-foot-deep drifts, but our steel-nerved driver, Ali Muhammad, feared the van would lose traction on the icy path and sit there, sandwiched in the snow, a fat target for a second avalanche.

So Asad Esker, our Pakistani guide, set out on foot for Gulmit to get a tractor that could pull the van through, and Ali backed the van up to a point on the road that looked reasonably secure. And we sat and waited.

Waiting for an avalanche or rockslide to sweep us into oblivion quickly lost its appeal, so after a while I decided to set out on foot for Gulmit, too. There wasn't much chance of making a wrong turn—the nearest intersection was about four hours away.

Scrunch, scrunch, scrunch went my feet, quickly along the snow-plowed path, then slowly when I reached the other side. There, beyond sight of the van, the notion of solitude took on a whole new, almost otherworldly dimension. It was just me and the mountains, and I tried to imagine what the traders and missionaries and adventurers who had wandered this way before me had felt.

Scrunch, scrunch, scrunch.

If I walk long enough, I thought, I'll reach the Chinese border. And if I keep walking after that, eventually this same road will take me to Kashgar, where right now wild-eyed mountain men are sizing up camels and crockery, bartering for boots and broadcloth.

Scrunch, scrunch, scrunch.

This is one of the most remote and desolate places I've ever been, I thought. If I were traveling alone, I would probably think I had come to the end of the Earth.

Then I took out my tape recorder and said: "It's not just that it's an inhospitable environment—which it certainly is—but also that you sense the forces of nature and time grinding on all around you, and you feel like a grain of sand on the slopes of one of the mountains."

My voice seemed like an intruder, and I stopped—and listened. The silence was so overpowering, so absolute, that it was almost like a vacuum of sound. Instead of sound, enormous waves of energy emanated from the mountains all around, so strong that I had to sit down.

Perhaps Marco Polo felt these same waves, I thought. Perhaps he called his fellow adventurers to a halt in this very spot, and sat on this very rock, and pondered—just like me—what an insignificant piece he was in the world's vast puzzle, how easily he could be bent, or lost, or simply worn away.

I walked all the way to the Silk Route Lodge, and the others eventually arrived by jeep and pickup truck. Gulmit's only tractor had been dispatched that morning to a town near the Chinese border, however, and wasn't expected back until the following day, so the van remained marooned on the road.

After a revitalizing night at the Silk Route Lodge—where the meals were indeed excellent, although the hot water ran out before I could run into the shower—we returned by jeep to the avalanche and walked through it to our van. Then we rode south for about an hour—until we were stopped by another avalanche. This one had smothered the road like an overturned sack of sugar—a sack of sugar in which each granule was the size of a bowling ball.

This avalanche was so recent that it had not yet been plowed, but somehow the wizardly Asad had heard about it before we left the Silk Route Lodge, and had called his office in Gilgit to request that vans be sent to meet us on the other side of the snow.

We disembarked and hiked up, up, and over the avalanche—and lo and behold, two vans white as angels awaited us. Cries erupted from them at the sight of our group, and porters scurried forward to transport our bags over the avalanche's hump. We chucked snowballs at each other in celebration.

On the rest of the long and winding road to Gilgit, we passed palaces, poplars, and petroglyphs, waterfalls and meeting halls, stupas and sheep, but for many the most exciting discovery was packets of British biscuits and chocolate cookies at a roadside stall.

After a heartening night at the Serena Lodge in Gilgit—heated rooms, delicious fried chicken, and custard desserts!—we journeyed on to Skardu. As it turned out, the weather began to clear during this all-day drive, and we were treated to spectacular vistas of brilliant snowcapped peaks and deep blue skies, puffy clouds and lush green terraced fields—the Pakistan of the guidebook pictures and tour brochure prose—before the end of the day.

This ride and the following few day trips to nearby villages and lakes afforded me ample opportunity to reflect on the trip, and on some of the complexities and contradictions of northern Pakistan and of adventure travel in general.

On the night before we were to leave Skardu, I tried to sort them out in my notebook:

The most troubling issue on this trip has been the role and presence of women in Pakistan. From the beginning, I have been surprised by how few women were to be seen in public places. Those we do see consciously avoid our gaze, and it is clear that we are not to speak with them or photograph them. By now this has grown into a subtle psychological oppression, a kind of spiritual heaviness; I feel worn down by the rough and rigid masculine energy that seems to pervade Pakistan, unleavened by any feminine softness or flexibility.

This creates special obstacles for women traveling in Pakistan, especially women traveling alone. The complaints I have heard range from the covert—the sense of constantly being on display—to the overt: being jostled or fondled in crowds, glared at in markets, and ignored in offices. "I can't wait to get out of this country," one Englishwoman told me in Peshawar.

Certainly women can lessen these problems by dressing like Pakistani women—wearing clothes that cover their arms and legs and scarves on their heads—and by adopting a certain aura of unaggressiveness. But the differences in attitude—and so the potential for problems—still remain.

Another fact that has become apparent is that despite the cost of the trip—more than $4,000 when you include airfare—rough conditions and travel unpredictabilities come with this territory, and so flexibility, tolerance, and good humor are absolutely essential.

Money does not buy certainty or guarantee comfort here. What it does buy is access, and that's why people are willing to spend a hefty portion of their salaries—to go places they would have great difficulty going on their own.

The situation becomes especially irritating if you get sick—and so end up paying thousands of dollars to shiver in blankets or shuttle between bed and bathroom in some remote hotel room. Yet the lower standards of hygiene and foreign foods and germs you inevitably encounter on such a trip make sickness an inherent possibility.

And finally there's the issue of mortality: I risk death every time I cross a San Francisco street or drive on a California freeway, I know, but the possibility of death by accident on Interstate 80, say, is familiar and so easier to ignore than the possibility of death by avalanche on the KKH.

Rugged, remote trips such as this one put the gift of life in a new perspective, and I guess that's what it all comes down to: Every day in our lives presents dangers of one kind or another; some we challenge because they are expedient, others because we judge that the rewards merit the risks.

This last notation took on new meaning two days later, when we sat around a table in the troubled town of Chilas debating what to do.

We had driven to Chilas the day before from Skardu, after learning that the Skardu-to-Islamabad flight would not operate that morning. Heavy rains had been falling for at least forty-eight hours, loosening the rocks above the highway and increasing the possibilities of avalanche or flood.

If we risked the road, we could reach Islamabad by midnight, giving us a full day to recuperate before the thirty-two-hour journey back to the United States. If we waited in Chilas, the rain might let up, allowing us to drive more safely straight to the airport the following day.

Tom Cole said he thought we should stay in Chilas. Asad said he thought it would be all right to go.

Rain pattered on the roof, and the grimy light of a cloud-covered dawn smudged the windows. If we didn't risk the road and the rains continued, we faced the distinct possibility of missing our plane in Islamabad and being stuck there for three days until the next scheduled flight—if we could get seats on that flight.

We thought of appointments and commitments, dangers and delusions, imponderables and percentages—and, most of all, loved ones anxiously awaiting our return. We looked at each other long moments and then, as if with one voice, said, "Let's go."

I have felt fear at various times in my life, but almost never as palpably and deeply as I did that morning. It sat round and heavy, a lead ball, in my stomach.

The van was silent as we drove slowly down the rain-slicked road out of Chilas. A coppery dryness parched my mouth, and for a while I had to grip the van seat to keep my hands from trembling. I wondered if there would be even a second of realization before the avalanche came, or if it would arrive in a cloud of instantaneous obliteration. I wondered if a search party would be able to identify our remains. I wondered why I had ever put myself in this stupid situation in the first place.

After some time, to take my mind off the slippery slopes, I took out my notebook and wrote:

> We left at 5:30 so that we could get into Rawalpindi before nightfall or shortly thereafter. Now we have been bumping along through the morning mists for about a half-hour. We have not seen one other car or truck, and that is spooky.
>
> The possibility of death by landslide is in the air, and the reality of the KKH hits home—it is not something to be trifled with. We are in an elongated life-or-death situation with no way of pinpointing if or when the life-or-death moment will strike. If we get through without incident, this will seem like so much groundless worry. If not, well.... Let us hope that at some point in the future I will look back at these notes and smile at the memory.

After about two hours the mists began to lift, and our spirits with them. A kind of exhilaration began to take hold, a feeling of exploring a world no one had seen before us. We were trailblazing, opening up the KKH. Adventuring!

Once again we began to exclaim at the vistas and peaks, at the trim stone houses and rock-bordered emerald terraces. The crescendo came at 8:07 A.M., when a red bus with "Rawalpindi" written on the front passed us going in the opposite direction. Cheers broke out in the van—the road was open!

From this point on, it was all downhill, so to speak. The sun shone, the peaks glistened, the clouds puffed, the road dried—occasionally waterfalls coursed across the pavement or we bumped over great gaping stretches where the road had been washed away, but these were trifles, good photo opportunities, footnotes to the epic of the KKH.

Morning slid giddily into afternoon, and at some point I took out my notebook and wrote:

> Three weeks ago Pakistan meant nothing to you. And now it is all around you. Pakistan is burros burdened with fodder and wood; it is lush green fields dotted with big blossoms of color that, as you get closer, turn out to be women in red, green, purple, or blue robes. It is children with dark hair and big shining eyes who smile and wave and cry out, "Bye-bye, bye-bye," and weathered men in white caps and dun-colored blankets, their stares like skewers until you smile and wave—and their wrinkles crease into smiles and they raise their hands in stately salute.
>
> Pakistan is a string of camels plodding down the highway; young men in spattered *shalwar kameez* playing cricket in the rain. It is women washing their clothes in a river, and naked children playing jacks in the mud nearby. It is tiny, musty shops crammed with old artifacts and new handicrafts; open-air stalls selling oranges and dates, carpets and cloth, jewelry, spices, guns. It is painted trucks, horse-drawn carriages, battered bicycles, mountain palaces, and muddy refugee camps. It is white clouds and gray clouds; green fields and snowy meadows; dusty plains and snowcapped peaks; pearly mist and blue sky. It is all Pakistan. Pakistan!

I put down my pen and thought: Little did I know, three weeks ago, that I was beginning a journey that would have no end.

⌒

Insights into Nice at the Musée Matisse

I turned forty when I was at the Examiner, *and to soften the blow of aging a full decade in one night, I sent myself on a hedonistic adventure to the South of France. I stayed at celebrated hotels and ate Michelin meals, but the most memorable experience of all occurred at the newly opened Musée Matisse. I love Matisse's work, so I was excited to see the museum, but what ended up impressing me even more was a vivacious trio of local women. My entire encounter with them happened so quickly that it felt almost like a dream afterwards, and when I considered writing about it, there seemed no other choice but to present our meeting as a scene from a play starring one haplessly enchanted American and three fabulous—and oh-so-ineffably French—citizens of Nice.*

I WAS SITTING IN A SECOND-FLOOR SALON at the newly opened Musée Matisse in Nice, France, scribbling in my notebook, when an attractive, middle-aged woman in an impeccably tailored peach-colored suit approached me and said in flawless French, "Excuse me, but do you speak French?"

I said I did, and she continued, "Well, forgive me for bothering you, but I'm wondering just what a foreign visitor thinks about this museum. You see, I'm from Nice, and I can't find anything worthwhile here, and I'm afraid that visitors who come all the way to Nice from far away to see this museum will be terribly disappointed.

"Whatever have you found to write about?" she said, gesturing at my notebook.

"Well," I began, hoping my trusty, rusty French was up to this adventure in art criticism, "there are certain valuable illuminations to be found—"

"Illuminations!" she exploded, her pearl necklace trembling. "Have you been to the Matisse show in Paris?"

"Well, no," I said, "but I did see the Matisse exhibition in New York last year."

"New York!" she pouted, as if she had been one-upped by a neighbor. "And how does this compare to that?"

"Well, you really can't compare," I began, but then another well-dressed woman who had been hovering near us burst into speech.

"But you can't compare the two!" she exclaimed, fire in her voice and eyes. "I too am a native of Nice, and I think this is a very interesting museum, an extraordinary achievement given all the obstacles that had to be overcome, all the planning and work that went into it.

"You know," she continued, turning to me, "this museum was six years in the making. As you can see"—and her fiery gaze directed my eyes to the ancient rocky walls on the museum's grounds—"this villa is set on an area of Roman ruins. There were all manner of political problems and personality problems, permissions to be obtained, regulations to be followed—the plan had to be meticulous, absolutely perfect! It is a miracle this museum was ever finished!"

I almost expected the room to burst into applause.

"Well, yes," my original questioner countered, "but now that it is finished, I ask you, What is there to see? Some half-finished drawings, studies; a scattering of canvases. Where are the masterpieces? Where is the genius of Matisse?" and she thrust one diamond-bedecked hand toward the sky.

"Well," I said, "that canvas over there—*Fenêtre à Tahiti*—is a powerful composition, with those great blocks of color one associates with Matisse's masterpieces."

"Bravo!" said the second woman.

"Oh, that," said the first woman, flinging a finger at the painting as if it were the bones of yesterday's fish dinner. "Yes, there are a few canvases of note here—but so few! Why cannot Nice, Matisse's home, produce a more distinguished tribute to an artist of such distinction?"

"But don't you know"—the second woman's friend now entered the fray—"how expensive it is to mount exhibitions these days? All the permissions that have to be obtained, and the shipping fees—and the insurance!" she exclaimed, her eyes rolling heavenward in horror.

"The insurance," muttered woman number one. "We are talking about art and genius and a suitable tribute—and you are talking about insurance!"

"Yes, I am. You have to be practical, realistic. I think this is a very charming tribute. It has a hometown feeling—"

"An intimacy," I said.

"Bravo for the American! Yes, an intimacy, that I think distinguishes it from larger, more impersonal exhibits."

"I agree," I said. "You feel closer to the soul of Matisse here."

"*Voilà!*" exclaimed woman number two.

"The soul of Matisse?" the first woman said, eyeing me suspiciously. "Are all Americans so kind?" She paused and smiled slightly.

"I still think I would be—how shall I say?—deceived, disappointed, if I flew all the way across the ocean to see this."

"Well," I began expansively, "no one will fly all the way across the ocean just to see this. They will fly all the way across the ocean to see this!"—and I pointed grandly to the sunny seaside city outside the museum's walls.

"Ah!" all three women said.

"So you like Nice?" asked woman number one.

"Oh, I love Nice," I said. "I love the winding alleyways in Old Nice, and the old shuttered buildings. I love the sidewalk cafés and the restaurants that have room for only four tables. I love the grand Promenade des Anglais and the fantastic hotels that look onto it."

"And the people of Nice?"

"Oh, yes!" I began—"well, actually, you are the first Niçoises I've had the opportunity to talk at length with, but all the people I've encountered have been very friendly and courteous. One thing that amazes me is that people are so willing to speak English here. In Paris, even if they know some English, shopkeepers or waiters will often refuse to speak with foreign customers."

"We are not Parisians here, my dear," said woman number two.

"Gracious no!" added woman number one. "We have a temperament of the south, wouldn't you say?"

"Exactly," said woman number three. "We are more relaxed, more passionate,"—did she smile discreetly at me?—"more... In Paris, they work now to enjoy life later. In Nice, we enjoy life now!"

"Yes!" I said. "I'm sure that is exactly what Matisse felt!"

I suddenly realized that the visitors in the salon were paying more attention to our little group than they were to the paintings and drawings on the walls.

"So you like art?" woman number one asked.

"Yes," I said, "especially modern French art."

"Then you must go to Antibes to see the Picasso museum, and Cagnes-sur-Mer to see Renoir's former residence."

"And of course you must go to the Fondation Maeght in Saint-Paul," said woman number two.

"And the Chagall museum down the street," said woman number three, "and the Cocteau museum in Menton."

"Oh, and have you seen the Rosary Chapel in Vence?" asked woman number one. "It is Matisse's triumph!"

"And you must see the Cocteau chapel in Villefranche!" said woman number three.

"Yes," I lamented, "there is so much to see, and I have so little time."

I was waiting for the women to offer to take me in their Mercedes from museum to museum over the next few days. Barring that, I was waiting for them at least to invite me back to their homes for dinner or a drink.

But life never follows a set script.

"Oh!" said woman number two, looking at her watch. "I have to pick up the children!"

And the other two women, as if on cue, looked at their watches and exclaimed, "The time!"

"How quickly time passes with pleasant company," said woman number one, and winked at me.

"Well, our new American friend," she continued with a broad smile, glancing at my still open notebook, "have you found something to write about now?"

As they made for the exit, she turned one last time and said, "*Au revoir!* Enjoy your stay in our lovely Nice!"

Then they were gone.

I walked once more around the suddenly intimate and enchanting museum, looked again at the artist's luminous, passion-filled pieces and thought: Ah, Matisse—now I understand even better what you loved about Nice.

Treasures of Dubrovnik

When I was writing a column for the Lonely Planet website, one of the subjects I tried to focus on was the special people we meet when we travel, people who come to embody and transfigure our understanding of a place. Usually these encounters are entirely unexpected, and often they become our most precious souvenirs from a trip. My meeting in 2000 with the woman I call T, in Dubrovnik, was one such experience. She brought the city's glorious past and tumultuous present to life for me. And to this day, when I think of that poignant place, I remember the moment her eyes shone with an indomitable light as she recalled the Dubrovnik of old.

I WASN'T SURE WHAT TO EXPECT on my first visit to Dubrovnik in the fall of 2000. On the one hand, I knew that the city had long been considered the jewel of the Adriatic and was a UNESCO World Heritage site. On the other hand, I had heard that it had been largely destroyed by bombs in the early 1990s. Was I going to find rubble or restoration?

Happily, the answer was the latter. While 68 percent of Old Dubrovnik's 824 buildings were hit by bombs in an eight-month siege during the Yugoslavian civil war—leaving holes in two out of every three tiled roofs—the damage is hardly noticeable now. Most of the buildings have been meticulously repaired. And the old walled city is again truly an extraordinary jewel.

But the tale of Dubrovnik does not have an unambiguously happy ending. While the city itself has been largely rebuilt, the tourism on which the city depends has not been restored. And in this sense, the damage done by the shelling remains.

I happened to arrive on All Saints' Day, 30 October, and people were walking through the streets with armfuls of flowers to be laid at their ancestors' graves. This seemed a particularly appropriate introduction to a place where the past is such a powerful presence.

I signed up for a guided tour, which began with a bus trip to the outskirts above the city. From that vantage, Dubrovnik's Old Town seemed an exquisite labyrinth of honey-tinted stone buildings with terra-cotta roof tiles of red and orange, preserved within thick stone walls. It was an astonishing, almost fairy tale sight.

Then we walked through those gates, and the tale darkened. One of the first sights greeting visitors to the Old Town is a map that shows the damage done by bombs and grenades from October 1991 to May 1992. It is thick with black dots and triangles. "The worst day of the siege," the woman leading my group said, "was 12 December, 1991. On the day, 600 shells fell on the city." Six hundred shells.

"See up there?" she continued, pointing to a green hill within easy eyesight of the town, not far from where our bus had stopped. "That's where the guns were set. For months and months they just kept sending bombs onto the town. In all, 200 people in Dubrovnik were killed during this time." Nine years later, her voice still quavered.

This woman—I'll call her T—proved a passionate guide to Dubrovnik past and present. She explained how, in the 15th and 16th centuries, Dubrovnik had been a commercial and cultural center that rivaled Venice. Extraordinary treasures had been created and collected here; merchants from afar passed through and marveled at its splendors. Ships were sent to Syria, Egypt, France, and Spain.

The city's fall from these heights began in 1667, when an earthquake devastated the area. But despite that destruction, T said, the plan of the city itself is little changed from the Middle Ages. She pointed like a proud parent to the geometric precision of the city: the six-foot-wide alleys that rise off the main street; the steep stairways between age-blackened stone facades and freshly painted wooden shutters; the strings of bright laundry festooned against the sky.

On one side street a shopkeeper was hastily stringing up an American flag. "This flag is to welcome the sailors from the USS *George Washington*," T said. "We are so grateful to the U.S. Navy for stopping here. The sailors are good visitors; they enjoy our town and spend money. We need more tourists!"

Later in the tour, she said that about 50,000 people live in greater Dubrovnik, but that in the Old City itself, there are only about 4,000 people. "I couldn't live here!" she said. "Everyone knows everything—where you went last weekend, what you're having for dinner, what you and your husband are fighting about."

The treasures of the town came to life through her descriptions—the beautifully detailed Franciscan monastery complex, and its 13th-century pharmacy, the third oldest pharmacy in Europe, where people still line up to get their medicines prepared; the 15th-century Onofrio Fountain, whose water is still drinkable; the 15th-century synagogue, the second oldest in Europe; and the 17th-century Cathedral of the Assumption of the Virgin. The treasury here houses Dubrovnik's most precious works, T said, leading us into a room filled with a giddying array of golden artifacts. In the old days, she added, this room was impenetrable to foreign invaders; to open its doorway, three keys had to be used simultaneously.

We walked on for a couple of hours, past so many architectural and artistic glories that I began to feel almost drunk. The ancient walls of the city seemed like a jewel box, and the buildings, streets, and artworks its gems.

But it was T herself who made the most lasting impression on me. She was probably in her mid-forties—though her sculpted face seemed older—with graying golden hair covered with a silk scarf. "We are poor," she said at one point, "but we are proud." And I noticed then how the hems of her meticulous suit were frayed and how the scuffed sides of her fashionable boots had been rigorously shined.

When our tour ended, I asked if I could buy her a drink and she sank wearily into a chair at the Café Festival.

She told me about her children and her husband, about her efforts to make ends meet—growing their own vegetables and fruit, sewing their own clothes, guiding when the tourists were in town. She told me how difficult it was to cope with the ravages of the war, how it had changed the atmosphere throughout the region. "Now the borders are open," she said with a sigh, "but it's not easy to get together again as neighbors after the war."

And she told me how it had changed the atmosphere within Dubrovnik itself. "I am tired of so much gloominess!" she exclaimed. "Before the war, everyone was so happy. There was music and dancing in the streets every night. And such laughter! We had the Mediterranean spirit. But now—bah!—everyone is so gloomy. I am tired of the complaining! We need to move on, you know?"

I pictured how her life might have been before the war: lifting a glass of wine in a café, dancing on the cobbled streets. She was laughing, and the ancient buildings of Dubrovnik were glittering.

When I looked at her again, she was staring at me. "Our women are famous for being very beautiful—perhaps you have noticed?" she said, and smiled. And for a moment the spirit of Old Dubrovnik shone again in her eyes.

It is easy for us as travelers to take from the world. We go somewhere and we eat feasts, visit monuments and museums, snap pictures, meet people. Over and over, we replenish ourselves. The challenge, often, is to figure out how to give back to the places that nourish us. But in the case of Dubrovnik, this challenge is easily answered. Just go there. Do it as an homage to the treasures of the past. Do it as a testament to the idiocy of war and the resilience of the human spirit. And do it as a tribute to wonderful people like T, who deserve so much more—and who offer so much in return.

Letters from Jordan

I traveled to Jordan almost exactly one year after Sept. 11, 2001. I went mainly because I was tired of TV commentators telling me about "the word from the Arab street." I wanted to walk the Arab street, and hear the word myself. And I believed firmly that human beings are bridges, and that in times of crisis, it is not only our opportunity but our duty to become the mortal bonds that bring the planet together again. So, against the well-meaning advice of virtually everyone I knew, I journeyed to Jordan. The ensuing encounters there created a complicated and compelling portrait of the place and the people that I would never otherwise have known. I gained—and I gave—more than I ever could have imagined from home. And the trip profoundly affirmed once again the incalculable value and essential importance of seeing the world on our own.

Part One: Ancient Treasures, Modern Trials

When I was preparing for this ten-day journey to Jordan, most of the people who heard about it responded with furrowed brows. "Do you think it's safe to go there now? Aren't you worried?"

Their alarm was so intense that I partly succumbed to it, and boarded the plane for Amman on September 17, 2002, more apprehensive than I have been about any journey in decades.

But five days later, as I sit on a fountain-fronted marble terrace in the southern resort town of Aqaba, flanked by graceful palm trees and overlooking the clear waters of the Red Sea, eating delicious yogurt and fresh black olives and steaming local bread and fanned by a just-warm-enough-breeze, those fears seem worlds away.

In the past five days I have never once felt even a trace of hostility directed at me; I have not thought for even a moment that I was in danger. On the contrary, the Jordanian people I have met both in tourist places and off the beaten path have been remarkably generous, friendly, accommodating, and honest.

Which is not to suggest that they are either ignorant about or happy with the current condition of the world. The Jordanians I have spoken with would like UN inspectors to return to Iraq and to monitor the country closely, but their greatest fear is not of Saddam Hussein.

"We do not think Saddam has the kind of weapons of mass destruction that your president insists he has," a shopkeeper told me, "but even if he does, we do not think he will use them unless he is backed into a corner. That is what we really fear—that your country will provoke him to act."

And as they ask for international forces to monitor Iraq, Jordanians also ask for the U.S. to recognize and renounce its own double standard. If the U.S. wants Iraq to comply with UN resolutions, the reasoning goes, then it should demand that Israel comply with such resolutions as well.

But the reality for Jordanians is that they are subject to forces far beyond their control. As a Jordanian tour guide said to me, "What can we do? We are not a big player. We can't call the shots. We have to try to get along with everyone."

Getting along with everyone seems to be an art the Jordanians have mastered on the personal level as well. Exploring the country from north to south, I have found the people to be exceptionally warm and welcoming, gracious and hospitable. So it is especially heartbreaking to see how geography has affected tourism here. Officials say that since last September, visitor arrivals have dropped by 60 to 80 percent. While tourism accounts for only 12 percent of the economy, a few days of stopping at virtually empty hotels, restaurants, and souvenir shops makes the loss seem far greater.

And this is a huge loss for travelers as well. In just four quick days of touring, I have had at least two magical experiences that I will never forget.

The first was visiting Petra. To reach this site, you have to walk for twenty minutes along a sinuous slit sliced between whorling sandstone walls. Your footsteps echo on stones laid two millennia ago, twisting in and out of sunlight, until you turn a bend and suddenly the rose-colored columns of the Treasury soar before you, carved in exquisite designs out of the red rock. You step into a broad plaza and the façade appears in full, heart-stopping grandeur, the intricate columns and statues still awe-inspiring in their artistry twenty-one centuries after Nabatean hands carved them.

And Petra is much more than its Treasury. I spent a too-short day wandering its ancient streets and marveling at its elaborate temples and tombs—and then returned at night for the candlelit "Petra by Night" program. Straggling behind as the tour group walked to the Treasury, I stopped alone in the *siq* that leads to the site. Candle shadows danced on the sandstone walls, then the strains of a sole flute player drifted through the air and swirled around me in the Nabatean moonlight.

The second was two nights ago when I slept under the stars in the southern desert of Wadi Rum. I was staying in a Bedouin-style campsite-cum-resort called the Captain's Camp. Guests stay in goat-hair houses—the tents that the nomadic Bedouin have sewn and lived in for centuries—and eat in an open-air pavilion or around a campfire listening to traditional Bedouin songs. When the manager of the camp asked if I would like to sleep under the stars, I imagined dragging a blanket onto the sand. Oh no, sir, he said, we will bring your bed outside.

And so it was that I slept on a mattress on a wooden pallet set into the rose-colored earth, between cool sheets, with two palm trees framing the stars in front of me and the full moon overhead, and in the distance, far beyond flickering torchlights, the slumbering silhouettes of the desert crags of Wadi Rum.

Waking in the middle of the night, I walked beyond the campsite and into the desert. There I looked at the stars and absorbed the silence and thought of all the rich and conflicting cultures around me—Syria to the north, Iraq to the east, Saudi Arabia to the south, Israel and Egypt to the west. And for one brief and precious moment, peace reigned in the Middle East.

Part Two: Exhilarating Encounters, Enduring Lessons

On the tenth and final day of my Jordanian adventure, I am back where I began, in Amman—only the place looks entirely different to me. On my first arrival, I had been struck by the capital's architectural monotony of hill after hill of beige blocks, and by the exoticism of neon signs in flowing Arabic script, blue-lit minaret spires, the heart-tugging calls of the muezzin, and the occasional sight of women covered in black burqa from head to toe and men in flowing white robes and traditional red-and-white or black-and-white kefiya head-covers. Now all these have become so familiar that I hardly notice them.

What a gift! This is how travel stretches us: For me, now, waking up to a dusty dawn wail to prayer, looking onto tiny streets crammed with shops topped with Arabic loops and twirls, where men in kefiya sip tiny cups of cardamom-scented coffee, is intimate and familiar; it has become a part of my world, and so it will remain forever.

And there have been many such gifts on this trip.

One of the things I have gained is a new appreciation for the reality of the Bible, and for the rich presence of Bible-related sites in Jordan and neighboring areas. Scattered throughout Jordan are places associated with Abraham, Moses, Lot, Aaron, Elijah, Joshua, Jesus, and John the Baptist, among other Biblical figures. A couple of days ago I visited two of the most famous sites—Mount Nebo, where Moses gazed upon the Promised Land and died, and Bethany beyond Jordan, where Christ was baptized by John the Baptist. This was heady stuff for a Protestant manqué who had pretty much relegated all such sites to the realm of Sunday School storytelling. It gave a new and vibrant relevance to the Bible and made me want to re-read it as a guide to the modern Middle East.

Another lesson has been realizing what deep-rooted characteristics the countries in this region share—despite their bitter conflicts. Yesterday, on a trip to the desolate, sun-baked, and wind-swept ruins of Umm Qais, near Jordan's northern border, I looked out on areas that now "belong" to Syria, Israel, and the Palestinian Territories. There was no huge white dotted line separating one from another; the landscapes were indistinguishable, all one geologically. And the people shooing sheep or buying melons and eggplants or making dinner plans on cell phones in these areas were not really so different either, I was sure.

The day before, at Bethany beyond Jordan, I walked down to a viewing site on the Jordan River. A rock in the middle of the river, my guide told me, marked the border with Israel. If I could leap from that rock to the other side of the river, I would be in Israel. I looked up at a wide platform on the Israeli side and saw some people looking over at us. I waved and yelled "Hello!" They waved and called hello back.

It was silly, I know, but it seemed very important at the time. The sense of some impenetrable and threatening Other looming on the far side of that placid riverbank seemed so absurd. Here were people whose ancestors had lived in this region for centuries, who shared linguistic and cultural roots. I reflected on what I had heard over and over from Jordanians in shops and on the street, that governments are the problem, not the common people. "People everywhere want to get along," the owner of a crafts shop had told me. "We like the Israeli people; we like the Palestinian people; we like the Iraqi people. People want to get along with each other. But the governments are bad. All governments. They just want power."

The region's age and shape took on a different face that day in the easy-going and altogether enchanting town of Madaba. Here, in the Greek Orthodox Church of St. George, are the remarkable remains of a mosaic map that dates back to the 6th century. The mosaic, which originally contained more than two million tiles, depicts the Holy Land as it was in 560 A.D., stretching from the Mediterranean Sea in the west to the desert in the east, and from the Phoenician cities of Tyre and Sidon in the north to Egypt in the south. It was spine-tingling to think of pilgrims and traders 1,500 years before standing where I stood, gazing at the exact same stones, remembering loved ones they had left behind in Jericho, or dreaming of the journey they would one day make to Jerusalem.

At the northern ruin of Jerash I stepped back even farther in time, to a 3rd-century Roman city of 20,000, with impressive theaters, temples, plazas, and broad shopping streets where the ruts of chariot wheels can still be seen. As I walked around the amazingly well-preserved site, imagining everyday citizens shopping and gossiping in Latin half a world away from Rome, I encountered a family of four in the amphitheater. There was a young girl and boy, perhaps five and seven years old, a husband in his mid-thirties, and a wife of indeterminate age—indeterminate because she was completely covered in a black burqa, with thin eye-slits her only exposure to the world. Yet here they were on a simple family outing. The children were scampering around the complex, and the parents were talking softly with each other, a typical young couple delighting in their children and occasionally reprimanding them when they threatened to topple down stone stairs. At one point a tour guide invited their daughter to step to the middle of the stage and test the theater's amazing acoustics. After much encouragement from her parents, she wriggled, all giggles, to the center of the stage and yelled out "Ahhhh!" Then her hands flew to her mouth and her eyes grew wide as her words echoed and amplified around the theater. We all laughed together.

It may seem terribly simple-minded to say so, but this little incident put the burqa in a different light for me. I don't mean to suggest that it made the principles behind the burqa seem more palatable or benign, only that it un-demonized and humanized the whole burqa issue for me. It gave me a human referent for what had previously been a de-humanized symbol, made me see it not simply as an icon of oppression. I have no idea what that woman felt about the burqa; she may have accepted it without complaint, or wished she didn't have to wear it, or never even considered other options. But she made me realize that there are humans under those symbolic layers, women who bear children and try to teach them not to fall down stairs and who enjoy long autumn walks with their families around centuries-old ruins.

Like so many other things on this journey, that encounter in Jerash made the whole Middle East equation more human and more complex.

And so we come back to Amman and the end of my journey. As I wrote soon after my arrival here, all the misgiving I had felt when I boarded the plane in New York on September 17 vanished once I set foot in Jordan. In ten days here, I have never—not for a single moment—felt threatened or even vaguely uneasy. People everywhere have been extraordinarily open and kind and hospitable, eager to talk about the world, warm and welcoming beyond all my expectations.

Time after time, wandering virtually alone around world-class ruins or deserted handicrafts shops, I have felt the heart-breaking toll of geography on this country of treasures. Two days ago, I walked into a beautiful carpet store in Madaba and the owner asked what kind of carpet I was interested in. I wasn't there to buy, I told him, I just wanted to learn about the carpets. That's fine, sir, he said, and proceeded to ceremoniously unroll carpet after carpet, giving me a concise lecture on the history and highlights of Bedouin, Persian, and Iraqi rugs. I had the feeling it had been quite a while since he had done this, and that it was a pleasure for him simply to be going through the motions of his trade. "How is business?" I asked at one point and he looked at me. "Sir," he said slowly, "business is not down; it is dead."

Still, when I finally said that I had to leave and that I really wasn't interested in buying anything, he didn't try to bully me into a purchase, as carpet-dealers in many other countries have. He simply smiled graciously and said, "That's all right, sir. Would you like a cup of tea before you leave?"

Despite all the fears from friends and family at home, and despite the sophistical saber-rattlings of Donald Rumsfeld and George Bush that are beamed here daily on CNN and the BBC, I haven't felt a moment of misgiving on this trip—that is, until this morning, when I awoke to find a slim white envelope slipped under my hotel door. I opened it, thinking the hotel had mistakenly compiled my bill a day too early, and found a letter bearing the seal and name of the Embassy of the United States of America. The note was from one Arnaldo Arbesu, Acting Consul, and it began:

"In keeping with our policy of making available as much information as possible concerning potential terrorist threats and targeting, we are distributing the following notice through the U.S. Embassy warden network. We note that it is consistent with patterns of information already discussed in previous worldwide announcements, including that of September 9, 2000.

"The U.S. Government has received uncorroborated information indicating that as of this summer one member of the Al-Qaeda organization was considering a plan to kidnap U.S. citizens in Jordan. There is no further information to determine the credibility of this threat, or indications of timing. The U.S. embassy is working closely with the Jordanian government, police and Security Officials on the basis of this information, and they are taking appropriate measures."

My first thought was: I'm glad I'm getting out of here tomorrow. My second thought was: Oh god, poor Jordan, this is the last thing it needs. For me, this message simply underlined the truth that had become so evident throughout my trip. As a tour guide had said on my first day in the country, "Jordan is a quiet house in a noisy neighborhood." Or to put it another way: Jordan is a victim of geography. It is a relatively peaceful and progressive country smack in the middle of a region dominated by dangerous despots and racked by age-old conflicts. It is an oasis, but the desert is vast and severe.

As I pack to leave, I am boundlessly grateful that the blank space labeled "Jordan" on my mental map has now been replaced by this vivid multi-colored mosaic. And I pray that the historical betrayals and antagonisms that delineate this region today will give way before the deeper desire of everyday world citizens—whatever their country, whatever their religion—to live side by side, in peace. For one thing, the monuments here can teach us all valuable lessons about the aspirations and achievements of our ancestors; but even more importantly and more urgently, the wonderful people I have encountered on this trip deserve nothing less.

Baja: Touched by a Whale

I had never seen a whale, much less touched one. And so, when the opportunity arose to travel to Mexico's Sea of Cortez on a whale-watching expedition, I jumped onboard. The journey was organized by Lindblad Expeditions, a founding member of a consortium of adventure travel companies called the Adventure Collection, whose Adventurous Traveler blog I had been asked to edit. I am normally more attuned to close encounters with cultures and peoples than animals, but whales are so enormous and at the same time seem to be so intelligent and benign, that I have always been irresistibly attracted to them. What eventually transpired on this expedition was so extraordinary and so moving that it vibrates within me still. And it made one more lesson clear: Not all the encounters that transform us are of the human kind.

I WANTED TO TOUCH A WHALE. At heart, that was my entire reason for traveling to Baja California Sur, Mexico, to cruise in Magdalena Bay and the Sea of Cortez in the spring of 2007. In thirty years of world-wandering and twenty-five years of living on the Northern California coast, somehow I had managed to miss seeing, much less touching, the largest animal on the planet. And on my life list of Things to Do, touching a whale was near the top.

Of course, it would have been foolhardy to predicate the success of an entire trip on such a mission; that would almost guarantee failure. So I told myself that just seeing a whale would be enough. And I told myself that even if the whales inexplicably failed to show up, there would be other rewards that would more than merit the trip.

But I have to admit that after my first morning's whale-watching excursion—motoring around the choppy seas of Magdalena Bay for two hours in a rubberized Zodiac peering whalelessly into a cool, cottony fog—my heart had sunk about as deep as a bottom-feeding gray.

These depths were plumbed again at lunch, when passengers from other morning excursions breezed in with tales of whales swimming right up to their Zodiacs; quickly an invisible divide grew between those who had and those who hadn't.

While this was only the second full day of our cruise, I knew that the Zodiac outings were the only opportunity we'd have on the week-long trip to get close enough to whales to touch them, and I knew that I had only two more Zodiac outings—at 4:00 that afternoon and 8:30 the following morning—to realize my dream. To pass the time after lunch, I tossed and turned in my bunk, stared blankly at my journal, and scanned the implacable horizon.

At 4:00, seven of us clambered into our Zodiac with a naturalist and a local whale guide on board. The local guides are essential: They know the waters and the ways of the whales, and they ensure that we are complying with rules established to protect the whales in the region. (In fact, these local guides are the only individuals who have the official Mexican government permits that allow whale-watching.)

As we bounced over the waves, the fresh air and sea spray swooshing our faces, Carlos, the broad-smiling, big-hearted, encyclopedic Mexican naturalist on board our ship, reviewed what we'd learned so far: Every year gray whales make a 5,000-mile migration south from the frigid waters of the Bering and Chukchi Seas to the comparatively tropical waters of Baja California. The whales arrive here around January, and in these gentle, protected waters, they give birth and raise their young.

"Blow at two o'clock!" he suddenly yelled, and Lucinda the Zodiac driver shifted toward the spout of whale-spray that had materialized on the horizon.

The area we were approaching—Carlos pointed toward the now invisible blow—is known as "the nursery," a protected stretch of water near the Boca de Soledad's narrow entrance from the ocean to the bay. This is a favorite place for whale mothers to give birth and to train their calves, Carlos said, teaching them how to swim against the strong currents at the mouth of the bay. When they're ready, they embark on the long migration north again, in March and April.

"Rolling!" Lucinda shouted, pointing ahead. In the distance we could see a massive gray arcing shape mottled with whitish spots slowly rising out of the water and seeming to turn over on top of an even larger gray mass beneath it.

"That's the baby rolling over the mother!" Carlos said. "They love to play like that. Whales are very tactile creatures, and touching is an important way for them to communicate and to bond."

As we bounced closer, Lucinda slowed the Zodiac and we could clearly see two massive humps—one twice the length of our Zodiac, the other so much larger we couldn't see its head or tail—swimming side by side. The mother spouted and with gigantic grace flipped her flukes up and then dove into depths we couldn't fathom. The baby dove after her.

We floated, scanning the blue sea surface for whale "footprints"—smooth oval stretches of water created when the whales propel themselves with their tails underwater. We searched for spouts or sleek gray humps breaking through the waves. Nothing.

"Carlos," I asked, "when a whale flips its flukes like that—can you call it fluking?"

He cocked his bald head, smiled. "You can call it that if you want to."

"Look out! Nine o'clock. Coming right for us!" Lucinda shouted, and rising toward the surface a huge gray-white shape sped toward our Zodiac. The baby!

"He's coming to check us out," Carlos said.

"Splash! Splash!" a passenger named Thuy said, and immediately she and another passenger bent over the side of the Zodiac and began to slap the surface of the water with their hands. "We learned this morning that this might help attract the babies," she explained.

Suddenly a four-foot-long gray head appeared just below the surface of the water a few feet off our Zodiac. The baby whale turned and swept its eye over us, then swerved away. "Keep splashing!" Thuy encouraged us.

So I got on my knees and leaned over the Zodiac's rubbery side and began pounding the water for all I was worth.

"Momma at three o'clock!" Thuy's husband Mitch said and nine heads simultaneously swiveled. A blue-white undersea giant at least three times longer than our Zodiac serenely swam by us.

"I think she's checking us out to see if we're suitable for her baby to play with," Carlos said. "Send out good whale vibes."

Our Zodiac erupted into cries of "Come here, Baby! We love you, Baby! Momma, your baby is so beautiful!" accompanied by a chorus of splashing.

"Here comes Baby!" Carlos said and the now familiar snout surged toward us, swimming right up to our Zodiac, lifting itself out of the water so it could touch us. I dove forward with the other passengers and stretched my arm as far as I could. Contact!

Sleek, smooth, soft, rubbery whale-skin—cool and pliant and living and unlike anything I'd ever touched before—was flowing under my fingertips. Baby seemed to give a little smile and then pushed away.

"Woohoo!" I shouted and high-fived Mitch and the Zodiac resounded with Woohoos and All rights and Wows. Even the two teenagers among us seemed impressed.

But Baby wasn't finished. It swam right under our Zodiac—I felt its bulbous back slide lumpily beneath my knees—then surfaced and made a run for our other side. Like cartoon characters, we all leaped to that side. And again, Baby swam right up to us, lifted its head out of the water and seemed to welcome—to initiate—our contact.

Again I leaned over as far as I could and trailed my hand in the cold whirling water and again the cool sleek touch of baby whale skin electrified me. Double whale contact!

For the next half hour we floated in an otherworldly orb of whale-ness. Baby and Momma circled around our Zodiac, spouting, rolling, diving, swimming side by side, skimming up to us and then plunging playfully under us. A few times Baby swam up to us as if we were a rubber ducky in its bathtub and pushed us along with its snout.

We were all whooping and laughing and calling out to Momma and Baby and for a half hour it was as if we were having an interspecies play date.

I didn't think it could get any better than that, but shortly before Momma and Baby swam away into the depths of the bay, Momma sent her own message. She had been swimming warily but serenely at a distance from the Zodiac the entire time, content to let Baby play with us, just monitoring that we all behaved.

But at this moment, she swam straight at us, a blue-white underwater mammal-bus hurtling our way. She swam right up to the Zodiac and turned gently over as she approached, so that her eye was out of the water, looking up at us. As she cruised under the bow of the Zodiac, where I was straining forward, she passed right under me. I arched and extended my arm and felt her cool, sleek cheek. I stroked it for a few seconds and in that time she looked straight into my eye and I looked straight into hers.

And plunged into a pool of understanding and wisdom older and more far-reaching and of a different order than anything I'd encountered before. She *knew*. She knew things I could never know—about the age and evolution of the earth, about her vast underwater world. And in that instant she communicated something that I can only convey as peace and understanding, and that surged through me as an all-knowing, and somehow pardoning, blessing.

Call it projection if you want, but I know what I felt.

And it flukes in the deep blue depths of my being, even now.

Building Bridges in Mostar

As I learned four decades ago in Paris, the world is the classroom. With this mantra in mind, in the fall of 2007, I decided that the best way to understand the perplexing problems, potentials, and politics in the Balkan region would be to go there, and I arranged to join a two-week Geographic Expeditions cruise to Croatia, Montenegro, and Bosnia-Herzegovina. On that journey I learned much more than I could have anticipated, not only from the onboard lecturer but from completely unexpected teachers, such as chefs encountered in markets and fishermen met on wharves. The priceless value of this worldly education was demonstrated most movingly in Mostar. As our engaging twenty-something guide took us around the town and described the heartbreaking history of that exquisite city and of her own young life there, the divisiveness and destruction of war became soul-piercingly clear. But what also emerged as she showed us her home was the irrepressible hope in her eyes.

I HAVE SEEN THE FUTURE, AND IT LOOKS like a bridge. In fact, it is a bridge, the very structure I am admiring right now: the Stari Most, or Old Bridge, in the Old Town of Mostar, in Bosnia-Herzegovina, which spans the Neretva River and connects the Muslim and Croat communities in this venerable and poignant place.

On hearing the word "Mostar," most people would probably not think "budding tourist destination" but rather "bombed-out war zone." Mostar was in headlines around the world when it was besieged during the Balkan conflict of the early 1990s. The once charming and harmonious place was first bombarded by Serbian and Montenegrin forces in April 1992; that attack subsided half a year later, only to be replaced in May 1993 by brutal, bloody fighting between the Croats and Muslims who had co-existed peacefully before. Ripped apart along ethnic and religious lines, Mostar became a haunting site and symbol of the war's destruction.

That destruction is still powerfully visible fourteen years later. Walk for fifteen minutes in the Old Town and you'll pass at least a few gaping, bomb-blasted, hulking shells of buildings and others with facades eerily pitted and pock-marked by bullet and shell holes. And you'll no doubt pass a cemetery too, as I did just now, with row after row after row of flower-graced tombstones bearing poignant photos of handsome young men, with a numbing litany of dates: 1912-1993; 1967-1993; 1967-1994; 1969-1994; 1972-1994. They give mute eloquence to the pain at the heart of this place.

But look beyond the cemetery and you'll see symbols of another kind: here a freshly painted restaurant with bright striped awnings and a red-tiled roof; there a meticulously reconstructed shop with elegant stone walls and flower-bedecked windows; and over there a cobbled terrace with immaculate wooden tables and benches arranged under new pine-green sun umbrellas.

The greatest symbol of all is the bridge. Originally constructed in the mid-16th century, for more than 400 years this ethereally slender, curving, 100-foot-long arch had been the icon of Mostar, a wonder people crossed oceans and continents to see. It had survived man's invasions and nature's earthquakes, but it couldn't survive the heavy shelling inflicted on it Nov. 9, 1993, when it collapsed into the river. So it was of singular importance that UNESCO undertook to rebuild the bridge—using the same Tenelija stone and 16th-century methods as the original—and was able to officially reopen it on July 23, 2004.

The Stari Most is important literally as a connector between the two communities of Mostar, the Croats who live on the western side of the river and the Muslims on the east; today foot traffic flows ceaselessly between the two. But its importance is even greater as a symbol of connection, of reconciliation and rebirth, of hope. And for me, it symbolizes the potential of this lovely, historic, and once all-embracing crossroads to again become a magnet for travelers from around the world, and for tourism to help heal the wounds of the war and to help cultivate a new economy and culture here.

On this September day, the sky is a deep blue, the branches of the trees that line the emerald Neretva are waving in a gentle breeze, and the sun is glinting gloriously off the white and gray stone walls and streets of the Old Town. As my tour group listens intently to our guide, six Italians smilingly settle in at a riverside restaurant, a procession of Russian tourists snap photos of domes and minarets, three UN soldiers in green-and-brown fatigues stride toward the produce market, and a phalanx of French visitors amble from alley-side stall to stall, fingering their brimming jewelry, copperwork, and other treats. Energy and optimism surge through the streets.

In the course of a morning walk through the eastern side of the Old Town, I have been touched by an exquisitely simple mosque and an exquisitely elaborate Turkish house that illuminates the life of a Muslim family here three centuries ago. But mostly I have been moved by the juxtapositions—the beautifully restored building next to the windowless shattered shell; the desolate cemetery two blocks from the bustling café; the tales of utter brutality and despair you hear and read and the laughter and hope in the eyes of the shopkeepers and students you meet.

All this is embodied for me here in the engaging form of Lana, the vivacious twenty-something tour guide who has been leading our group through the Old Town, and who is now unfolding her own extraordinary tale. Lana was raised as a Muslim in Mostar, but before the war, she says, no one knew or cared about the religious beliefs of friends and neighbors; everyone got along. Then the war came and suddenly religion took on an inexplicable and chilling importance. One day, Lana says, she looked out her window and watched a soldier come and take away her bicycle. She cried and cried after that, she says. A few days later, soldiers came and took away her father.

He was imprisoned in a concentration camp. After a harrowing period of separation, as their world collapsed around them, they were able by good connections and good luck—eventually hidden in the bowels of a UN convoy—to escape as a family to Norway. There they were able to live out of harm's reach, but they were determined to return to Mostar as soon as the hostilities ceased.

And return they did, Lana continues, only to find that their apartment had been taken over—by a judge. The only way to reclaim a dwelling at that time was to go through the legal system—that is, through the judge. So this situation posed a serious problem. But after a while, Lana finishes, a smile lighting her face, the judge moved out on his own and her family was able to move back into their apartment and begin the long task of rebuilding their lives.

As she relates all this, Lana radiates a youthful energy and optimism and innocence that are astonishing and uplifting. Somehow, she has not been scarred by this; her dreams have survived intact.

"Among my friends," she says, "we don't even ask what our religions are. We don't care. We want to move on with our lives. We want to live in peace with each other." She pauses, then opens her arms to the city around her. "We want to rebuild our beautiful home."

I look at Lana, and at the Stari Most behind her, and suddenly tears fill my eyes. How could people do such atrocious things to one another? And then, how could such a glorious flower take root and bloom in that wretched soil?

I had thought the Stari Most was the great symbolic bridge here, a bridge between Muslim and Croat, past and present, but now I think that Lana is a bridge too, between Mostar and us, and between present and future.

And as I stand on this cobbled square, watching the frothy flow of the Neretva below and the human flow above, watching the passion flame in Lana's eyes, I realize that we are all bridges here—bridges from horror to redemption, from intractable history to unbound possibility—and that every single one of us visitors also plays a crucial role: Through the money we have the privilege to spend and through the values of tolerance, understanding, peace, and goodwill we have the opportunity to embody and extend, we rebuild Mostar; we buttress all the Lanas of this beautiful, poignant place—and become in ourselves bridges across the divide of despair.

I have seen the future, and it is here.

Into Africa

On the same adventurous summer when I climbed Mount Kilimanjaro, after my year teaching in Greece, the family of my Greek students also organized a safari for me and a fellow teacher. This was an actual shooting safari, led by a grizzled guide described as one of the last of the great white hunters, and while all I shot was a tree, I ended this experience with profoundly mixed feelings. Three decades later, I was able to return to East Africa with pure, unadulterated anticipation on a photo safari choreographed by Micato Safaris, another Adventure Collection member. That exploration of Kenya and Tanzania bestowed lessons on many levels, but deepest of all was my sense of being a guest in the majestic home of the lion and elephant, cheetah and giraffe. I felt exhilaratingly small, alien, and alive, and I tried to recreate these feelings—and the gifts they gave—in this five-part series I wrote for the Adventure Collection blog.

Part One: The Kiss of the Giraffe

My introduction to the wildlife of East Africa was a kiss from a giraffe. No, this isn't a metaphor. We're talking about a real wet lip-smacker here, a come-here-big-boy-and-let-me-give-you-a-taste-of-my-long-black-tongue kiss.

But let's back up a bit.

I arrived in Africa from London at about 8:45 on a humid Nairobi night. Almost immediately on exiting the plane, I was greeted by a smiling woman from the safari company that had organized my tour, and whisked through Immigration to the baggage claim area, where she introduced me to two fellow safari-mates who just happened to be on the same flight: Jennifer and Benjie, exuberant thirty-somethings who, she explained, were celebrating their new marriage with a safari honeymoon. Ah, romance!

We gathered up our green duffle bags and before long were rolling through the night toward the Norfolk Hotel, a grand colonial-era establishment on the outskirts of the city, where I tumbled into a deep sleep.

Early the next morning we met the fourth and final member of our party—Jill, a lively Southern Californian—and then met Duncan, the company's director of safari programs, and our safari leader, Lewela. Pointing to a large map, Lewela presented an overview of our itinerary: We would spend the first day touring Nairobi and the surrounding area, then fly south the following day to Amboseli, where we would spend two days; in successive two-day stays, we would visit the Mount Kenya Safari Club; Masai Mara National Reserve; Serengeti National Park in Tanzania; and finally Ngorongoro Crater before returning to Nairobi. Duncan then introduced a tall, thin man splendidly attired in bright red traditional Maasai garb, who told us in a soft voice about the history and culture of his people, and said that as part of our stay in Masai Mara, we would be able to visit a Maasai village; he said the villagers welcomed this opportunity to teach us about their traditional ways of life.

After that we scrambled into a minivan for a day-tour of Nairobi and surrounding towns. On first impression, Nairobi is a daunting city, a big, bustling, car-crammed and pedestrian-crammed, choking-air capital that seems to uncomfortably combine elements of the first and third worlds. On the one hand, there are shining skyscrapers, headquarters of international corporations and organizations, and businesspeople striding in sleek suits as they talk urgently on cell phones; on the other hand, there are potholed streets, broken-up sidewalks, and endless strings of people walking, walking, walking along the roadways, crossing haphazardly in the midst of perpetual-rush-hour traffic or threading a ragtag path between cars. In some places we passed small plots of lovingly tended community gardens and bright brand-name boutiques; in others, trash fires burned where sidewalks should have been, and muddy, tin-roof shanty towns sprawled and spread. While experience tells me that a sustained stay would open up the idiosyncratic wonders of the city, on first glance Nairobi seemed an intimidating, impenetrable place.

Soon a very different Kenya revealed itself as we drove into the suburbs of Karen, past posh mansions and rambling walled estates to the gracious former farmhouse of Karen Blixen. A Danish aristocrat and coffee planter who settled here from 1914-1931, Blixen wrote the passionate memoir *Out of Africa*, which has probably introduced more Westerners to the country than any other single tome. On her expansive estate Blixen lived what was considered a life of luxury, but it's illuminating to tour the farmhouse, now a museum, and see what kinds of cooking and cleaning contraptions constituted luxury in those days.

We also drove into the green, tea-growing highlands of Limuru, where we visited Fiona and Marcus Vernon's Kiambethu

Tea Farm. This excursion presented another and even more unexpected view of Africa—lush green rolling hills of tea plants, punctuated by farmsteads with broad pastures and bright gardens. The Vernons are descendants of one of the original Kenya tea farmers, who settled here in 1910, and they opened their home to us, describing the process of tea cultivation and production in their living room and then serving a splendid lunch—featuring vegetables grown in the backyard gardens we had just toured—under sun umbrellas on their lawn.

But the most memorable moment of that first day for me occurred at the Giraffe Center in the suburb of Langata. Founded by Betty and Jock Leslie-Melvile in 1979 as a refuge for endangered Rothschild giraffes and supported today by the African Fund for Endangered Wildlife, the Giraffe Center makes exemplary efforts to educate Kenyan schoolchildren about their wildlife and environment. Part of that effort includes the opportunity to feed the giraffes and, for a brave and foolhardy few, to kiss a giraffe.

When Lewela asked our adventurous foursome if any of us wanted to be kissed by a giraffe, I felt sure someone else would volunteer—wouldn't a giraffe kiss make that honeymoon even more memorable? But when no one stepped forward, I felt a professional obligation to put my lips on the line. Lewela laughed and slapped me on the back, then placed a long thin stick of some sweet treat—a kind of giraffe Tootsie Roll—between my teeth and instructed me to pucker up. Sure enough, within a few seconds, a Rothschild beauty was swinging her patched proboscis toward me and unfurling her prodigious leather-black tongue. With a swift tickle of chin hairs and a sloppy slippery scratch of the tongue, she took the Tootsie from my lips. Wow! Talk about interspecies communication.

As I blinked in disbelief, Lewela draped an arm over my shoulder. "Don't worry, Don, the giraffe's saliva is extremely antiseptic." Ah, I felt much better.

So what did it feel like? Make a dish of tapioca pudding and spread a thin layer over a sheet of very rough-grained sandpaper; now take that sheet and smoosh it across your lips. Mmmm. The kiss of the giraffe.

That night we were treated to a festive feast at a private home in another gracious Nairobi suburb and I was able to regale the table with my tale of the giraffe's kiss. Sometimes adventure travel takes you places you never expected to go. And this was just the beginning!

Part Two: Dramas in the Bush

We've just stepped off an eighteen-seat Air Kenya propeller plane onto the airstrip at Amboseli National Reserve. Vast brown savannah surrounds us. A nearby herd of ungainly, big-horned wildebeest stares at the noisy, propeller-beaked bird that just disrupted their grazing. Beyond them sleek-striped zebra munch, flanks twitching, on the grass. To their distant left a trio of Thomson's gazelles leap toward the green foothills of Mount Kilimanjaro, whose flanks disappear into masses of gray clouds.

I look at the three others on my safari and blurt out the only words that come to mind: "This is so—Africa!"

We climb into our minivan and set off for the tented camp where we will spend the next two nights. We've been driving for about fifteen minutes when we come upon a swamp. Lewela, our safari director, suddenly points to the far shore, "Look! Over there!"

Four heads swivel. And there it is: Three feet from the water's edge, a lioness is lying next to the bloody half-carcass of a zebra, the remains of the pride's dinner. "They had a big party last night!" Lewela laughs as we stop to absorb the scene.

Another lioness is lying down about twenty feet away, sated, so exhausted from the effort of eating and digesting that we can hear her labored panting and see the bellows of her tawny body moving in and out. Soon a great African drama begins to unfold. First wiry jackals come on the scene, cautiously approaching the carcass, smelling the air, anxious in their hunger, waiting for an opening when they can dash in and make off with some lunch. Then two hyenas come loping across the savannah, eyeing the lions, warily working their roundabout way toward the glistening kill.

For a long time the lioness lets them approach, head on paws, eyes closed, seemingly oblivious. Then she slowly raises herself, turns, and begins a purposeful stride in the direction of the jackals and hyenas. After a few taut seconds they scoot away, followed closely by the lioness's eye. Then she returns to her resting place and curls up again next to the carcass. One of the jackals gives a disappointed yelp. Lunch will have to wait.

Another drama begins to play out in the swamp as the wildebeest and zebras start to cross. They enter the water in a line, following the leader across the depths and out to the opposite shore. But suddenly, about a third of the way into the swamp, one of the wildebeests begins to flail wildly. It has strayed off the path into deeper waters and bucks in terror for a few seconds before it finds its footing and splash-charges into shallower waters and onto the land.

"During the Great Migration a lot of wildebeest die this way," Lewela says. "Either they drown or they get separated from the herd and become easy prey. The lions wait by the rivers like they're at a buffet."

As he speaks, the next wildebeest in line hesitates, confused, then looks around, snorts and gallops back onto the land he'd just left. The one behind him stands still for a second, then belligerently wheels around and follows him back. Soon the entire line of wildebeest and zebra has beaten a retreat onto land, and the animals graze and gaze placidly, now on both sides of the water, as if nothing has happened.

In the foreground a flock of long-beaked, white-winged great white pelicans erupts as one into the sky, swerving over the sweeping brown-golden grass-plains and toward the line of hazy green-purple hills beyond. Acacia trees thrust their thorny branches into the sky, and giraffe, elephant, and Cape buffalo materialize in the distance. The smell of fresh dung carries on the breeze, mixing with the dry dusty earthy smell of the land. And Kilimanjaro broods over it all, massing in the clouds.

Africa!

We continue our game drive to Tortilis Tented Camp. When I had been preparing for this trip, the words "tented camp" had conjured visions of summer family camping trips, lightweight tents pitched by the campfire, and freeze-dried meals cooked on camp stoves. So I am more than a little nonplussed—and delighted—when we pull up to the gracious, thatch-roofed main building at Tortilis and I am taken to my luxurious tented room. This is definitely not your typical summer family camp-trip site....

Now it's 3:15 and I'm sitting on my verandah, looking out on the snow-topped crown of Kilimanjaro—well, I would be, if the mountain would deign to appear—and the dry swaying grass of the savannah. A mid-afternoon torpor has settled over the scene. A slight breeze barely stirs the branches of the Acacia tortilis trees that tower around my tent, casting long shadows over a dense tangle of green, insect-loud vegetation. The most energetic beings are the buzzing flies and the calling birds. There's an amazing, sweet cacophony of bird calls—one that has a sandpapery grate to it, others high branch-strung tweets, others that woo-woo-woo.... To the east of cloud-massed Kilimanjaro, rain sheets down in the distance.

A whiff of wetness is borne on the breeze, and the insects shrill with even greater intensity.

I look around and shake my head: It's almost impossible to believe that this is just our first day in the bush. Who knows what wonders await?

Part Three: Under the Elephant's Spell

On our second day in the bush, as dawn is just beginning to light the world outside my tented room, I hear a shuffle of feet and then *"Jambo!* Your tea, sir." One of the Maasai staffers at Tortilis Camp places a tray with a pitcher of tea, heated milk, sugar, a china cup and saucer, a spoon, and two biscuits on my verandah. I throw on my clothes, down a quick cup of tea, and hustle up to the main lodge, where our safari van awaits.

Lewela, our safari director, greets us with a broad smile. "Are you ready to see some wildlife?"

We hop into the van and set out as the rising sun starts to streak the sky. Bouncing on dirt tracks through the dry brown savannah, we soon spot a herd of elephants in the distance. As we approach, the classic Amboseli photo composes itself in my mind: a line of huge gray elephants standing in the foreground among swaying, lush green elephant grass, with snow-crowned Mount Kilimanjaro rising massive and majestic in the background.

All the elements are there, except one—the lower flanks of Kilimanjaro are visible, but the top remains tantalizingly hidden within a dense gray camouflage of clouds.

"The elephants are probably walking toward a waterhole for their own version of morning tea," Lewela says. Their path parallels the dirt road we're on, and we're able to drive alongside them for about ten minutes. Then the lead elephant veers to the right, directly onto our road. We stop and watch in awe as a parade of elephants lumbers unconcernedly in front of us, less than 15 feet from our van.

There are twelve in all, ranging from mature adults nearly twice the size of our van, with two-foot-long tusks, to babies about as tall as a bicycle. They plod slowly, deliberately, delicately across, a surprising combination of girth and grace, then plunge unhesitatingly into the dense tangle of trees and brush on the other side of the road. Immediately the air rings with the sound of tearing and scraping as they break and uproot their breakfast, grabbing great trunksful of branches and bushes and curling them into their mouths, where they methodically chew them.

"In fact," Lewela says, watching the elephants feast, "elephants spend about three-fourths of their lives eating. Adult elephants generally eat between 200 and 400 pounds of vegetation a day. About 70 percent of their diet is grass; the rest is leaves, fruit, branches, roots, and bark. As you can see, the elephants grab the food with their trunks and stuff it into their mouths; then they grind the food down with their molar teeth. They use these teeth so much that in its lifetime, an elephant will grow six sets of molars."

Suddenly Lewela pauses. The next to last elephant in the road-crossing parade has stopped, and is now turning toward us. Ears extended, tusks pointing our way, eyes staring straight at us, he ponderously maneuvers his tree-sized legs so that he faces us squarely.

"Don't worry," Lewela whispers, "he's just curious about us. He's checking us out."

For an electrifying moment, we stare at each other, and rather than fear, I find myself falling under the spell of the elephant. There's something so gracious, dignified, and wise about him. I know these are personifications and projections, but still—look at him! His big round eyes curiously, peacefully staring, his Dumbo ears ever so gently flapping, his foot-long tusks just starting to curl, his tail swishing, he's a big gray embodiment of curiosity and self-assurance combined. We hold our breaths in taut suspension, and I feel a kind of primordial gut-tug, like some spirit-understanding is leaping from me to the elephant and from the elephant to me. An inexplicable, irrefutable connection is fused, then the enormous tree-legs start to slowly turn, heroically bearing that wrinkled gray bulk, and the elephant slowly shifts course, heavy footstep by heavy footstep, and ambles off into the brush.

Elephants are a good example of the complexities of conservation in Africa. "They are enormously destructive," says Lewela. "Look at how much they eat! If they're confined to an area, they can strip it of its trees and other vegetation. They can even transform a wooded area into a grassland. But they also open up dense forests so that all kinds of animals and plant life can thrive there. They have a role in the cycle. And of course they're good for tourism, too. But as local people want more and more land for their livestock and farms, the elephant's territory gets smaller and smaller. It's a very complicated situation."

We drive on and see our first hippopotamus, a brown blur slowly stepping through the bush. "He must have been out late partying and now he's headed back to the swamp," says Lewela.

Then we see elegant, impossibly elongated giraffes nibbling on tree-top leaves, and two tawny, big-maned lion brothers walking magisterially through the elephant grass. We come upon a herd of big-nosed, crinkly-skinned Cape buffalo—"a face only a mother could love," Jennifer says—and wildebeest and zebras placidly grazing. Our drive climaxes with a rare view of two lions mating in the grass. (We share this sight with a van full of peach-skinned Scandinavian teenagers; one especially cherub-faced girl turns to us breathlessly, flashes a thumbs-up, and exclaims, "Lion sex!")

The wonders continue. But that night, as we review the day over a sumptuous meal on the Tortilis dining verandah, it's the elephant—full with a wisdom that seems to stretch through centuries—that stands, stolid and wide-eyed, in my mind.

Part Four: Kenya Connections

It's 10:40 P.M. on our second night at the Mount Kenya Safari Club. I'm sitting on my verandah, staring into the light-less night and up at the star-spattered sky, more full of stars—in this high-altitude African blackness—than I have ever seen before.

Yesterday morning we rose early and drove back to the Amboseli airstrip, where we caught a flight to Nairobi. In Nairobi we transferred planes and flew north to Nanyuki, gateway to Mount Kenya National Park and the Mount Kenya Safari Club.

The Safari Club is a storied place, founded by the late actor William Holden in 1959. Sir Winston Churchill and Lord Mountbatten were members, and guests have included Clark Gable, John Wayne, Ernest Hemingway, Robert Redford, Sean Connery, and Catherine Deneuve. The lush, rambling lawns and gracious buildings lend it a colonial atmosphere, and you still half-expect to see Hemingway and Holden drinking port in the plush sitting room.

Our stay here is something of a lull in the itinerary. After the bouncing and jouncing of our Amboseli game drives, it has been rejuvenating to take a leisurely dip in the pool, amble along the fairways of the deserted golf course, and sit on the verandah reading, pausing now and again to gaze at the snow-capped crag of Mount Kenya.

We did make one relatively sedate game drive today at nearby Sweetwaters Game Reserve, where we spotted two massive white rhinoceros. "The rhinoceros is one animal we are always careful to stay well away from," Lewela said. "They have excellent senses of smell and hearing, but their eyesight is extremely poor, so they will charge almost anything that gets too close and poses a threat." As he talked, they walked slowly through the grass and toward our vehicle. We waited, watching, wondering exactly when "close" becomes "too close." Then, when they were about twenty feet away, they veered to the right and walked slowly, placidly, over the track we'd driven in on.

One fundamental factor that has set the trip apart has been Lewela, our safari director. He has proved to be an astonishing fount of information on just about everything, from the intricacies of the wildlife, plant life, and bird life to the history and political situations of Kenya, surrounding countries, and the larger world outside them. He is an incredible encyclopedia—and best of all, a human encyclopedia, which gives us a human connection to the countries and the cultures that we just wouldn't have if we were traveling on our own. In addition to all that knowledge, Lewela is invariably smiling, efficient, and sensitive to the idiosyncrasies of the group; it's a privilege to be able to see Kenya and learn about Africa with him.

At dinner tonight, talking with Benjie, Jennifer, Jill, and Lewela—and fueled by four truly splendid gin and tonics—the other thing I re-realized is how travel makes the world local. We were talking about Somali politics and the Somali warlords, and how chaotic the situation in the country is now. I knew this vaguely from headlines I'd seen in the States, but being here on the ground in Kenya, which has a long border with Somalia, brings that situation so much more vividly to life, gives it a personal presence and connection that it wouldn't have for me otherwise.

And that's one of the great gifts of travel: It localizes the world, so that wherever you are becomes of intense interest and palpable presence by your being there. For us, Uganda, Somalia, Tanzania, Africa as a whole, have suddenly taken on a vivid, vibrant reality. Just like the giraffes, lions, and elephants we've encountered on this trip, they're a part of our world now, with a presence and importance they never otherwise would have. This is how travel makes world citizens of us all.

I know I won't come away from this trip understanding Kenya's complicated, rich history in depth, just as I won't understand in any depth all of the wildlife we see. But I also know that when I leave, they will be a part of me.

Part Five: Cheetah Time on the Mara Plains

Just as we were finishing breakfast this morning in Masai Mara National Reserve, Sammy our driver and Lewela arrived in our van. Perfect timing.

We set off on a game drive. During the course of the drive we saw big brooding Cape buffalo, mud-caked elephants, tree-top-munching giraffes, and a young hyena emerging from the hole that led to its underground home. But the wildlife highlight of the day occurred about a half hour into the drive, when Sammy spotted a yellow flash in the grasses to our left. He crept closer, slowly and steadily, until a mother cheetah and her two children suddenly emerged into a wide area of lower grass. What a sight! There was something breathtakingly sleek and elegant in the way they walked, the lean rippling lines in their flanks, the sloping spotted back, the slim, quick, powerful legs. Speed personified—or rather, cheetahfied.

We followed them for a while. They were scouring the plains for their breakfast. They would walk slowly, majestically, for a few paces, then lift their heads to smell the wind and look at the plains. At one point they froze—a herd of Thomson's gazelles was grazing in the near distance, and a couple who weren't paying attention seemed to have strayed from the others.

Suddenly the mother cheetah went into stealth stalking mode, sinking into the grass so that she virtually disappeared, slinking forward long taut leg-stretch by stretch. We could make her out now and again, low to the ground, her belly almost touching the soil, sliding ever closer to the gazelles. The gazelle closest to the cheetah looked up and around, ears twitching; the breeze was blowing toward the cheetah. Closer. The gazelle went back to its grazing, and was soon enrapt again in the grass. Closer. My throat was dry; my palms were wet. Closer.

Then the air went electric. In a bright yellow blur the cheetah leaped up and pounced toward the nearest gazelle, which shot off as soon as she noticed the spotted blur. The gazelle vaulted through the grass and the cheetah gave chase, bounding forward in time to the gazelle's leaps. The chase continued for twenty seconds that seemed like an eternity, then the gazelle suddenly veered to the left and leaped into a waterhole, high-stepped through the water and scampered out onto the other side. The cheetah bounded into the water but was slowed by it and stopped in the middle of the waterhole, abruptly giving up the chase. The gazelle bolted on to the safety of the herd.

We resumed breathing, and continued to follow the cheetah, who had returned to her two cubs. Would they find breakfast? Who was the good guy and the bad guy in this drama? Neither, of course. On some gut level I felt simultaneously relieved and disappointed. Life in the wild.

The cheetahs strode to the shade of a tree, and before long the two cubs had climbed up into its branches. Their mother continued to search the plains. Was there a kind of desperation in her manner or was it just my projection? Her children were hungry; there must be breakfast out there somewhere. She spotted another herd of gazelles and began to crawl toward them. We followed slowly behind. She neared them, heading toward one loner who was lingering over a patch of grass while his mates had nervously scattered away.

Suddenly a couple of bush bird beauties—the regal crested crane, the national bird of Uganda, adorned with a flamboyant golden crown—flew into the air and settled near the gazelle, where they began to emit a distinctive cry.

"Look at that!" Lewela said. "See how the prey work together? The birds are trying to warn the gazelle that the cheetah is approaching. We see this often here—the prey work together to keep each other safe."

Alerted by the birds' cries, the gazelle leaped away to re-join his herd.

"I bet that cheetah would like to get her paws on those birds right now," Jennifer said.

Now it is 10:00 P.M. After dinner I was escorted by a gun-bearing guide along the pathway back to my tented camp. Happily, no buffalos or other inordinately scary things appeared in the arc of his light. For a moment on that dark path, though, I had been the gazelle—and now that I am back safe in my tented camp, I feel simultaneously relieved and, in an odd way, disappointed.

Life goes on, and so, I now understand, will this safari, long after we have left, in the savannah of my soul: Africa has gotten under my skin.

∼

Making Roof Tiles in Peru

The encounter described in this essay took place on the same trip during which I visited Machu Picchu. I especially love this experience because it was such a grounding counterpart to Machu Picchu. Making roof tiles—sinking my hands into wet clay, molding it, then leaving it to bake in the sun, knowing that in a few days it would be part of a villager's home, protecting it from the wind and rain—forged a deeply moving, visceral connection to the people and the land. I wrote this story for the blog of Geographic Expeditions, the same company that took me to Pakistan along the Karakoram Highway in the 1980s; I have been editing and writing for the GeoEx blog, which I re-named (of course) Wanderlust, since 2007.

ON MY FIRST VISIT TO PERU, I spent an expanding and enlightening week wandering through the Sacred Valley. The highlights were almost too numerous to mention—the resonant ruins of Machu Picchu, of course, plus other soul-stirring sites such as Ollantaytambo, Moray, Pisaq, Tipon, and Pikillacta; the amazingly varied and delicious cuisine; the uniformly hospitable people; the intricate textiles, transporting music, and other cultural and artistic riches; ancient and cosmopolitan Cusco.

But one completely unexpected highlight was a chance to experience firsthand—literally—the fine art of making roof tiles.

On the next to last day of my journey, after exploring as far as Racchi, halfway to Lake Titicaca, we were returning along the road to Cusco. On the way we approached a site I had expressed interest in earlier in the day—a roadside area where a team of workers was making roof tiles; that morning we had seen the tiles arranged in semi-circular columns by the side of the road.

Throughout the Sacred Valley I had been expressing admiration for the mud-brick and roof-tile houses that we saw everywhere, and as we passed the site, my guide Manuel turned to me, "Do you want to see how roof tiles are made?"

Of course, I said.

OK, he said with a grin, then instructed our driver to make a U-turn. Suddenly we veered off the main road onto a dusty driveway. We bumped past a one-story mud-brick house and a startled grandmother sitting on its porch, then rolled to a dusty stop at the edge of the tile-maker's lot.

Manuel and I descended from our van and walked over to the work crew, under their bemused stares.

"Hello!" Manuel said. "My friend here would like to learn how roof tiles are built. Would you mind showing us?"

"With pleasure," said a strong, compact man in a white baseball cap, orange shirt, and mud-spattered apron. He approached us with a big smile, and when I extended my hand to shake his, shyly indicated his own mud-lined hands. He didn't want to dirty my pristine palms.

He explained to Manuel, who translated to me, how roof tiles are made. First you get clay from the local quarry and heap it in a big pile to dry in the sun. Once it is completely dry, you wet it thoroughly with water and then mix sand with the clay, so that the mixture is about 20 percent sand. You have to check this mixture very carefully, the foreman said, to make sure that there are no bubbles because bubbles will cause cracks later.

Then you leave the clay mixture to dry in the sun and the shade for two days. After that, you cover it with a plastic tarp and dry it for one more day.

"That's the clay you see here," the foreman said, pointing to a muddy mound under a sky-blue tarp. "This is the material we use to make the roof tiles." Then he looked at me and grinned, "Do you want to try?"

I looked at Manuel, who smiled at me. "Why not?" I said.

The three workers broke into broad grins and one lifted off his own mud-layered apron and handed it to the foreman, who gingerly draped it over my neck and tied it behind me.

Then we went to work.

First, under his careful direction, I scooped a big handful of clay from the slick mound under the tarp. Placing that handful on the dirt ground just in front of the mound, I kneaded it into a sausage shape. Then I transferred this mud-sausage to a rectangular metal mold roughly six inches by ten inches, with sides about a half-inch high.

I placed the sausage at the end of the mold closest to me and then began to spread the clay the length of the mold. The foreman showed me how to work my hands along the clay, almost as if I were massaging it, making sure that it filled every crack, crevice and corner entirely.

By this time, five kids ages four to fourteen had come to watch the show. We all inspected my work to make sure that I had filled the mold evenly and uniformly, with no air bubbles anywhere. Finally the foreman gave a smiling thumbs-up. Then he told me to take a thin, smooth piece of wood, about three inches by eight inches, from a pail of water. I slowly slid this piece the length of the clay, skimming off any excess, to make sure the surface was absolutely smooth.

Next I carefully lifted the molded clay out of the mold and placed it onto another mold curved in the shape of a semi-circle. I left it there for a few minutes, just enough time for it to assume the curved shape of a finished roof tile. Then I slid it off the curved mold and carefully carried it—trailed by the ever-growing gaggle of kids—to an area where hundreds of roof tiles were laid in neat rows, drying in the sun. With a little flourish, I placed mine at the end of the closest row, then posed with it, surrounded by the giggling kids and smiling workers.

As Manuel and I went to leave, we thanked them all profusely, especially the foreman, who had so graciously and generously interrupted his day to teach a stranger his everyday art.

I extended my now mud-caked palm. He looked at it and then at me, and clasped my hand into his own.

～

Living-History Lessons in Berlin

This story came from a Baltic cruise I took with my wife in the summer of 2014. I wasn't expecting to get any material for great stories on this cruise—the trip was supposed to be a vacation—and this piece is a good example of why a travel writer should always have his/her mind open and alert. Before we docked in Germany, I had arranged for a private half-day tour of Berlin with a guide. As we approached the capital on the train from the port, I imagined we would have a pleasant four hours seeing the city's main sights and monuments. But as soon as we met our guide and she began talking in a deeply personal way about the day the Berlin Wall came down, everything changed. Goosebumps rose all along my skin as she told her impassioned tale, and we felt transported through time with her. Sometimes the world delivers the deepest connections when we least expect it—and that's why we have to be alive to every moment.

IT'S ONE THING TO STAND IN A PLACE where a historic event transpired a thousand years ago. It's entirely different to stand in a spot where history was made during your own lifetime.

This lesson resonated for me on a mind-expanding cruise around the Baltic Sea in the summer of 2014. Our voyage included day tours in Stockholm, Tallinn, Helsinki, St. Petersburg, and Copenhagen. In each city we gazed at grand, centuries-old cathedrals and statues commemorating epoch-making events. And yet in each, history remained somehow cerebral and out of reach—until we reached Berlin.

My wife and I traveled by train from the port of Rostock to Berlin's central rail terminal, where we met a wonderful guide, Sabine Mueller, who immediately took us to the Brandenburg Gate.

As we stood in the shadow of the iconic arch, Sabine said, "I want to tell you about the night the Berlin Wall came down."

She recalled that in a news broadcast aired at 8:00 P.M. on November 9, 1989, the East German authorities announced that the eastern borders, including the borders between East and West Berlin, would be opened. She was twenty years old at the time and had been living in West Berlin since she was a toddler.

"People in East Germany listened to these broadcasts, too, and as soon as they heard this news, they streamed to the borders," she said. "The East Berliners were afraid that the decision might be reversed at any moment and wanted to take advantage of it while they could.

"The next morning I was awakened at dawn by a phone call from my friend. 'We have to go to the Wall!' he said. 'Why?' I asked, still half asleep. 'Because they're tearing it down!'"

Sabine paused and goosebumps ran along my body. I was in two places simultaneously, one foot in modern-day Berlin and the other in the newsroom at the *San Francisco Examiner* that long-ago November day as the first reports streamed over the wire.

Standing in Berlin in 2014, I felt the same exhilarating breeze I'd felt in 1989 as I read eyewitness accounts from the German capital and marveled that changes beyond my comprehension were sweeping across the planet.

Sabine pointed at our feet, where a trim line of light gray concrete perhaps eight inches wide ran down the street. "This marks where the Berlin Wall stood," she said. "My city was divided."

"Think of it," she continued. "Twenty-eight years earlier, in 1961, barbed wire had been erected overnight. Some East Berliners who had spent the night in West Berlin woke up unable to return home, or faced the decision of whether to stay in the free West or return to loved ones in the East, knowingly giving up their chance for freedom. Some people who lived in East Berlin but worked in West Berlin suddenly couldn't go to their jobs. Families and friends who lived on separate sides of the Wall were torn apart."

Sabine explained with photographs that the Berlin Wall was actually two walls separated by a no-man's-land that varied in width from about 30 to 500 feet and was punctuated at regular intervals by watchtowers and guards. Anyone attempting to cross was shot, she said.

"So you can imagine the euphoria I felt, we all felt the next morning when my friend and I raced to the Wall," she went on. "There were crowds of people drinking and dancing and celebrating. Some people had hopped on top of the Wall; others were chipping away parts of it. No one knew what the future would bring, but in that moment no one was thinking of the future— we were just intoxicated by the sense of history happening under our feet, in front of our eyes."

Three hours later, Sabine ended our tour at one of the most substantial sections of the Wall still standing. Alone, isolated, stretching about a city block, it seemed such a frail confection—a long drab wafer of a wall, perhaps ten feet tall and less than a foot thick, that looked as though it could be toppled with a good kick.

I stared and thought of all the lives that Wall had ripped apart, the dreams that it had buried. It was almost impossible to grasp the authority it had once imposed. Indeed, Sabine said her own school-age children found it hard to believe the Wall had ever existed. It seemed so absurd, so impossible.

It was an equal challenge to reconcile the privations of the Communist past with the prosperity of the capitalist present, proclaimed in the bold, corporate-branded buildings and brisk, besuited businessmen we'd seen on our tour. And that was a good lesson, too—that Berlin was resolutely not mired in its past, but had moved on to embrace a once inconceivable future.

As we surveyed that symbolic slice of concrete, Sabine smiled broadly, her eyes alight, and I thought anew of how travel can connect us to history—and to the people and stories that compose it—in the most visceral, heart-pounding way.

I thought, too, of another truth, fundamentally related to travel but soaring beyond it: that no wall can subdue forever the human will.

And as I imagined Sabine dancing and hugging her newly freed countrymen in this very spot in the fall of 1989, these words formed in my mind: Walls fall; people rise.

Berlin's living history had opened my eyes.

⌒

CALIFORNIA

PARIS

AITUTAKI

EL SALVADOR

PART THREE:
Illuminations

SHIKOKU

SAINT-PAUL-
DE-VENCE

PYTHION

ITALY

CAMBODIA

BALI

PRAMBANAN

N

At the Musée d'Orsay

I visited the Musée d'Orsay in Paris on the same momentous return trip where I had the epiphany in Notre-Dame Cathedral which I wrote about earlier in this collection. Both of those pieces were the product of a lesson that was just beginning to crystallize for me: the importance of focus. The closer you focus on a place or a thing, the more you notice, and the more you have to say. When I began this essay, I wanted to write about the extraordinary richness of art in Paris, and how that richness added layers to the life of the city and to my interaction with that life. I first tried to write about three museums, but in my 750-word Examiner *column, I could barely begin to say anything about each museum. Then I tried one museum, then one gallery in one museum, then five paintings in that gallery. Each time, the essay seemed too superficial, just glancing the surface of the topic. Finally I realized that the only way to do this topic justice would be to focus deeply on one painting and re-create my interaction with that painting. And that's what I tried to do in this essay. After it was published, an art professor at San Francisco State University wrote to me that she was making it required reading in all of her courses—so perhaps I did something right!*

I HAVE BEEN LOOKING AT MONET'S *Les Coquelicots*, the painting of two women and children walking through a field of bright red poppies on a sunny, cloud-dappled day, for about forty minutes. It moves me just as profoundly now as it did when I was last in Paris twelve years before; it still tugs deep within me, cuts through all the layers to something fresh and fundamental and childlike.

At first I stared at it closely, my nose within a foot of the canvas, so close that I could see the black-dot eyes of the child in the foreground—something I had never seen before, or at least never remembered seeing.

Get that close and you reduce the painting to its elements: layers of oil paint on canvas, brushstrokes, dabs, tiny tip-tips with the brush. You realize just how fragile a thing a painting is, and just how common.

And you realize too that it was made by a man—fragile, common—who stood at the canvas and thought: "a little more red here," dab, dab; "a cloud there," push, push; "how can I capture that light?"

Look at the painting closely this way for a few minutes and you break it down into an intricate complexity of colors and textures and forms.

Then step back and—*voilà!*—all of a sudden it is a composed whole, a painting: a cloud-bright sky and poppy-bright field, a woman with a fancy hat and a parasol and a child almost hidden by the tall grasses in the foreground, and in the background another woman and a child almost obscured against a distant stand of trees. They are on a walk, or a picnic—a story begins to compose itself, to take on a life inside and outside the canvas.

And you realize that this is a kind of miracle, that colors and shapes dabbed on a piece of cloth 115 years ago have somehow reached across time and culture to touch you.

Look long enough and feel deeply enough, and your eyes fill with tears.

And when you feel these wet, cool, unexpected tears, you look around you suddenly as if waking from a dream, and see men and women in shorts, blue jeans, dresses, and sportcoats, holding guidebooks and pointing at the canvas and sighing, or whispering in passionate appreciation.

You feel strangely displaced—for a moment it was your painting, or rather, you were a part of it, and now you are outside it again—but then you think, "This too is part of the miracle, that one painting can touch so many people."

You think of art's extraordinary power, that a scattering of people and poppies in a field can push age, despair, fatigue, and cynicism away, can focus you so intensely on this time, this place; that time, that place.

You stand close to the canvas again and see the complexity of colors—the fields all gray, brown, green, yellow-green; the poppies red and pink; the sky a mixture of light and dark blues; the clouds gray, purple, white.

You see that the forms are simple: a gently rolling landscape; smoothly, sparingly suggested people. And that the child in the foreground holds flowers that are almost the same color as the band in his (her?) hat.

You step back one last time and see peace, lightness, a sense of infinite wonder and potential, a childlike purity.

And when you return to the luminous streets you know you will hold that vision in your head, like a handful of flowers on a country-bright day.

You know that you have returned to Paris. You know that, deep inside, you were never away.

California Epiphany

When I became Travel Editor at the Examiner, I quickly realized how little I knew about the region in which I lived, and how much there was to do and discover right in my own backyard. There was a reason why people flew halfway around the world to explore Northern California! My daughter was born the same year I became Travel Editor, and while my wife and I enthusiastically took her around the world from the moment she could fly, her presence was one more important incentive for me to travel close to home. So I began to explore California. I made the journey described in this story on an October weekend in 1988, setting out with no clear idea of what would befall me or what I would write about, just trusting that the world would deliver. And as always, it did.

WHILE I LOVE WANDERING THE FAR CORNERS of the globe, I'm continually amazed by the range of riches our own region has to offer. I re-learned this again one October weekend when I explored a spectacular stretch of my favorite California road, Highway 1, from Bodega Bay to Leggett.

At the trip's beginning on the outskirts of Bodega Bay, the road wound through green and brown hills, dotted with purple, red, white, and yellow flowers like drops from a pointillist's brush; then ribboned along the coast, offering soul-soaring views of crashing white waves, ragged red-brown cliffs, and craggy black rocks at every turn. I passed trim clapboard galleries, boutiques, and souvenir shops, and peaceful houses of brown weathered wood tucked into the green folds and creases of the hills, smoke pluming from their chimneys.

FOR SALE signs and fences demarcated the land, and satellite dishes symbolized reality, but more impressive were the profusions of wildflowers lining the road like nature's bridal bouquets.

My first stop was in Point Arena, whose downtown displays just what a downtown really needs in Northern California in the 20th century: a post office, bank, deli and grocery store, telephone office, gas station, liquor store, movie theater and video rental place, café, natural foods store, and tribal office (the Manchester-Point Arena Indian Reservation is located just inland).

I drove to the Point Arena Fishing Pier and had my first close encounter with coastal life: the salty smell of the sea, the slap of the waves and the sight of fishing boats bobbing and bewhiskered men in messy blue jeans and flannel shirts casting off the pier. They caught only seaweed while I was there, but we all knew it didn't matter: They were catching the sunshine and the bracing wind, the deep blue sky and the screeches of the birds, the weekend company of each other and the summer lusciousness in the air. Behind them a signpost at the Arena Cove Bar & Grill pointed the way to Acapulco, Berlin, Anchorage, Pebble Beach,

Las Vegas, Honolulu—and I had a feeling that was about as close as any of them wanted to get to the outside world.

Beyond Point Arena proper, I followed a winding road to the Point Arena Lighthouse. This singular structure is lovingly maintained by a dedicated group of volunteers who call themselves the Point Arena Lighthouse Keepers, Inc. One of the keepers greeted me at the entrance and filled me in on some of the lighthouse's history: how the original lighthouse began operation in 1870 and functioned until 1906, when it was effectively destroyed in the great earthquake; how the new 115-foot steel-reinforced concrete tower debuted in 1908 with one extraordinary addition: a first order Fresnel lens over six feet in diameter and weighing more than two tons, with 666 hand-ground glass parts and a brass framework, all built in France and shipped to California.

In an adjacent museum another volunteer pointed with pride to the old artifacts—plates, lanterns, tins, and other treasures recovered from shipwrecks; historical information about and photographs of California's lighthouses, the 1906 earthquake, and the Point Arena area; and an enchanting exhibition of poems and drawings by local elementary school students.

The views from the lighthouse were inspiring: undeveloped, free-flowing countryside dotted with sheep; wild, unbounded water. But even more inspiring was the love these volunteers clearly felt for the tower and its surroundings. Call me a meandering mystic if you will, but I think that kind of love, concern, commitment adds a special quality to the landscape—it imbues it with a spirit that becomes a part of what you see and sense when you visit there. And if you are lucky enough to feel that spirit, not only do you carry it away with you, but you also leave some special part of yourself behind that enhances the area all the more.

In this sense, I thought, the lighthouse keepers are preserving much more than the lighthouse itself; they are keeping a vital piece of the state, and of ourselves, and deserve all the support they need.

After Point Arena, my next stop was in Mendocino, where something remarkable happened.

I had spent half an hour wandering among the galleries and boutiques, the upscale clothing and kitchen utensil places, the coffee and burger stops, and ice cream and sandwich shops. Despite its tourist orientation, I already liked Mendocino very much; for some reason, it reminded me of Lenox, Massachusetts, a resort town near the Tanglewood concert area where I spent many a youthful weekend trying to absorb symphony music and starlight.

I liked the feel of the town, the attention to gardens and benches and decks, the neat inns and wooden houses, the arts and crafts places, and then, in the opposite direction, the crashing white waves and magnificent, wind-slanted trees and wildly swaying grasses. It felt like what I once upon a time imagined much of California to be—or, more precisely, it felt like New England in California. Well, most precisely: It felt like me.

I sat on a bench outside the Presbyterian church, which could have been transplanted from a New England town, looked at the ocean and felt the world slow down a bit; I was beginning to get back in touch with what's really important, like peeling paint and buzzing bumblebees, the feeling of sunshine and a salty breeze on your face, the surprise of wild roadside blackberries.

And then I came upon a gentle bookstore called The Book Loft, where Windham Hill music drifted through the air and books on yoga and Zen and new age science greeted fervent readers. It felt like a portal to another time, and so it became. I was standing in the back of the store, in the used books area, when I saw some old, well-thumbed, and obviously lovingly read copies of the J.R.R. Tolkien trilogy, *The Lord of the Rings*.

This was the same trilogy that my brother had persuaded me to read more than two decades earlier because he had loved them so much, the same books I had inexplicably been thinking of earlier in the day—after not having thought of them for years. Suddenly I was aware of tears filling my eyes.

I don't know quite what it was: the conjunction of youthful idealism and older-age reality, perhaps, a sudden and overwhelming sense of times past and distances traversed. It was not only sad, but a combination of happiness and astonishment and sadness; it was like something had tapped a spring in my soul, and all the waters burst out from within. I thought of my brother and parents on the East Coast, and then of my wife and child, equally far away, it seemed, in Oakland. And I wondered: What happens to our youthful dreams, our fantasies about what life will be? How can I reconcile the glories of the present with the goals of the past? Where do they come together?

I had no answers, but somehow in The Book Loft, among the blooms and benches and boutiques of Mendocino, that was all right. And when I resumed the trip, I realized that that moment had transformed everything: The world around me seemed stunningly beautiful, had taken on a deeper life.

I spent the night at an inn overlooking the sea in Elk. After an excellent dinner at Harbor House, I walked down Highway 1 to my cottage. From my balcony, there was only the wash and scrape of the waves, the vast slumbering outlines of rocks against the sea, and the intricate puzzle of the stars.

In the morning, soft sunlight lent the visible world a magical quality. Bumblebees flitted patiently from flower to flower, hawks turned and glided in the air; trees bent in the wind, water broke over the rocks. I felt calm and far, far from the city.

After a hearty breakfast highlighted by fresh blackberries and thick cream, I was back on the road. Above Fort Bragg, the scenery alternated from opulent open vistas of sea and sky to the surprise of sand dunes, to dense green groves of evergreens. On one side I passed flower-bright meadows and rolling hills, on the other broad white-sand beaches with picnic tables and ample parking lots, where the only litter was driftwood.

I passed through Westport in the time it took me to say "a couple of inns, an all-purpose general store and gas station, and not much else" into my tape recorder and then began to look for Rockport, which I had been told was the last checkpoint before the unmarked turn-off to the wilderness area known as the Lost Coast.

The road turned steep and twisting, and soon the sea seemed only a memory. Massive white birches, redwoods, and other leafy trees I couldn't identify towered beside and over the road, giving it a kind of gloomy enchantment. To complete the effect, a gentle rain had begun to fall, and clouds were covering the trees like soft white comforters. Plush pine needles and green gossamer ferns carpeted the floor; the only signs of habitation were rotting, abandoned farmhouses and cabins.

And where was Rockport? Suddenly I came to a sign for the "Drive Thru" redwood tree in Leggett, which was well beyond Rockport on my map. Since I was so close to the Drive Thru tree, I decided the only thing to do was to drive through it, but my mind was on Rockport and the Lost Coast.

But first I drove to the end of the road, literally, the non-descript intersection where the forlorn green signs say End California I. Then fate led me well. The ticket-taker at the Drive Thru Tree Park said she loved the Lost Coast, had once spent ten months camping there—"and one week when I didn't see another soul"—and told me exactly where to find the dirt turn-off twenty-five minutes back toward Westport.

"Rockport?" she echoed when I asked. "Oh, that doesn't exist anymore."

Back along the winding road through the towering trees until there it was, ten minutes after the sun came out, a dirt road charging uphill with a tiny, virtually illegible white sign indicating

Mendocino County Road No. 431, the pathway to either disaster (what if my reliable rented Reliant got stuck in the mud?) or paradise.

Six muddy, bumpy, grass-graced, vista-vibrant, lupine-lovely, heart-stoppingly beautiful miles and half an hour later I came to the end of another road, a dirt trail off the county road that stopped at the Usal Camp beach. I felt like I had stepped into an undiscovered world: Waves tumbled and roared; seabirds wheeled and screeched. Before me and to my left was sand, rocks, seaweed, driftwood; to my right, rocky cliffs plunged into the sea; behind me, grassy hills rose into a blazing blue sky. I sat and watched, and these lines drifted into mind: "The sea moves in white waves toward the shore; the wind moves—white waves toward the sky." I saw bright orange poppies, purple thistles, blue and white baby's breath, exquisite tiny white flowers with yellow centers.

The day moved, but I didn't.

Thirty minutes that seemed like hours later, it was time to leave sea and seaweed, wave and wood, behind, but one adventure was left.

As I was driving back along Road No. 431, I came to a particularly tempting trail, stopped the car, and ran under the trees into a grassy expanse with a precipitous view of the glimmering sea. I was running through this meadow, exulting in the sunshine and pure, pristine freedom of the place, when I saw what looked like horse's hoofprints in the grass. I knelt over them to get a better look, and as I was absorbed in wondering what a horse had been doing in that isolated place, a cool shadow passed over me.

I looked up to see one red-tailed hawk, and then another, spectacularly silhouetted against the sun. Wings outstretched, they were dancing in the air, riding its thin highway, swooping and soaring, wheeling with wordless grace out toward the ocean and then back over me. They performed this pas de deux for perhaps ten to fifteen seconds, hovering motionless in the air, wing tips almost touching, then soaring away, until they sailed out of sight over the trees.

I knew then that this was really the end of the road: This was where things, in some obscure way, came together—up in the air, catching the current and gliding, circling, swooping, hovering with ruffled tips on the wind. And even as I write these words, those hawks are still in my mind, swooping, soaring. The breeze freshens; the ocean glints below. They are dancing, dancing. I see them dancing. Still.

Japanese Wedding

I wrote this essay for a special quarterly travel magazine that the Examiner *published in the 1980s and '90s called* Great Escapes. *The theme of this issue was Extraordinary Journeys, and so I wrote about the most extraordinary journey of my life, when Kuniko and I traveled from San Francisco to her home village of Johen, in the southwestern corner of Shikoku, to get married. The trip alone required two planes, two trains, a ferry, and a bus, and took thirty hours door to door, but the truly extraordinary journey was simultaneously moving from one world to another and from one state of life to another. In the heart of rural Japan, I realized that our marriage represented much more than the union of two people—that it was a bridging of cultures and lifetimes as well as souls, and that the most extraordinary journey of all was just beginning.*

OF ALL THE JOURNEYS IN MY LIFE, the most extraordinary occurred in the early 1980s in Japan, when my wife, Kuniko, and I traveled to her hometown of Johen to observe and celebrate our marriage in the Japanese Shinto style.

The journey to Johen, a tiny village located in the southwest corner of the island of Shikoku, was a revelation in itself, a trip through layers of modernity into the heart of the country.

We flew first from San Francisco to Tokyo's Narita airport, then switched planes to fly to Osaka. From Osaka, we traveled by train past steam-belching factories and concrete-block apartment buildings into suburbs where two-story wooden houses were set irregularly among rice paddies the size of tennis courts, and beyond them to the port of Uno.

We spent the night with friends in Uno, then rose early to catch the ferry that traverses the Inland Sea to Takamatsu, the principal city on Shikoku. The ferry set off in a thick mist, and soon we were plowing by tiny islands—a stand of pines and a solitary cabin or two—that hovered uncertainly, as in a *sumi-e* painting, in the fog.

Kuniko said that this particular ferry was famous for its noodles, so we bought two big, steaming bowls and settled inside. There we were surrounded by a veritable symphony of slurping: Construction workers in sweatshirts and headbands, schoolkids in shorts and baseball caps, grandmothers in somber kimonos—all were vigorously sucking away. In Japan, it's considered bad form not to, so after a few hesitant attempts, I began slurping happily away as well. (As I always suspected, the noodles do taste better that way.)

At Takamatsu, we transferred to a rickety local train that wound along the rugged northern and western coasts of Shikoku, where the mountains plunge to the sea, past forests of pine and scatterings of houses tucked into the hills, with smoke pluming from their chimneys.

We could tell the time by the ebb and flow of passengers: the housewives returning home from shopping in the late morning; the schoolchildren in their white shirts and dark skirts or shorts in the early afternoon; the farmers, factory workers, and fishermen around sunset. As we got farther and farther into the country, other differences became discernible as well: The clothing was less sophisticated and stylish, the faces rougher, the postures more relaxed. Tangerines were eaten and their peels thrown onto the floor, tiny glass bottles of *sake* were lined up along the windows, and men slouched back with their feet on the opposite seat.

When groups of men got on, the train turned loud with laughter and reverberated with clipped, guttural talk far from the genteel sounds of Tokyo. And when schoolchildren got on, they stared and giggled behind their hands at me.

We rode that train for six hours, to the end of the line in a town called Uwajima, about forty miles from Johen. There we caught the Johen bus, and after an hour's ride in darkness punctuated only rarely by house lights, we arrived in Johen—a full thirty hours after we had left San Francisco.

Johen sits among thickly forested hills and lush green fields in a rugged and virtually untouched region of Shikoku. Very few foreigners have ever visited there, and sometimes wandering its streets—seeing adults stop in their tracks to gape at me, and little children turn away in terror or, conversely, run up to touch this strange being's skin—I felt like a medieval European explorer. It is a quiet village of fishermen and farmers, a place of wooden houses arranged along roads that follow the contour of the land, of rice fields and vegetable plots and shops open to the street where housewives in kimonos gather every day for groceries and gossip.

In the days before our wedding, we visited Kuniko's friends and relatives in the area, bringing small gifts, and explored the country around the town. Certain memories stand out:

197

a conversation over tangerines and green tea at one relative's house, about the "other foreigner" who married a girl from the town across the hill; random nods and smiles from grandmotherly shopkeepers; a thatched-roof farmhouse in the middle of distant rice paddies; fishing villages with their nets strung out to dry, and men and women in white sunbonnets sitting under tents surrounded by oysters and seaweed, beckoning to us and smiling great gap-toothed smiles while they patiently planted pearls; the quiet streets and wooden houses after sundown, lit from within; a gathering of mothers and children in the late afternoon, flying long-tailed kites in a field; and a Chinese lion dance a group of elementary school students put on in a garage in our honor, the kids in shorts and crew cuts beating the drums with all their might and the lion thrashing about under the garage's single bulb.

It was in the accumulation and sharing of such experiences—of the meticulously tended gardens outside even the simplest houses, of mornings loud with wind and rain and birdsong, of the wooden steps at the local shrine grooved by centuries of soles—that I first began to understand the Japanese sense of richness in simplicity, of vitality in the unadorned.

The climax of the journey was the wedding ceremony itself—a glorious gathering of friends and relatives in Kuniko's family home for five hours of eating and drinking and laughing and singing. At the end of that night, after we had made a wedding pledge to each other by drinking sanctified *sake* three times from three different cups, after we had danced a long and lingering waltz around the room, after I had sung the one Japanese song I knew and discussed in liquor-loosened Japanese all manner of things from Johen's social mores to Soviet-U.S. politics, I was sitting back holding Kuniko's hand and listening to everyone clap and sing an ancient folk song. I looked at her gorgeous kimono, and the lavish feast, and the animated faces—and suddenly the simple and the elaborate seemed joined, rounded, in celebration, and it was then I felt that one journey had been accomplished and another had begun, and that I had found a home in the heart of the country.

Prambanan in the Moonlight

I visited Indonesia in the summer of 1978, when the university where I was teaching in Japan was on summer break. I traveled to Singapore, Malaysia, and Indonesia, and the world expanded in seductive sensual overload all around me: So much to do, so much to learn! Princeton-in-Asia provided a ready network of friendly Fellows all around the region, who offered couches for crashing and immersive introductions to their respective regions. The "American teacher living in Yogyakarta" mentioned in this essay was one of these, and I'm indebted to him for excavating the layers of Indonesian culture. For me, this essay captures the enchanted, almost intoxicated sense of wonder and surprise that I was feeling—and still feel today—as the world opened up before my mind and eyes.

THE INDONESIAN NIGHT WAS SO HOT and humid that when you walked, the air seemed to part around you, like a curtain of exquisite filaments.

There was more to the night's dense weave, too—the liquid harmonies of an unseen gamelan wrapped around you, and the spicy scent of skewered chicken sizzling on a roadside grill, blue smoke curling toward a fat full moon.

The moon wove a gossamer scene: people in flowing batiks stopping at sidewalk stands, exchanging wadded bills for charred skewers; barefoot youngsters kicking up dust as they skittered through the streets; men and women ambling side by side, chattering in anticipation of the Ramayana performance at Prambanan.

Two days earlier you had visited Prambanan in the undiffused light of midday—the forests buzzing with insects, the heat bouncing off the hard-packed road and scythe-cut fields—and been staggered by the sight of its main temple soaring out of the fields like a stone thunderbolt carved by the gods.

An American teacher living in Yogyakarta had taken you there, and had told you that the monument was built between the 8th and 10th centuries, when a Hindu dynasty ruled the area.

He had guided you through the Shiva Mahadeva temple, the most fully restored, tracing the temple's intricate, encircling scenes from the Ramayana.

And when you had come upon Shiva, the Hindu god of destruction, on a giant lotus petal straight out of Buddhism, you had thought about the Buddhist monument at Borobudur, less than twenty miles away, and about the intricate interlayerings of religious practice and belief you had found in Asia.

Later, in the cool of the afternoon, you had talked about the layers of Indonesian society, and other layers, too—in gamelan music, and ikat dyeing, where the threads are dyed before being woven, and the epics themselves, in which the heroes have vices and the villains unexpected integrity.

Prambanan in the moonlight was an entirely different place, but layered, too—the top layer a festive scene of shouting kids and laughing families and, somewhere behind that, a more solemn place of ghostly footfalls and consuming faith.

On the moonlit stage, seductions and battles, entreaties and flights unfolded in an exuberance of color and costume: the stylized movements fierce, precise, poetic; the music as sinuous and sensuous as the dance—the whole encircling your soul and transporting you.

You thought about the places you had been in Indonesia—the rice paddies and horn-shaped houses of Sumatra; the Makassar schooners in Jakarta's old harbor, bound for the Straits of Malacca crammed with flour, cement, and timber—and about Bali still to come, all terraced fields and bright smiles in your mind.

And for a moment you did not know where you were, how you had gotten there or why—you were one deep gong in the gamelan of night, one tiny note in a harmony so profound and all-encompassing you could not possibly comprehend it. And for a moment it was enough simply to resonate in the Indonesian moonlight.

As you resonate in moonlit memory, even now.

⌒

In the Pythion of Time

I began keeping a journal in high school, when a wonderful friend and fellow poet presented me with a birthday gift of a big black hardbound journal. Since then, I've always had a journal close by; it was—and still is—an essential and trusted companion, in whose pages I can pour out everything I am doing, feeling, and wondering, and try to make sense of it all. When I moved to France and Greece after college, my letters to my parents began to serve a similar function. I didn't report everything I was doing or feeling, of course, but my parents were astonishingly understanding and supportive—now that I'm a parent myself, I'm even more deeply appreciative of this—and I took delight in describing for them my adventures exterior and interior. "In the Pythion of Time" was written in 1993, but it refers at length to a letter I wrote to my parents in 1976, describing a singular predicament I found myself in on the Greek-Turkish border; reading these words now, almost forty years later, I'm immediately transported back to that unlikely way station, and the philosophical ramblings that it inspired.

HAVING JUST "CELEBRATED" THE KIND of birthday where you go to bed in one decade of your life and wake up in another, I have found myself the past few days leafing wistfully through old letters and journals, dreaming of other times and other places.

This is a dangerous pastime, of course, but sometimes it turns up one of those little seeds that blossom into a whole world you had forgotten. So it is with a letter I have just come across, written seventeen years ago to my parents from a Greek border town called Pythion, where I was waiting for a train to Istanbul. Sometimes it is just such global synapses—way stations—that unencumber and inspire us.

Here is part of what I wrote:

"I took the 10:00 P.M. train on Tuesday from Athens and arrived in Thessaloniki around 11:00 A.M. the next morning. In Thessaloniki I was informed that the Istanbul train had left earlier that morning, but that I was in luck—there was another, special Wednesday-only train leaving for Istanbul at 13:10. When that one arrived, I learned that it traveled only as far as the border.

"Still, that seemed better than nothing, so I had a very pleasant ride through Thrace with a compartment all to myself, and arrived at the border—poetic Pythion—at 2:30 A.M. Pythion being off-limits to foreigners, I was invited by the sole stirring being to sleep in the station's waiting room, which I did rather comfortably until 8:30, when I was awakened simultaneously by a policeman demanding to know who I was and someone shouting in German that the train for Istanbul was leaving in five minutes.

"I scrambled down the platform to the train, the policeman chasing after me, only to discover that the train had come from Istanbul and was bound for Athens.

"And so I sit in the Railroad Buffet at Pythion, eyed by a suspicious policeman who can't imagine what a foreigner would be doing here if not trying to uncover state secrets, and contemplating ten hours of warming my toes and fingers by an old pot-belly stove in one of the more obscure of the obscure corners of the world.

"Situations like this make me question the nature of reality. I am sitting on a hard wooden bench at the end of a long, stained table in a dirty, cold, deserted Greek border town, scratching out letters under a layering of turtleneck, work shirt, sweater, rain-coat, and scarf, and eating peanuts and figs to keep warm.

"This is certainly one kind of reality, but is it any more real than that envisioned for me by my friends in Athens, who imagine me right now walking under minarets through crowded streets from Hagia Sophia to the Blue Mosque, or than the pic-ture you may have of me right now (discussing me halfway across the globe even as I write these words) walking through sunny Athenian streets to the gleaming pillars of the Acropolis: Is my here any more real than that there?

"I am here, but in a few weeks I will be at the Acropolis, and in twenty-four hours I will be wandering Istanbul's alleys. Maybe all three are concurrent realities?

"At any rate, last night, when I was sleeping happily some-where in northeastern Greece, I had a dream that all my traveling was just a dream, and that I was actually still living in Connecticut, and in my dream I woke up from my dream (of traveling) and felt this tremendous relief and joy to be home and still so young as not to have to worry about being out and alone in the world.

"Then, a split second later, I woke up from that dream—and found myself sweaty and disheveled in a humid train compart-ment speeding somewhere through the Grecian night.

"And so I wonder about this pithy waiting room in Pythion—is this too a dream from which I am about to awake? And who/what/where will I be then?"

I read these words, and life's border towns and way stations come back to me: the raggedy, muddy-streets-and-strung-light-bulbs place where I spent an itchy night between India and Nepal; the misty, barbed-wire swamp between Hong Kong and China; the snow-locked sentry post between Pakistan and China; the dusty honky-tonk of Tijuana and Nogales.

I think of a one-café town in the middle of Malaysia where I was stranded between buses, and a patch-of-grass "taxi stand" in Indonesia where cicadas serenaded me for hours while I waited for a ride; I think of a slumbering French railroad station where I passed an afternoon reading Proust and pondering the tall grasses that waved dreamily in a drowsy breeze, and a high Swiss village where I ran out of gas and francs, pitched a tent in a frosty field, and watched the moon dance to the music of Van Morrison.

As I think back on all these places, one truth becomes clear: They were all way stations to adventure. They were the gathering of breath and coiling of muscle before the great leap into the unknown. They were the portals to wonders unimaginable and unforgettable.

And so I find myself in the Pythion of time again. Just now the station master has come and checked my ticket, stamped my passport, waved me toward the platform. And here comes the train—I can see it now, all steam and gleam!

Already the pulse quickens, the mind races ahead once more: What lessons lie ahead, I think; what wonders are in store?

Finding Salvation
in the South Seas

As on most of my journeys, I didn't know what to expect when I arrived in Aitutaki on assignment for Islands *magazine. All I knew was that Tony Wheeler had said it was the quintessential South Pacific island, the perfect place for someone who wanted to reconnect with tranquility, sensuality, and a sense of things as they used to be. As a travel writer, I thrive on these uncharted journeys, stressful as they may be. On the one hand, as I'm traveling around the place, my mind is always thinking, "What's the story? What's the story?"—and that's stressful. But on the other hand, my adrenaline is flowing, I'm keenly aware of everything happening around me, and I'm inspired to ask questions and forge connections that I might otherwise be too intimidated or reserved to concoct. On Aitutaki, my desire to understand the essence of the place for my story inspired me to do things I would never normally do—and in retrospect, momentarily transforming into a Cook Islands warrior on the dance floor was one of the best things I have ever done.*

FOUR DRUMS POUNDED A DEEP, INCESSANT RHYTHM through the sultry South Pacific night. A ukulele plunked plangent notes into the air. A smiling-eyed young beauty with copper skin and flowing hair, wearing a palm frond skirt and coconut bra, took me by the hand. "Will you dance with me?" Retire flashed a grin and winked. "You want to be Cook Island warrior, right? This your chance! Go!"

She led me unsteadily onto the sandy stage. I swallowed my pride, and suddenly my legs were doing things they'd never even tried.

An eternity later, the pounding and plunking stopped, the two dozen foreigners watching the weekly Island Night performance burst into applause, and my lovely maiden disappeared with a fleeting smile down the beach.

Retire slapped me on the back. "You make good Cook Island warrior someday! How old you live to be?"

By now I knew Retire well enough to understand what he meant to say: Maybe if I lived into deep old age and practiced dancing every day, I'd finally win the maiden—or at least the warrior's lei.

I'd met Retire four days earlier at the Aitutaki International Airport, a charming one-room, open-to-the-breezes terminal where taxi drivers, tour operators, and resort managers met the two dozen visitors who deplaned on the morning flight from Rarotonga. Mutual friends had arranged for Retire to play reception committee, driver, and tour guide for my five days on the island. I was trying to spot someone who looked "Retired" when a rotund, deeply tanned, thirtyish man in khaki shorts, a blue and white floral shirt, and a broad, beaming smile approached me. "Are you Don? I'm Retire. Welcome to Aitutaki!"

Soon after we had piled my bags in his car and set off on the ten-minute ride to my hotel on the island's northwest coast, Retire turned to me.

"You like diving, right?" Before I could even tell him I wasn't a diver, he continued, "Tomorrow we go deep-sea diving. That good for me. Sharks like white meat!" And he broke into a loopy, high-pitched laugh. Welcome to Aitutaki.

I had come to this tiny South Seas island on a quest, but not one I could easily define. Eighteen hours before, I had been befuddled, beleaguered, bedraggled, and altogether benumbed by 21st-century stress: too many projects, too many deadlines, too many demands. I longed for quietude, simplicity, and a sense of things as they used to be. I was pining for qualities I associated with islands and with the South Pacific in particular: a lush, slow, wild beauty, a barefoot tranquility, a balmy, palmy, sea-scented sensuality.

But did such qualities even exist? I asked the most well-traveled person I know, Tony Wheeler, lifelong wanderer and co-founder of the global guidebook company Lonely Planet, if he knew of such a perfect island. He didn't pause for a moment. "Aitutaki," he said.

Where? Wheeler explained that Aitutaki belongs to the Cook Islands, a vaguely S-shaped scattering of fifteen islands roughly halfway between Tahiti and Fiji. Rarotonga, with a population of about 8,000, is the main island. Aitutaki, 150 miles north of Raro, is the second most-populated, with 1,500 residents. It's also the second most-visited of the islands, with some 25,000 arrivals each year. Shaped like an upside down fishhook, Aituaki is the clasp in a necklace-shaped lagoon, about nine miles long and seven and a half miles wide, that is set with fifteen idyllic islets, or *motu*, all of which are uninhabited. Aitutaki is compact—it takes less than an hour to drive the paved road that circles the island—but its effect is clearly expansive. "This may well be the friendliest, sexiest, and most beautiful island in the entire Pacific," Wheeler said.

Late on the afternoon of my first day, I was admiring that beauty outside my thatched-roof hotel hut—a long powdery white-sand beach lapped by crystal-clear waters, with schools of silver fish darting through infinite gradations of blue and green; tall palm trees slanting over the sand, fat yellow coconuts hanging under their rustling fronds; white clouds billowing in a deep blue sky, and the sun sliding mango-slow toward the horizon—when Retire returned.

"You like to dance, right?" he asked as soon as I climbed into his car. I started to protest, but he cut me off. "Then you are very lucky, my friend. Because tonight is the Aitutaki Dance Competition! And I signed you up!" Before I could say anything, he plunged on. "But first, we eat!"

As we drove, Retire gave me a crash course in the island's history: Aitutaki was settled around 1,100 years ago by Polynesian Maoris who sailed from present-day French Polynesia. According to legend, the first settler was Ru, who arrived with his four wives, four brothers and their wives, and twenty royal maidens. Ru divided the island into twenty sections, one for each of the maidens, and completely forgot his brothers, who stormed off to settle New Zealand. As other settlers arrived from throughout the South Pacific, they had to be accepted by one of the twenty maidens or their descendants to be able to live on the island. This family system of land ownership, where plots of land are accorded by birthright and bestowed by family consent, and where money never changes hands, continues to this day.

Fifteen minutes later, on the road to the inland village of Tautu, we stopped at Café Tupuna, a four-year-old eatery under the impeccable hand of artist, chef, and entrepreneur Tupuna

Hewitt. Set in Tupuna's glorious garden, with a sandy floor and, as dusk comes on, tiki-torch lighting, Café Tupuna features the chef's own vivid paintings of island scenes on the walls and equally artful concoctions from the back-room kitchen, which is hung with well-used pots, pans, woks, and woven baskets. My meal began with a corn and seafood chowder that offered a delicious marriage of tastes—not just corn but other local vegetables like *rukau* and *kumara*, plus generous helpings of shrimp, crab, and mussels. For the main course I had reef fish stuffed with shrimp and onions, doused with a pesto sauce and served with rice. The combination of flavors and textures was exquisite and illuminating, like a master course in island tastes, but I was distracted.

"Retire," I began, "about this dance competition—"

"Oh, can't talk about that over dinner!" he interrupted and began joking with the kitchen staff.

Tupuna chatted with the diners and Retire traded quips with everyone. When I remarked that it felt like one big family, Retire replied, "That's because it is!"

Tupuna smiled from the kitchen. "Yep, these are all my nieces helping out," she swept an arm toward the waitresses and the young women cleaning and preparing in the kitchen, "and the food you just ate—I learned those recipes by experimenting in the kitchen with my mother and grandmother."

By the end of the meal I felt like family, too: When one niece asked if we wanted dessert and I said I was full up to here, indicating mid-throat, she replied, "Good! You can still go up to your nose!"

After dinner, we scuttled like overfed crabs back to the car and hurried on to the main town, Arutanga, a classic sleepy South Seas port with a funky market, a historic limestone church, a scattering of souvenir stalls, the tourist information center, post office, and bank—and the only stop sign on the island.

The dance competition was being held in the open-air court-yard at the Orongo Centre, right on the wharf. This was the biggest event of the year, Retire announced, and would determine which *hura* dancers—*hura* being the Cook Islands Maori word for the islands' singularly sensual dance—would represent Aitutaki in the annual Cook Islands Dance Competition the following month on Rarotonga.

"So you didn't really sign me up, right?" I said.

"No, not tonight," he said. "But I think you dance before you leave."

The competition was due to begin at 7:00, but when we arrived at 6:50, a calm chaos reigned. Lights had been strung up and a stage open to the stars and surrounded with green plants had been erected; in front of this stage, row upon row of folding chairs waited, empty. One sumo-sized man in a bright red and white floral shirt was plugging things in, checking wiring and sound systems. Elegant islanders in flowing floral dresses and shirts, wearing green, white, and yellow leis around their heads or necks, were wandering in and out, hugging and joking. Children skidded and screamed gleefully in the background, and to my weary, wondering eyes they were like personifications of the island—their eyes as limpid as the lagoon, their skin as smooth-brown as polished coconut nuts, their smiles as bright as frangipani.

After about a half hour, six musicians appeared with drums and ukuleles, and positioned themselves to one side of the stage. Then one by one lights came on. At about 8:00, everyone bustled into their seats, the lights went down, and the emcee sauntered into the spotlight. The competition began with the youngest group, the Juniors aged 10-13. Next came the Intermediates, ages 14-16, then the Seniors, ages 17-39, and finally the Elders. Each competitor performed two dances—one long and elaborate, accompanied by a singer, and the second a very quick and intense minute of non-stop leg-pounding and hip-shimmying.

The entire island was there, it seemed, and everyone knew everyone. When the younger dancers performed on stage, the children in the crowd mimicked them, and I began to understand how these competitions kept the ancient culture alive, how these *hura* dancers became the freshest link in a centuries-old lineage of legend and craft, designed to pass traditions and tales from one generation to the next. And when the oldest dancers took the stage, the entire crowd sang along with their songs, applauded artful moves, and laughed at their audacious hip-sways. The men enacted tales of fierce warriors, stomping their feet, booming their greeting, telling their story with out-thrust arms. The women were nubile maidens, their arms floating fluidly through the air, their hips swaying and shaking with an intoxicating mix of innocence and sensuality. And at some point as the drums pounded, the hips swayed, the stars sparkled overhead, and the hibiscus-scented breeze blew through, a timeless piece of Polynesia settled like a breeze-blown seed in my soul.

The next morning, well before dawn, I heard a tap-tap-tap on the slatted doors of my hut.

"Good morning, Don! Time for fishing!"

Fishing?!? Oh, right, at one point during the jet-lagged night, Retire had told me he had arranged a fishing expedition. Somehow I'd forgotten that it was for the next morning, and that he'd said he'd come by to get me at 5:30. Ah, paradise.

So I scrambled into some clothes and we set off to a friend's house, where we attached a small motorboat to Retire's car and drove to the Arutanga wharf. Retire and his friend maneuvered the boat into the water, and Retire steered through an imperceptible break in the reef to the deeper waters beyond. When we stopped after a half hour to drop our lines, the sky blazed with more stars than I'd ever seen, and the night was absolutely still. We tried two favored lagoon locations with no luck, but at the third spot, as I was savoring the stars, the rising breeze, and the salty tang of the sea, my pole began to bend.

"You got one!" Retire shouted. "Pull it in, pull it in!"

For a moment I stared dumbly at the pole, then childhood muscle memory kicked in and I began to pull up and reel in, pull up and reel in.

"That's right!" Retire said. "Another twenty minutes and you have fish!"

Pull up, reel in, pull up, reel in. It seemed like forever and my arms felt like stone but eventually I got the fish to the side of the boat and Retire swooped down with a net and hefted it in. It was a modest-sized queenfish, but big enough to keep, Retire said.

"Make good dinner for my friend," he winked.

Before the morning was over, I'd reeled in two more queenfish and a rainbow-colored parrotfish.

"Big party tonight!" Retire beamed.

Later, back on land, Retire took me for a drive along the coast. A lush green tangle of vines, bushes, and trees climbed into the interior; bright yellow and white blossoms and plump papaya, banana, pawpaw, coconut, and mango hung heavy from boughs; simple one-story cinderblock houses, painted in tropical reds, greens, and blues, showed immaculate lawns and vegetable plots—with here and there stately granite family tombs set among them; goats and chickens and baby pigs wandered heedless by the road; on a palm-strung clothesline, multi-colored pareus wafted in the breeze like Polynesian prayer flags; children in crisp red-and-white and green-and-white uniforms played volleyball in a school yard; and always the blue-green waters glinted in the lagoon.

About fifteen minutes into our tour we passed a group of houses set back from the road. An elderly man sitting on the stoop of the middle home waved toward us. Instinctively I looked toward Retire, but he was watching the road. I glanced behind us to see who he was waving at, but there was no one. Then I realized—he was waving at me! I waved back. A few houses later, a young mother with a plump pink-dressed toddler at her knee was standing outside. Would she wave? Yes! We passed a couple of kids kicking a soccer ball on a lawn. Yes! A white-haired woman pedaling in the opposite direction; three middle-aged men in a truck. Yes and yes! Soon I felt like the mayor of Aitutaki, waving at everyone I passed and being waved at in return, with smiles as bright as the sun all around.

We swerved inland, bouncing along wild boar trails under ponderous branches and past slapping vines to the summit of the central hill, Maungapu, the island's highest point at 400 feet, which legend says was brought from Rarotonga by Aitutaki warriors who decided the island needed a mountain. Retire showed me the plot of land where he planned to build his "Retire-ment" house someday, and took me to a number of *marae*, the traditional pre-Christianity meeting and ceremonial sites which are marked by elaborate arrangements of massive boulders. Retire showed me one set of blood-chilling rocks where he told me human sacrifices were performed.

"See," he said, pointing to one peculiarly chiseled stone, "this is where the man's neck was held for the sacrifice, and this"—he pointed to a slithering rivulet of rock—"is where the blood ran down and was collected." He looked at me appraisingly. "What size neck you have?"

In ensuing days I met woodcarvers and pareu-makers, schoolteachers and hotel owners, chefs and tour guides and Internet entrepreneurs. I met thirty-something Maoris whose parents had emigrated to New Zealand and Australia and who had moved back for the grounded values and saner pace; teenage Aitutakians who planned to head for the bright lights of Auckland or Sydney as soon as they could; Westerners who had visited on holiday and never left. Some people worried about the influx of travelers and the ongoing building boom, which was evident: When I compared the tourist maps for July-December 2004 and January-July 2005, four new hotels had opened, plus a new tourist shop and a dive operation, and on my island explorations I saw a half-dozen new hotels in various stages of completion. Some complained that outside money was going to seep into the economy and unbalance the place; others lamented the islanders' dependence on canned goods from New Zealand and the youngsters' indifference to preserving local ways and words. Clearly, the island was not without its anxieties, yet to this 21st-century refugee, the place seemed as close to peace, plenty, and paradise as I'd ever come.

Those feelings crystallized one day on a visit to the motu known as One Foot Island. Through a serendipitous arrangement a skipper dropped me alone on the motu in the morning and said I could hitch a ride back with a lagoon tour group that would arrive in the afternoon. In my mind I immediately became a Cook Islands castaway, the lord of my private island. Surveying my domain, I turned a corner to a scene that simply took my breath away: a brilliant scimitar of white-sand beach washed by a transparent lagoon, green near the shore, then green-blue, then blue-black as it deepened. Arcing palm trees lined the beach, their fronds green, yellow, and brown against a deep blue sky. It was so beautiful I wanted to cry. I waded into the baptismal sea, the air warm and swaddling, the water buoyant and serene.

I began my last day on Aitutaki by attending the 6:30 A.M. service at the main church in Arutanga, the oldest in the Cook Islands, a majestic limestone structure with stained-glass windows and painted ceilings. Aitutaki was the island where the pioneering 19th-century English missionary John Williams, of the London Missionary Society, entrusted a Polynesian convert, Papeiha, with the conversion of the locals. Papeiha was so proficient that he was later moved to Rarotonga, where he was similarly successful. By the start of the 20th century, virtually all Cook Islanders were Christians. A double-sided monument to these two persuasive preachers graces the weathered churchyard.

On my visit the main church was closed for restoration, but when I entered the spare, humble side building where the service was being held, about two dozen people nodded and smiled at me. The women wore fancy woven-pandanus hats and bright floral muumuus and the men were in crisp polo or aloha-style shirts. The room itself had cloud-white cinderblock walls, sky-blue windows, about two dozen plain wooden benches, and a varnished wooden ceiling. At 6:30 precisely a preacher in a suit and tie began to speak in Cook Islands Maori. As he spoke a gentle breeze blew through the unscreened windows, a choir of cocks cock-a-doodle-doo'd, the wind swayed in the trees, and the mingled scents of tropical blooms and moist earth wafted in. After a while the preacher stopped speaking and the congregation rose all together. Suddenly a torrent of song surged forth; all two dozen parishioners were singing at full voice, pouring all their bodies into the song. The melody soared, subsided, soared again, the voices pounding, straining, merging, lilting, rising, falling, filling the humble space and seeming to lift the entire building, the entire island, with their force.

Later that day, as dusk was falling, Retire rejoined me. "Big surprise tonight. Island Night. Buffet and performance. Perfect for you!"

We drove to an open-air, thatched-roof restaurant called Samade, a stone's throw from the lagoon on the placid powdery stretch of Ootu Beach. Tourists sat at about fifteen tables set in the sand. The evening began with a sumptuous buffet featuring more than a dozen platters: pork cooked the traditional way in an underground oven, tuna, chicken, beets, tomatoes, cucumber, papaya salad, and *ekamata* (raw fish marinated in lime and coconut)—all washed down with cold Steinlager beer.

After we had feasted for an hour, a half-dozen musicians trooped in bearing ukuleles and wooden drums, then groups of young dancers stepped onto the floor in pandanus skirts and coconut bras and began informal, enthusiastic renditions of the dances I'd watched four nights before. Their passion and energy were infectious, and with the warm, caressing air, the delicious food, the music mingling with the stars, and the dancers' supple limbs and exuberant smiles, it was easy to get lulled into the spirit of the dance. At one point, I returned from getting seconds at the buffet table to find Retire gone; then I spotted him with the musicians, banging away on a homemade drum. And at the end of the evening, when a young beauty with copper skin and flowing hair materialized before me and invited me to dance, I found myself suddenly on that sandy stage, hips swaying and legs pounding as they never had before.

Thumpa-thumpa-thumpa-thumpa! Pumpa-pumpa-pumpa-pumpa! My feet were pistoning as fast as they could, trying to convince the ancient gods—and my undulating partner—that I was a worthy warrior. In my mind I was barefoot and dressed in green *ti* leaves with black tattoos on my legs and arms and a crown of white and yellow flowers on my head, and I was fending off all enemies with a long spear and a menacing glare.

Time slowed, and all the discoveries of my five-day stay coursed through me: the island's slow, stately pace, the warmth of the people and their fervent faith, the soul-soaring beauty of the place, the bountiful humor I had encountered in all, the sense of plenty in papaya, mango, and pawpaw, the sense of peace in palm tree, lagoon, and beach, the answering power of pure belief. The leg-thumping, heart-pumping rhythms reached my deepest core like a key, turning and turning, unlocking mysteries that seemed even older than me.

And suddenly I found myself in a place I'd never been but knew instinctively. Drums pounded, hips swayed, gardenia perfumed the balmy, palmy, mango-slow scene. In an instant I recognized this South Seas culmination: I had found the island of Salvation.

The Intricate Weave

When my dad passed away in November 2007, it took me half a year to begin to come to terms with his passing and many more months to feel "normal" in the world again. I didn't realize it at the time, but in retrospect, the journey described in this piece, which took place eight months after his death, was an essential part of that process. I was in the Lake Garda region of northern Italy leading a travel writing workshop. As part of our activities, we were making daily excursions in the area, to wineries, markets, and museums. My dad had served in Italy during World War II, and so I had been thinking about him throughout the trip, but he wasn't explicitly in my mind the day we decided to visit the violin museum in Cremona. As a result, what happened there, and the lessons it imparted about the special people in our lives, seems all the more powerful and precious to me.

MY DAD PASSED AWAY IN NOVEMBER OF 2007. He enjoyed a long and full life and died after a relatively swift and painless decline, so I have no unfinished longings or regrets about his life. But there are still times when I wish he were by my side so we could share something we both exulted in.

In his waning months, I understood on some level the inevitability of his demise, but no matter how I tried, I could not prepare myself for his death, or the gaping hole it would leave in the fabric of my life. Eight months later, I realized that I couldn't prepare myself for something else that would happen after he passed away: how the intricate weave of his life would continue to thread through my days.

I was on a two-week tour of northern Italy. I was with a small group of people who had never met before the trip, and we were bonding and braiding and dissembling as such groups do— fussing over idiosyncrasies and annoyances, sharing deep-rooted passions, planting and watering dreams that were just beginning to bloom.

One of the many riches of the trip was a visit to the violin museum in the city hall of Cremona, where priceless violins hundreds of years old are reverently housed. Each day, some of these violins are taken out and played as a way of keeping them in their finest condition. We were privileged on our visit to hear the exquisite "Il Cremonese" built by Antonio Stradivari in 1715. As we sat in that simple hall, surrounded by 17th-century paintings and 13th-century stones, I lost myself to the strains of the violin. With heart-plucking clarity, they swooped, descended, spiraled, and soared until at one point I was at the apex of the room, just a shining sliver of sound reverberating.

My dad loved music; he sang in our church choir and regularly attended the local symphony's concerts, and afterwards he would speak glowingly about how this pianist or that flutist, that violinist, had played. He also had served in Italy during World

War II, and one of the memories that had stayed in the forefront of his mind was how as an aide du camp, he had navigated his beloved general through Italy without harm. So he had been with me throughout my Italian journey—and from Venice to Verona, I would catch myself wondering if he had looked at the same vine-yard-latticed hills or cobblestoned squares sixty-five years before.

But it was at that moment in Cremona, at the apex of that room, that I felt his presence most powerfully, felt that his spirit and mine were intertwined in the music of those strings. And I realized that people, from new-made friends to life-long family, inevitably come and go in the composition of our lives, but that once they have appeared, they never really leave.

And I realized too that the people we love—the memory of the people we love, their enduring, pulsing presence in our lives—is like those violins. Every day, in one form or another, we take them out and play them, if just for a while. We become them, swooping, spiraling, soaring to the apex of our minds. We honor them and keep them alive—as they do us, intertwined.

Unexpected Offerings on a
Return to Bali

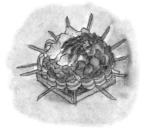

I first visited Bali in 1978, on the same trip where I encountered the layers of Indonesia at Prambanan, which I described in a piece earlier in this collection. This essay describes my return to Bali thirty-four years later. Much had changed in those thirty-four years, of course— inside me as well as inside Bali. And yet much remained the same. Bali is one of those rare places that seem charged with a special energy, where the shields/layers/skins that separate us from the spiritual core of the universe seem thinner, more porous. As a result, magic seems to happen more readily there, more easily. I've been to Bali a few times since that first visit, and something unexpected, magical, has happened to me every time—some gift that fundamentally rearranges and reinvigorates the way I live in the world. In the journey described here, the quest to see a gamelan orchestra led me to a resonant lesson in desire and fulfillment.

IN THE FALL OF 2012, I SPENT a week on the Indonesian island of Bali as a guest of the Ubud Writers & Readers Festival. This was my first visit to that blessed place since I'd fallen in love with it thirty-four years before.

Like me, the island had lost some of its innocence in the intervening years. Unlike my earlier trip, when the Balinese I met had simply welcomed me with wide eyes and hearts, this time most immediately asked me if I'd been there before. When I answered, "Yes, thirty-four years ago," their eyes opened wide for a different reason and they smiled and shook their heads. "Oh, Bali has changed much since then!" they'd laugh, though many of them couldn't say exactly how because they hadn't even been born thirty-four years before.

Of course, to my eyes too, Bali had changed. The streets were much busier, clogged with trucks and motor scooters, than I remembered, and the towns were more built up; the road from Denpasar to Ubud was lined with many more buildings and fewer rice paddies than I recalled.

But in a deeper sense, the spirit of the place seemed hardly changed at all. During a few free days of wandering, I passed a number of festival processions flowing through the streets. Every day I was enchanted as I had been three decades before by the sweet, simple *canangsari* offerings—hand-sized compositions of colorful flowers on green coconut leaves, some graced with a cracker—that were meticulously placed outside my door and on bustling sidewalks, off-the-beaten-path foot trails, temple thresholds, and business entrances alike. And while I realize I know nothing about the difficulties of being Balinese—the need to scrupulously follow rigorous traditions, for example, or the unpredictabilities of relying on a tourism economy—the people I met exuded a gentleness, tranquility, contentment, and sense of sanctity in the everyday that was as exemplary, expanding, and restorative for me as it had been thirty-four years before.

But it wasn't until my last day in Ubud that Bali's soul-binding offerings really came to life for me.

I began the day with a mini-pilgrimage to a paradisiacal place I had visited earlier in my stay. I had been introduced to it by a local expat who had taken my all-day writing workshop. During the workshop lunch break, she had described a beatific organic restaurant perched among the rice paddies, a short walk from central Ubud. She kindly offered to take me there, and the following day we met at Tjamphuhan bridge, walked a few minutes uphill along Jalan Raya Campuhan, then turned left up a wide paved driveway. At the top of this driveway was a sign neatly hand-lettered: TO RICE FIELDS SARI ORGANIK.

After a few minutes following this narrow path, and frequently having to step aside for a seemingly endless succession of motor scooters, we entered what seemed an enchanted land of rice paddies, palm trees, and, here and there, one-story "villas" with red-tiled roofs. As we threaded through the paddies on this narrow path, we passed a spa, an art gallery, a couple of "house for rent" signs-of-the-times, and a fledgling neighborhood of new homes called Dragonfly Villas. After about twenty minutes, we came to a sign and a stone pathway that led to Sari Organik.

An open-to-the-breezes restaurant of some two-dozen tables blossoming in the middle of verdant rice paddies, Sari Organik has one of the most exquisite settings of any restaurant I've ever visited. We sat in this tranquil place sipping juice from fresh-cut coconuts, and as sunset slowly gilded the paddies, the centuries seemed to slip away.

I went back on my last day to pay homage to Sari Organik and to see if it could possibly be as magical in the harsh light of midday. Happily, it was equally lush and glorious and vibrant at noon, pulsing with the peaceful energy of the land around it. I savored an omelet of organic mushrooms, tomatoes, and onions, fresh-squeezed orange juice, and delicious strong coffee, and struck up a conversation with a smiling, energetic woman who turned out to be the restaurant's extraordinary founder and owner, Nila, who told me that her goal is to help the local farmers grow a diversity of crops organically, so that they can preserve the environment and become economically self-sustaining.

After that serendipitous encounter, I walked back through the rice fields, feeling singularly content. I had gotten to do just about everything I had been hoping to do on Bali, I was thinking. There was just one exception—I hadn't heard a gamelan orchestra. I'd caught snatches of gamelan music at a couple of different performances during the festival, but I hadn't had that soul-transporting immersion in the music that I remembered vividly from my first trip to Indonesia.

Just as I was having these thoughts, approaching the end/beginning of the path, the sounds of a gamelan orchestra drifted on the air! I could hardly believe it—it was as if my thoughts had conjured those notes.

I reached the sign for Sari Organik. To my right was the wide, paved driveway that led to the main street, but then I noticed to my left a narrow, hard-packed dirt path that paralleled a rock wall twice my height. The sounds of the gamelan were coming from somewhere beyond that wall. The wall disappeared into a densely vegetated interior, with a couple of red-tiled roofs visible in the distance. I figured that if I followed the path, eventually it would lead to a break in the wall where I could enter and discover the source of the gamelan music. I wanted to see the orchestra with my own eyes.

So I set off down this winding path, following the sinuous curve of the wall and the music's tantalizing rise and fall.

I startled two workers who were on their way to restore a magnificent old house set among the paddies on the other side of a stream that paralleled the trail. They laughed and welcomed me to the forest. A few minutes later, a lone and lanky Western woman with a backpack passed me and pressed on into the green. After fifteen minutes of ambling, I came to a lush setting where palm trees, twining vines, giant ferns, and slick bushes with propeller-like leaves tangled the air. Still there was no break in the wall, and the gamelan music was sounding fainter and fainter.

I stood in the shade of that jungly patch, puzzling over what to do, wondering if I would ever find the break in the wall, when suddenly it hit me: I had already found the break in the wall; it was in my mind. Listen! I didn't need to see the orchestra—my wish had been to hear the gamelan. And there it was, all around me. What more did I want?

I walked back down the path and the sounds of the music swelled in the shadowed air. When I reached a point where it seemed loudest of all, I stopped and closed my eyes. Gongs, flutes, and drums gonged and trilled and boomed in layered patterns, lapidary high notes skipped like diamonds across a pond, bong-gong-gong-booming low notes reverberated in my ribs, rising and falling and rising, staccato and slow, each note like a drop of water from heaven, submerging me in a pool of otherworldly harmony. Time stopped.

After a while—ten minutes? twenty?—the music ceased, and the forest echoed with its silence.

Then the harmonies flowed anew, and suddenly I felt released. It was time to move on; I had a taxi to catch, a plane to board.

I realized that all day I had been regretting my imminent departure, despairing at having to lose this blessed place. Now Ubud had answered that need, bestowing one last *canangsari*-lesson that would allow me to leave: I didn't need to see the gamelan to hear its music, and I didn't need to be in Bali to have Bali in me. It was already there, gonging and trilling and booming, rice paddy blooming, and it always would be.

Spin the Globe: El Salvador

Because I've been a travel writer and editor all my life, I like to think I have a pretty good grasp of the world—which is why the assignment described in this story was especially confounding. AFAR magazine has a regular feature called Spin the Globe, where they dispatch a writer to a place with only twenty-four-hours' advance notice. In my case, I was told two weeks in advance that I would need certain immunizations, one of which was for malaria, so I ignorantly assumed that I was going somewhere in Africa. Twenty-four hours before my plane was to leave, I received the email announcing my destination: El Salvador. I'm supremely embarrassed now that my initial reaction was, "Where?" I knew nothing about El Salvador—and that, of course, is precisely why travel is so wonderful. Once again, the classroom of the world had much to teach me, and not just about El Salvador, as I hope this story shows.

EL SALVADOR. THIS WAS EMBARRASSING. Despite twenty-five years as a travel writer and editor, I was barely sure the country was in Central America. Yet in twenty-four hours I would be headed there on an impromptu magazine assignment. My ignorance, it turned out, was shared by all my supposedly worldly, well-traveled friends. None had any information for me.

Except one. "Don!" wrote an executive consultant who works in San Francisco. "That is my country! My sister still lives there. I will introduce you!"

So, on my first morning in El Salvador, I found myself sitting across from a kind-faced woman who told me, "Actually, I've put together about a dozen books on many aspects of El Salvador—the ruins, the nature preserves, the flora, the fauna." We were in my hotel's open courtyard, looking onto a garden of green vines and red and yellow blooms—unexpected fecundity and tranquility in the mostly grimy, clattering capital, San Salvador. My visitor swept an arm toward the green highlands and volcanic peaks far beyond. "I love my country, and I would be very happy to introduce you to its riches over the next few days."

I soon learned that my breakfast companion, Claudia Allwood, not only had published books about El Salvador but also had been the first secretary of culture after the civil war ended in 1992, and later served in the Ministry of Foreign Affairs for years. In other words, by sheer serendipity I had gained one of the most knowledgeable people in all of El Salvador as my Spin the Globe guide. For the next two days, Claudia led me deep into the countryside and culture of her homeland. On that first afternoon, she drove me south to the port of La Libertad, where we walked past stalls selling lobsters, crabs, and a dozen varieties of flopping fish.

Later, as we gazed over a sweeping—and noticeably tourist-free—sandy beach near El Sunzal, Claudia sighed, "One thing you must know is that our recent history has been very difficult.

In the 1930s, the government massacred the indigenous people. In the 1970s and '80s, the rebels and the right-wing government forces waged a devastating civil war. These were very dark times, and virtually every family in El Salvador was affected in some way. But now," she continued, her face softening as a smile broke through, "we are looking ahead. We are determined to make the future better than the past."

The legacy of that brutal war underlay every encounter during my weeklong stay. It cropped up in my conversations with Carolina Baiza, the environmental projects manager of Árbol de Fuego, the wonderful eco-hotel where I stayed in San Salvador. Almost everyone in her hometown, located in the worst of the war zones, had fled or gone into hiding during the war, she told me.

"My grandmother was one of the few people who kept their businesses open," Carolina said with a rueful shake of her head. "She had a general store, and she was a master of discretion. One week she would sell to the leftists; the next week she would sell to the partisans of the right. Her business was booming! But even for her, those years were awful."

I met a taxi driver who had lost a brother, a shopkeeper who had lost a son, a waitress whose brothers had fled abroad. On a visit to Suchitoto, a colonial town of about 25,000 people, an hour's drive north of the capital, it all became real to me in a new and personal way. A one-room exhibition in the Centro Arte para la Paz showed an enlarged photograph of a dozen teenage boys standing in a semicircle and grinning widely. Immediately I thought of my son's high school soccer team, who had struck just such a pose, all excitement and hope, before a championship game—except instead of soccer balls, these boys were holding automatic rifles.

And yet, despite the heartbreak and horror of that period—which ended with the signing of a peace treaty in 1992—brilliant smiles greeted me virtually everywhere I went. From hotel clerks and office workers to backcountry cooks and wizened weavers to the everyday entrepreneurs who walked the streets selling fresh-plucked papayas in woven baskets and handfuls of cashews in neatly tied bags, everyone I met exuded resiliency, determination, and hospitality. In every interaction, there was visible pride in El Salvador today and a resolve to show the country in its best light.

Embodying this effort, Claudia—who seemed to know every person of importance ("I'm so sorry the minister of tourism is away," she said at one point, "I would have loved for you to meet him.")—had arranged for me to meet with Fernando Llort, an artist revered throughout the land for his simple, buoyant paintings of rural scenes and for the gift of art and hope he has given to his fellow Salvadorans. On my third morning, we met in the living room of Fernando's humble one-story home in San Salvador. It was just around the corner from his two-room museum, where I had immediately fallen in love with his primary-color, Picassoesque renditions of animals, birds, flowers, women balancing baskets on their heads, and white adobe houses with terra-cotta tiled roofs.

"I get my images from the Savior," Fernando said, "and I think I am his instrument to bring hope and joy, inspiration and healing to the people."

As part of this healing, Fernando created a series of workshops to teach the residents of his wife's hometown, La Palma, how to paint in his vivid, childlike style, and also how to create intricate colored carvings in wood and on seeds of a legume called *copinol*. Those same workshops now employ hundreds of artisans who turn out folk-art bowls, plates, tiles, and, yes, refrigerator magnets. From the craftspeople who make the art to the shopkeepers who sell it and the restaurateurs and hoteliers who serve the tourists who come to see it, Fernando has sparked an entire town's economic revitalization.

That's one tile in the mosaic of modern El Salvador. I discovered another that evening in Suchitoto, when I joined the weekly Friday procession of the Stations of the Cross. Some 350 townspeople, ranging in age from elementary school kids to bent-over elders, gathered in the cobbled streets of the town center.

A half-dozen boys in medieval cassocks, one swinging a smoking censer, others holding flaming torches, led the procession. Four sturdy young men carried a wooden figure of Christ bearing the cross. Drawings depicting the stations were hung on different street corners, and the faithful shuffled slowly from one illustration to the next, chanting as they walked. When they reached each station, they stopped, and a nun or priest read the relevant verses from scripture. Then all intoned the Lord's Prayer.

As we walked in the torchlight through the darkened streets, I felt like I was moving back through centuries—until I noticed some bored teenagers surreptitiously checking their cell phones. Still, the sweep and resonance of the past carried us into the cathedral, where the ceremony swashed into an incantatory sea of prayer.

After the procession, I stopped for a Pilsener beer at the only bar still open on the town square and joined three U.S. visitors, who were volunteering locally, and one of their Salvadoran friends. The volunteers' idealism was inspiring, but what stayed with me was the very end of our conversation, when I asked the Salvadoran what his dreams were for his life. After a pause, he spoke haltingly: "I want to have a wife. I want to have a family. I want to give my children an education. I want to have a stable income. I want to have a home." He stopped. That was all. Suddenly the night was suffused with gratitude and hope and despair and pain and wonder. Five bottles clinked; five voices rose in a single cheer: "El Salvador!"

As I walked through the silent streets to my hotel, the Salvadoran man's aspirations mingling in my mind with the timeless prayers of the torchlit parade, I remembered the night before in San Salvador, when Carolina had taken me for a ten-minute walk to her favorite pupusería. As we approached the neighborhood square, we came upon a group of mostly twenty- and thirty-year-olds in shorts, T-shirts, and running shoes, stretching and jogging in place.

We watched, amazed, as more and more people, old and young, all dressed to run, joined the crowd. Carolina asked a passerby what was going on.

"Ah!" she said when she heard the response. "Of course! A couple of nights a week, people gather in the square and run together through the town. The police accompany them to make sure one lane of traffic is open for them to run."

She paused for a second and then turned to me. "I love this!" she said, and her face glowed with a moon-bright light. "During the war years, people couldn't even go out at night. Now, look at this! This is the new El Salvador."

French Connections in Saint-Paul-de-Vence

*I've been in love with France since my first visits in the 1970s.
Something about the French language, culture, and approach to life
connects on the deepest level with me. As the site of my first infatua-
tion, Paris will always occupy the primary place in my heart, but the
region that has enchanted the (slightly) more mature me is the Côte
d'Azur. When I explored Nice, Cagnes-sur-Mer, Villefranche-sur-
Mer, and Saint-Paul-de-Vence in the mid-1990s, these seemed like
heaven to me—and they still do. The climate, the landscape, the art,
the sensual ease, the abundance of fresh fruit and vegetables—the
light! The Côte d'Azur embodies so many of the quintessential riches
of life for me. And that's why my stay in Saint-Paul-de-Vence meant
so much, because for a day I was able to indulge a deeply held dream,
and make a home in that fabled place.*

I OPENED THE WINDOWS OF MY THIRD-FLOOR hotel room in Saint-Paul-de-Vence. Before me spread a view of green hillsides dotted with straw-colored, terracotta-roofed homes, sloping toward the distant, glinting Mediterranean Sea. I took a deep breath and the faint scent of lavender wafted over me like a balm. Suddenly it hit me that one of my deepest fantasies was coming true: "For a day," I proclaimed to the stony square below, "I'm a resident of Saint-Paul!"

I'd visited this rocky hilltop village in the hinterland of France's Côte d'Azur twice before, but both times I'd been forced to stay well outside the medieval ramparts and to explore the town only on day-trips. This visit was different: I had procured a room in the elegant hotel Le Saint Paul, a 16th-century Renaissance mansion in the heart of the village.

I had fallen in love with this region's rare mix of sun and sea, herb and bloom, art and architecture, craft and cuisine, soul and sense, as a fresh-out-of-college wanderer more than thirty years before, and it had enchanted me ever since. Now I resolved to make the most of my time in Saint-Paul.

Immediately I took to the cobbled streets, now *my* streets. Visitors thronged them, but no matter. "*Bienvenue à Saint-Paul,*" I graciously greeted them in my mind. *Welcome to my village.*

As on previous visits, I quickly realized that the real magic of Saint-Paul unfurls when you simply wander without plan or destination.

I began at the 17th-century Place de la Grande Fontaine, a market square distinguished by a monumental urn-shaped fountain. The town market used to be held here, and for centuries residents would come to fetch fresh water for their drinking and cleaning; as I watched, two children ran up to cup a sip from the dripping spigots and a trio of backpackers gratefully filled their bottles. From this square I ambled up winding alleys to the town hall, located in the medieval castle and in whose stony hush

French movie stars Yves Montand and Simone Signoret married in 1951.

My wanderings took me beyond the ramparts and through the Porte de Nice to the cemetery, where an Iron Age settlement thrived more than 2,000 years ago and where I paid homage to the simple stone tomb of artist Marc Chagall, who lived in Saint-Paul from 1966 to 1985. Then I re-entered the ramparts and came upon the stunning Chapelle des Penitents Blancs, a spare 17th-century chapel that was luminously re-decorated by Belgian artist Jean-Michel Folon and re-opened in 2008.

These routeless ramblings revealed the village as a happy marriage of old and new: a meandering medieval maze of cobbled lanes and well-preserved battlements, whose dwellings now house galleries, restaurants, crafts shops, and cafés. While the ramparts don't dissuade the hundreds of tourists who squeeze through the narrow streets, because cars are limited to residents, Saint-Paul still seems supremely livable. Green vines arch over alleyways, jasmine clambers up sun-splashed walls, crimson flowers burst from window boxes—and visitors and residents come and go in easy harmony. The village seems to embody tranquility and tastefulness: The galleries are artful compositions of colorful canvases and provocative sculptures; in the shops, the platters and bowls, scarves and shawls, reflect the rich, earthy tones of the hills and gardens outside; and in the alleyways, the fragrances of herbs and perfumes mingle with the scents of garlic and pizza.

As a temporary resident, I had a schedule-free afternoon and evening to explore Saint-Paul, so I was able to spontaneously accept when a last-minute cancellation liberated a luncheon table at La Colombe d'Or, a place where I'd dreamed of dining. This restaurant-inn was founded in the early 1920s by the perspicacious and congenial Paul Roux, son of a local farmer, who befriended many of the painters who moved to the region for its salubrious climate, sunlight, and clear air. When these painters didn't have money to pay for their meals or nights at his inn, Roux is said to have accepted paintings instead. Over the years, he accumulated a museum-quality collection of works by such artists as Bonnard, Dufy, Utrillo, Chagall, Picasso, Braque, Matisse, and Miró, which are still on display for diners to savor.

Lunch at La Colombe d'Or proved as enchanting as the restaurant's history. Ensconced under a white parasol on a sun-mottled terrace, with a Leger mural wrought into the wall on my right, I admired the living landscape before me: rolling verdant hillsides lush with vineyards and cypress, olive, orange, and fig trees, and pastel villas the color of wheat and sand and rose. Then, amid a choreography of weaving waiters and seductive smells, an artful succession of specialties appeared: fragrant truffle salad followed by savory grilled sea bream with green beans, ending with plump red raspberries.

As I feasted, time slowed and I lost myself to the symphony of silverware on china, the splash of wine into glasses, and the mellifluous, multilingual chatter of diners in summery clothes.

After lunch, I sat on the sprawling Jeu de Boules just outside the restaurant and watched four gentlemen in berets and vests play a lively late-afternoon game of *petangue*. Then I whiled away a couple of hours, first talking troubadours and textiles with an exuberant twenty-something salesclerk and later talking clothing and canvases with café connoisseurs who became relaxed and talkative as the tourist crowds thinned.

Toward evening, as the slanting sun painted the hills in warm golden tones, I savored a pizza and a glass of *vin rosé* on a vine-shaded terrace, then set off for the opulently updated comforts of my 16th-century home, where Provencal fabrics, elegant artworks, and house-made madeleines awaited.

As I walked through the peaceful streets, a different Saint-Paul sprang to life, now that the tourist throngs had departed. The jewelry-maker who'd fashioned the necklace I'd bought that morning walked by, touched me lightly on the shoulder, and murmured a friendly *"Bonsoir,"* two children skittered by in answer to their mother's dinner call, a trio of neighborhood cats meowed, and the salesclerk who'd shared her passions an hour earlier waved to me from her doorway.

"I was hoping you'd pass by!" she called. Then she skipped forward and pressed a lavender sachet into my hands. "This is for your souvenir of Saint-Paul," she said smiling, and her cheeks took on the color of rosé.

Dusk's grainy light softened the chiseled walls; the cobbled streets echoed with ancient footfalls. Lamplight shone through windows here and there, and the music of laughter and clinking glasses floated on the air. I looked up at the tower silhouetted against the darkening sky where a few pin-prick stars had begun to shine. I lingered and lingered as the village quieted into night, until the moon lay a veil of Provencal lace over the scene and a whiff of lavender rose in the breeze.

I stopped and sighed and closed my eyes. Then I opened my arms wide to embrace it all: *my Saint-Paul.*

Piecing Together
Puzzles in Cambodia

This is the most recent story in this collection. I visited Cambodia in the autumn of 2014 and spent the month of December working on this piece. I wrote it for a new section of BBC Travel that I had been hired to edit and that had launched in July of 2014, called Words & Wanderlust. The goal was to present high-quality long-form articles that grappled with the rigors as well as the rewards of travel, and that ultimately were about falling in love with the world. Cambodia hit me in the gut—and the heart, and the soul—in ways that I never anticipated. It was a deeply multi-layered experience for me, making me question my views of humanity on one level, expanding my understanding of Cambodian history and culture on another, reconnecting me with the adventurer at my core on still another, and finally, teaching me something precious and irreplaceable about the journey we all share.

AS MR. KIM NAVIGATED HIS CAR onto the puddled, potholed road that led to Banteay Chhmar, he turned to me. "Where are you staying?" he asked.

"I don't know," I said.

He looked at me out of the corner of his eye. "There are no hotels in Banteay Chhmar."

"I know," I said. "I arranged a homestay. On my computer."

"OK. Where is the home?"

"I don't know."

He swiveled to face me. "Where should I take you?"

This moment seemed to symbolize my entire Cambodia trip: Where was I going? Why was I here?

I had arrived in Cambodia after a week-long tour consisting of lectures, book readings, and writing workshops in Melbourne and Singapore. When I was planning that tour half a year earlier, I realized that Siem Reap was just a short flight from Singapore. I had been wanting to visit Siem Reap since childhood, when I had seen a photo of Angkor Wat in a *National Geographic* magazine. Some kind of seed had been planted then, and over four decades, its stony tendrils had blossomed into an irresistible longing. I had to see that place, touch its ground, smell its air. Now it would be just two hours away by plane. I booked a one-week visit.

Over the ensuing months, as I was researching Siem Reap, I discovered a village about 100 miles to the northwest called Banteay Chhmar, where an organization named Community-Based Tourism (CBT) arranged homestays. There was scant information online, but what I found promised amazing ruins and kind people. At first I thought I would base myself in Siem Reap and spend one night in Banteay Chhmar. Then I decided to make it two nights. As time passed, the image of going off the map to little-visited Banteay Chhmar took hold of me, and I ended up reserving a three-night stay through the CBT's website.

Mr. Kim met me at the airport to take me to my Siem Reap hotel. During the twenty-minute drive, he spoke easily and impressed me with his knowledge, English fluency, and calm, kind air. I asked him about getting to Banteay Chhmar. A few years earlier, he said, the drive would have taken most of a day, but recently a paved highway had been built almost all the way to the village, and now the journey would be about three hours by highway and just thirty minutes along bumpy, unpaved paths. "Of course," he added with a wry smile as a sudden downpour turned the windshield into a washing machine, "it's the rainy season, so it might take longer." I asked if he could take me, and he said sure, that he liked that part of Cambodia and had served in the army there.

Over the next two and half days, I immersed myself in a giddy, deluge-dodging round of ruin-hopping and restaurant-gorging in Siem Reap. I saw Angkor Wat at dawn and dusk, mysterious strangler-figged Ta Prohm, the benevolent, beguiling faces of Bayon, and exquisite Banteay Srey. I slung back Indochine Martinis at the seductive Miss Wong bar and savored a six-course seasonal feast at acclaimed Cuisine Wat Damnak. I was exultant to have reached the place I had dreamed of for decades, but somehow among the thousands of balloon-panted, sarong-wrapped, selfie-snapping foreigners, I sensed the essence of Cambodia eluding me. Even immersed in the cultural heart of the country, I felt somehow distanced from the place.

So it was that on my third morning, filled with a mixture of apprehension and anticipation, I set off with Mr. Kim for Banteay Chhmar. The drive was spectacular—palm trees, rice paddies, cassava fields, stilt houses, bright-eyed children waving and calling "Hello!"—and it was only when we arrived at the outskirts of the village that I realized I literally had no idea where I was going. The emailed reservation confirmation had said to check in with the CBT office when I arrived in Banteay Chhmar, but I had been too distracted in Siem Reap to think about re-reading emails, and the only thing I could remember was that I had arranged a meeting the following morning with a man at the Global Heritage Fund (GHF), an international organization that was working to restore the main ruin in Banteay Chhmar.

"So you are staying at the Global Heritage Fund house?" Mr. Kim asked.

"No, I don't think so."

"Anyway, we go there," he declared and turned back to the road. A few minutes later we saw a sign for the GHF and Mr. Kim pulled into a fenced, two-building compound. A dignified man strolled toward us and asked if he could help. This, it turned out, was Sarun Kousum, the assistant director of the GHF project and the man I was supposed to meet the following day.

"Is Mr. Don staying with you?" Mr. Kim asked Sarun.

Sarun looked uncomfortable. "No, no, he is not staying here."

"He says he made the reservation on the computer."

"Oh, that must be through the Community-Based Tourism office," he said. "You need to go there."

After bouncing, sloshing, and skidding along the main street for another ten minutes, we reached the two-room, thatch-and-metal-roofed CBT office, where a smiling young man named Sokoun Kit greeted us.

"Ah, I have been waiting for you!" he said. "Welcome! Please fill out some paperwork and I will take you to your home. It's just a short walk from here."

As I wrote, Sokoun explained that since my host family was not equipped to serve meals to guests, I would take all my meals at the CBT office. The village had electricity from 6:00 P.M. to 11:00 P.M. each night. He would be happy to lend me a flashlight.

"How about Internet access?" I asked.

"I'm sorry," Sokoun said. "There is no Internet access."

A few minutes later, Mr. Kim parked at the edge of an unpaved road outside a muddy compound of stilt houses, and sloshed my suitcase on his shoulder through the muck and around the puddles, scattering chickens as he walked, to the two-story home where I would be spending the next three days.

Sokoun joined us in the spare, open-air, concrete-floor living area under the second story of the wooden house, where a middle-aged couple stood to greet us.

"Don, these are your hosts," he said, gesturing to the man, who was wearing a polo shirt and shorts, and the woman in a bright patterned sarong. They both smiled and bowed slightly, and the man said something to Sokoun. "They don't speak much English, but they are very happy to have you here," Sokoun said. I smiled and bowed in return, and said the one word I had learned in Khmer, "*Agung!*"—thank you.

Their eyes brightened momentarily, then the man gestured toward a wooden staircase that led to my bedroom. Mr. Kim kicked off his sandals and carried my bag up the stairs. I sat on a child's red plastic chair that had been placed at the bottom of the stairs and laboriously liberated my feet from my muddy shoes. With a quick nod, I ascended with my backpack.

Sokoun and I had arranged to meet later that afternoon, and after calling out, "Make yourself at home," he left to take his lunch. Mr. Kim had said he would stay with a friend who lived nearby, and we confirmed that he would meet me at the CBT office four days later for the drive back to Siem Reap. He left too. Then I was alone.

I sat on the edge of the mosquito net that covered the queen-size four-poster bed that occupied most of my room. The noontime sun blasted through the room's barred windows. The humidity hammered on my head. Outside I could see a half dozen wooden stilt homes surrounded by muddy patches and palm trees, a clothesline hung with shirts and sarongs, tree branch kindling stacked under a storage shed, a scrabbly vegetable garden where smoke plumed from a dying fire. Roosters strutted and crowed, dogs barked, babies wailed, adults called from home to home.

Suddenly I felt utterly overwhelmed: What had I gotten myself into? My hosts didn't speak English. I was cut off entirely from the outside world. The roads were a muddy mess. I had no means of transportation and no idea what I was going to do for the next three days. Sweat poured down my face. Was there a shower, or even running water? And what about the toilet—where, and what, was that? What had I been thinking when I booked three nights here?

It took all my energy simply to lift my mosquito net and crawl into its cocoon.

The next morning, over coffee in the GHF courtyard, Sarun Kousum told me he had first visited the main Banteay Chhmar ruin in 1997. "It was a huge surprise," he said. "Only a little bit of the dirt and trees had been cleared at that time, but already you could tell from the size of the ruin and the quality of the work that it was an important site." GHF began its efforts there, under the directorship of John Sanday, in January 2008. "I have been a part of this project from the beginning," Sarun said, and his face glowed with a quiet pride.

After coffee Sarun grabbed a couple of umbrellas and took me on a tour of the site. As we walked toward the ruin, Sarun explained that the Banteay Chhmar complex had been commissioned in the late 12th century by King Jayavarman VII, the architecturally ambitious ruler who had also commissioned the magnificent Ta Prohm, Angkor Thom/Bayon, and Preah Khan complexes. When it was completed in the early 13th century, Banteay Chhmar was one of the largest and most important religious sites in the kingdom, rivaling Angkor Wat in size and grandeur.

We reached the spectacular 180-foot-long wall that greets visitors who approach from the eastern entrance, now the principal entry to the site, and Sarun said, "One of our first projects was to secure, stabilize, and restore this wall."

The restoration showcases a stunningly detailed bas-relief depicting battles between the Khmer and their long-time enemies, the Cham. In one section, long ear-lobed Khmer soldiers bearing spears and shields march over a battlefield under the command of their larger-than-life-sized king. The Cham soldiers, identified by their curious headwear, which looks like lotus flowers plopped upside down on their pates, flee from the advance. As the narrative unfolds, the Khmer offer the heads of their now vanquished enemies to the king. Later, musicians and dancers perform in a palace celebration.

"The builders in the 12th century were very skilled," Sarun said. "Even though their tools were unsophisticated, the quality of the carvings they did is astonishing."

A gentle rain began to patter on the leafy boughs that covered much of the site, and Sarun led me along a muddy path to an area where a concrete-floored, metal-roofed storage and work space had been built; beyond that a portion of wall about thirty feet long had collapsed into a jumble of stones.

"I was here in January when this wall fell down," Sarun said. "There was a big wind during the night, and the next morning when we came to the site, we were surprised to see this toppled portion. In all, 214 stones fell over, and we are using computer imaging to put the wall back together. We paint a number on each stone, then we carve the number on the stone. Then we take pictures of each stone, do hand-drawings, and put the pictures and drawings on the computer. Then we begin to put the pieces back together on the computer. It really is like a puzzle, based on the shape of the rock and any carving on the stone. The experts know what they're looking at and are very skilled in reconstructing."

We toured the ruins for an hour without encountering any other visitors, and this poignant place—sculpted stones scattered as though a giant had smashed the temple with his club—cast a spell on me. As we exited by the western temple wall, Sarun showed me perhaps the greatest of Banteay Chhmar's master-pieces: two breathtakingly detailed depictions of the Buddhist god of compassion, Avalokitesvara, one with thirty-two arms and the other with twenty-two arms. A gaping hole in the wall next to one of these marked the spot where looters made off with two other Avalokitesvara reliefs. Happily, Sarun said, these were intercepted near the Thai border and are now on display at the National Museum in Phnom Penh. Unhappily, another sto-len section with two more reliefs has never been found. Sighing, he said, "We must preserve these for our culture, our heritage."

Sarun's pride in these ruins was so evident that before we parted, I couldn't resist asking him one last question. "You've been working here non-stop since January 2008. These ruins must be so deeply a part of your life by now, do you ever dream about them?"

He looked at me with smiling eyes. "Oh yes, sometimes...." he said, and then he looked away with a shy laugh.

That afternoon I met Sopheng Khlout, the slight, smiling, twen-ty-something CBT president. Sopheng had kindly arranged to be my guide for the rest of my stay, and over the next two and a half days, through an ever-changing flow of sunshine, light showers, and deluging downpours, he went far out of his way to give me an exceptional tour of Banteay Chhmar. We began by visiting two of the region's nine satellite temples. The first was Prasat Ta Prohm, just a few minutes' ride by motorbike south of the main temple. Ta Prohm is a four-sided tower, elaborately reinforced by modern carpentry, that soars about forty feet out of the sur-rounding vegetation, with Bayon-style faces—a prominent, wide nose; thick lips upturned into a slight smile; and protruding almond eyes—on each side. It looked to be entirely overgrown, but Sopheng knew a trail that wound through the vines, bushes, and branches to a hollow under the tower itself, where I was surprised to find not only ancient inscriptions but also fresh incense and candles. There was a red cloth wound around the tower, and Sopheng said that the cloth showed that this was a living temple where locals came to leave their offerings and to ask the gods to answer their prayers.

Next we motored eight miles south past tranquil rice paddies and simple stilt houses to Banteay Torp, a temple built to honor Jayavarman VII's troops for their defeat of the Cham. The most impressive feature of this sprawling, densely overgrown, crumbling complex was three towers that rose teeteringly over the ruins. For me, the place poignantly pictured the destiny of all ancient temples, and it gave me an even deeper appreciation for the dedicated efforts of John Sanday, Sarun, and the GHF—and other individuals and organizations like them—to rescue and restore these sites.

"It's hard to imagine what this must have looked like 800 years ago," I said to Sopheng.

"Yes," he replied, gazing over the ruins. "Mostly people come here to picnic now. I think this temple has become a place to worship nature."

Finally we visited a reservoir formally known as Boeung Cheung Kru, but more popularly called the Pol Pot Baray (*baray* means reservoir), because it was built during the reign of the Khmer Rouge under Pol Pot. The scene was blissfully beautiful: a placid expanse of water with patches of lotuses floating here and there, birds swooping and settling, children splashing, adults wading with fishing nets. On the horizon, green hills marked the border with Thailand. The peacefulness of the scene entirely belied its past.

"Yes," Sopheng said with a pained smile. "It is hard to believe how much suffering took place right here, to build this *baray*. We hear the stories. People worked at least twelve hours a day, every day, and they were fed only a little rice or soup. People were killed without reason."

For a moment his face darkened, and he turned away. After a long silence, he said, his voice tight, "We don't understand these things."

Immediately I recalled a moment in Mr. Kim's car, on the ride from Siem Reap. We had talked about Siem Reap's main tourist sites, ancient Cambodian history and Khmer culture, Buddhism and Hinduism, and the Cambodian economy. Now he was telling me about current politics and how the government was seeking to unify the country and focus on the future after being brutally ripped apart during the Pol Pot years from 1975 to 1979.

I had been reluctant to bring up the subject of Pol Pot, but this mention seemed to open a channel in Mr. Kim's mind. Suddenly the words streamed from his mouth.

"You can't comprehend what it was like during those years," he said, shaking his head. "No one who didn't live it can understand. Before the civil war, nine million people lived in Cambodia. After the war, there were six million left. Pol Pot killed one-third of the people. One-third!

"I was lucky. I was a commander in the Cambodian Army against Pol Pot. But I know so many people who were not so lucky.

"They took all the people from the cities—educated people, teachers, office workers—and put them to work in the fields. Then in the fields, if someone got sick, they would be killed. If someone wasn't working hard enough, they would be killed. Sometimes even if you just looked at a soldier the wrong way, you would be killed. These were Cambodian people, killing Cambodian people."

He stared straight ahead and his tone barely changed, but his words spewed with an almost terrifying urgency.

"Pol Pot wanted to break up all the families. The Khmer Rouge would separate children from their parents. And to break them, to make them loyal only to the Khmer Rouge, they would make them do terrible things. Do you know what they did? They made them kill their own parents. They would bring the parents before the children, and then tell the children, 'You must kill your mother. You must kill your father. From now on, your only loyalty is to the Khmer Rouge.' If the children hesitated, they would threaten to kill the children.

"You are a father. Can you imagine? These were children!" he said and his voice suddenly broke.

And then I broke too. Huge convulsive waves of sobbing shook my body, coming from some deep well I didn't even know I had, the tears streaming down my face, sobbing and sobbing so hard that I shook the car and the air writhed in agony around us.

Mr. Kim kept driving steadily, in silence. He never looked at me but simply exuded what felt like a kindly calm.

I covered my eyes but the tears kept pouring and the deep sobs kept racking my body. After what seemed an eternity, I finally stopped, embarrassed.

"I'm so sorry," I said. "I'm so sorry.... I just don't understand how any human being could do that to another fellow human being. I just don't understand how people could do that. I don't, I don't...understand," I said, and I started sobbing again.

"I know," Mr. Kim said quietly. "We don't understand either. We think, 'How could our fellow Cambodians do this?'

"This is why I don't tell my children about this," Mr. Kim continued. "I don't want them to think about this and to feel such sadness. I want them to feel happy. I want them to think about the future, about what they can do with their lives. Cambodian people don't want to think about this. Life is better now. We have human rights and freedoms. We don't want to dwell on the past. We want to focus on the future now...."

At the Pol Pot reservoir, Sopheng was silent, staring at the water and the horizon beyond. When he finally turned back to me, his smile seemed somehow refreshed, lightened, as if he had buried some burden in the landscape.

"Now we use the *baray* to water the fields and for fishing. The *baray* is giving back to the people," he said. "We can't change what's past. We can only make sure that the future is better."

On the first night of my homestay, I ate dinner at the CBT office and then slipped and sloshed back down the road toward my house. It was supposed to be about a two-minute walk, but in the unfamiliar dark I missed my house and continued on past more stilt houses. I could see families gathered by fluorescent light or lantern light in the paved, open-walled, under-stilt portions of their homes. In some, multiple generations were gazing at the television. In others, adults were eating, drinking, and talking around picnic tables. Here a mother carefully combed a child's hair. There an older sister bathed a sibling, both erupting into peals of laughter. When thickets of trees appeared on my left and rice paddies stretched away on my right, I knew I had walked too far. I walked back and finally discerned the small "Homestay" sign that marked my house.

At about 4:00 A.M. one of the most torrential rains I have ever experienced drummed on the metal roof above me. As it went on and on, I felt like I was living under a waterfall. It was unsettling being in an unfamiliar place, with unfamiliar weather, at the mercy of strangers. After about twenty minutes, men's voices shouted from house to house and footsteps scrambled on stairs. Then I heard splashing and urgent cries outside. I didn't know what they were doing or what I should be doing. So I simply fretted. After another twenty minutes, the voices stopped and peace returned, but still I couldn't sleep under the percussive pounding. Then I thought: This is not an unusual occurrence. This has been happening for decades, centuries, millennia even. You're just part of some cycle so much older and bigger than you that there's no point in worrying about it. This village has survived for centuries. These people have survived for decades. You've just become part of some huge natural whole that you were never aware of before. Lucky you. Now just surrender to it and go with the flow.

The next thing I knew, cocks were crowing and sunlight was streaming through the window.

On the second night of my homestay, as I walked back to my house, children waved and called, "Hello! Hello!" Mothers holding babies smiled and laughed. Teenagers nodded as they passed on their bikes, and the men talking around the picnic tables saluted me with their beers. Even the renegade dogs yapped in a more friendly way.

On the final evening of my homestay, I lay in the hammock in my home's ground-floor living area. Behind me Mom and Grandma were sitting on their haunches, chopping dandelions and radishes by a boiling pot, and Dad was rocking three-month-old Baby to sleep. I took out my journal and wrote:

> I can't believe this is already my last night here. I don't want to leave. I feel so comfortable here now, so completely at home. There's so much to love. The super kind and innocent people. The beautiful landscapes. The simple stilt house life. The kids running around playing with their makeshift stick-and-cloth toys; one kid has a red truck and that's as sophisticated as it gets. There's such a community feeling, everybody talking with everybody,

sharing with everybody. When a huge rain poured my first afternoon, everyone worked together to carry plastic buckets of rainwater to the ceramic storage vessels and to construct a temporary dam so the soil wouldn't erode so quickly.

And my god, the smiles! There are smiles everywhere, especially the kids with their big smiles and their incredibly bright, innocent, hopeful eyes.

The village cocks started their incongruous round of evening calls. Dogs barked. Frogs croaked. In the distance a tractor rumbled, and scratchy music wafted from speakers at a nearby Buddhist festival. The seven-year-old from the house across the way raced by on her bicycle and gave me a big wave. The boy with the red truck suddenly appeared carrying a coconut and held it out to me. Baby issued a blissful burp, and we all laughed.

"Thinking about leaving tomorrow," I wrote, "I feel like I could cry...."

For our last tour, Sopheng told me he was taking me somewhere very special, a place he didn't usually take visitors. I hopped behind him on his trusty Honda motorbike, and he maneuvered onto the rain-mucked road once again. The road to this temple was the worst yet. There were deep pools of water separated by thin islands of exposed road that looked too slick and mucky to even attempt. But like a moto magician, Sopheng turned the handlebars this way and that, minutely steering a course between puddles, somehow avoiding the slickest spots that would have sent us flying, gunning the engine moments before we got stuck, fording fathomless puddles when that was the only way, and all with a serene smile. Against impossible odds, we didn't topple over even once.

When we reached an especially submerged section of road, for the first time Sopheng stopped and said, "We'd better walk here."

So we dismounted. I must have been quite a sight: I had rolled up my trousers to my calves, showing a patch of alarmingly white skin between my blue socks and khaki convertible trousers. My walking shoes were thickly caked in mud. I had a red bandanna on my head and another around my throat, and I was wearing an electric blue T-shirt under a long-sleeved blue work shirt. We sloshed along on foot for about 100 feet until we had passed the worst section.

We re-mounted the motorbike and slow-motored down a series of ever narrower, branch-littered paths, between groves of lush green trees and rice paddies. Prickly bushes grasped at us. We passed a couple of stilt houses, and a bent woman with a leathery lined face suddenly crinkled into a smile and called out a greeting. The trail ended at a dense patch of jungle, where Sopheng stopped the engine and parked. One narrow, crushed-grass walking path led to the left through high grasses and bushes. Another led to the right through similarly forbidding growth.

Sopheng took neither. "Follow me," he said, and plunged straight into the impenetrable jungle. As I followed him, silently cursing, the barest brushstroke of a path materialized, a muddy, leaf-strewn depression. After a few steps, that depression disappeared and all I could do was try to exactly match Sopheng's footsteps as he burrowed into a world of densely overhung, intertwining vines, bushes, and branches, sharp rocks and slick tree trunks, all crawling with slimy insects, I was sure.

Soon the trail led onto a jumble of moss-covered stones with sharp sides. As sweat poured down my face, neck, arms, and legs, everywhere sweat could pour, I gingerly picked my way over the rocks, noting the fat brown millipedes on all the smooth surfaces. We crossed into deep green shadows, heavy with the weight of damp branches, dripping ferns, wet leaves and grasses. The air smelled of earthy wetness, a musky, primordial scent.

We stepped over another jumble of rocks—me slipping on one and missing a millipede by a millimeter as I grabbed a rock to steady myself. Then we turned a corner and the foliage gave way to a clearing and Sopheng smiled. "Look!" he said.

Just behind him rose a stone tower with a huge carved face—smiling lips, bulbous nose, protruding eyes. Its appearance was so unexpected, so hallucinatory, that for a moment I couldn't process what I was seeing.

Then it all came into focus: a single tower, thirty feet high, topped with a massive magnificent carved face, surrounded by the jungle, with no one else around for miles. We scrambled a few feet forward, then Sopheng said, "We can't go closer than this. It's too dangerous."

I stopped and tried to freeze the moment: There I was, gritty, grimy, and exhausted from a day of clambering and bumping and sloshing through the jungle, surrounded by bulbous leaves and drooping, dripping branches and vines, balanced precariously on mossy, vine-woven rocks, gazing at a tower of stone blocks, placed painstakingly block by block, hand by human hand, some eight centuries before.

I laughed and Sopheng laughed, and I took out my phone and snapped some sweaty photos. "This is incredible!" I said. "This is like a dream!"

"I found out about this temple only in 2009," Sopheng said. "The people who live nearby told me about it. Just a few foreigners know it. If tourists don't have a local guide, they cannot find this temple. It's too complicated to find on your own. Even if you are standing right in front of it, you won't see it." He paused. "I don't usually take people here," he said, and flashed a wide smile.

My last grand adventure of the trip occurred as Mr. Kim drove me from Banteay Chhmar to Siem Reap. Mr. Kim knew this was my final full day in Cambodia, and after I had waved a long and lingering farewell to Sopheng and Sokoun at the CBT building, he looked at me and asked, "When do you have to be back at

Siem Reap?" Not until dinnertime, I said, and his eyes shone. "Do you want to go to the Thai border? There are two temples there I want to show you. Twelfth century. We go?"

"Of course, of course!" I said, and off we went.

We drove north through heart-stoppingly idyllic landscapes—glistening, rainwater-filled rice paddies and lush cassava fields, towering palm trees and groves of green deciduous trees, interrupted occasionally by settlements of a few dozen wooden stilt houses. For a change, the sun was shining and the sky was a deep blue backdrop for a spectacular succession of pure white clouds—streaks and puffs and mounds upon mounds.

Mr. Kim was pleased. "I was here during the war," he said. "I was a commander here. There were many Khmer Rouge soldiers in this area." Looking out at a landscape that moments before had seemed the very picture of purity and innocence, I struggled to absorb the idea that Cambodians had been torturing and killing Cambodians here just a few decades before, that corpses almost certainly underlay parts of this pristine scene. My mind was spinning.

"We go to the temples on the border," Mr. Kim said. "Even just a few years ago, there was fighting there with the Thai soldiers. Many people died."

In the spring of 2011, he explained, Thai troops had seized the temples' grounds, claiming the areas belonged to Thailand. Cambodian troops had rushed to repel them, and for a month, artillery shells and gunfire from both sides had claimed at least fifteen lives.

"Now it is peaceful," Mr. Kim said, "but still, there are many Cambodian soldiers there, just to make sure the Thais don't try to move the border again."

We reached the first temple, Ta Moan, in less than an hour. The last section of road corkscrewed into almost unimaginably dense jungle mountains that marked the border. This was the territory where Pol Pot's troops had been based, Mr. Kim said, close enough to scurry into Thailand when necessary, and in vegetation so thick that it would be almost impossible to spot an encampment until you had literally walked into it.

Ta Moan turned out to be a sleepy site, about the size of a football field, with brown rock remains of walls that outlined one central building with some still visible decorated doorways and corridors, and half a dozen subsidiary structures. A couple of Thai soldiers sat on stones at the far end of the site, and a Cambodian border policeman and soldier stood at the near end, talking quietly. It was surprising to see these soldiers from both countries simply strolling around the grounds, and even more surprising when they sat down together and talked like old friends; a breath of hope seemed to rise in this peaceful air where blood had been shed just three years before.

The second temple, Ta Krabey, was even more moving. Mr. Kim knew the commander here, and we were accompanied by a military escort of a half dozen soldiers up a winding jungle trail to the mountainside temple grounds. Ta Krabey was essentially a single tower in a clearing about 100 feet square, surrounded by massive trees and jumbled, moss-covered stones. There was a much larger military presence here. Eight Thai soldiers were lounging on the site when we arrived. The soldiers nodded and smiled at each other, and one of the Thais greeted the Cambodians in Khmer. As they shared cigarettes and talked easily with each other, the Cambodian commander showed us bullet holes and scars from artillery fire in the temple stones.

"Now, we are friends," he said, gesturing toward the mingling soldiers. "But a few years ago, we were shooting at each other."

He then walked down and clapped his Thai counterpart on the back, and before I knew what was happening, I was being herded along with a contingent of Thai and Cambodian troops to a prime photo spot in front of the tower's entrance.

One Thai and one Cambodian soldier were dispensed to take photos, and the rest of us put our arms around each other's shoulders and smiled.

"We'll call this 'Tourist at the Peace Temple,'" the commander said, and as his words were shared and translated, the soldiers nodded and laughed.

After a half hour of cigarette-sharing and photo-snapping, the commander led us back down the trail to a roofed, open-walled meeting area with a table where he bade us sit and brought us tea. He then disappeared for a few minutes and reappeared with a dozen of his soldiers, including the six who had accompanied us to the temple. When all had been seated, he stood and gave a speech, which Mr. Kim translated, welcoming us and telling us what an honor it was to have a foreign guest among them. He also spoke about the history of the conflict over the border temples and how happy everyone was to have peace in the area now, and how they hoped the only visitors in the future would be tourists—he smiled at me—and not soldiers.

He sat down to applause and I rose and gave a brief speech, through Mr. Kim, saying how very honored I was to be welcomed at this ancient and important site, and how tremendously moved I had been to see the Cambodian soldiers talking so harmoniously with the Thai soldiers. I told them how very inspiring that was to me, and how that kind of peace and understanding between people was the prime reason I traveled and why I believed so fervently in the power of travel to transform the world. I said I would always treasure my photo of the Peace Temple and my visit with them.

I sat down and all the soldiers burst into smiles and applause, and then, quite unexpectedly, a very young-looking soldier at the end of the table got up and began to speak. His voice quavered at first, but as he continued to speak, the words flowed out of him with a pure passion.

"I am just a simple soldier," Mr. Kim translated. "I have not traveled far or seen much in my life. But today is a very special day for me." He looked directly at me. "Our honored guest is the first foreigner I have ever seen in my life, the first foreigner I have ever met. I am so excited and happy to have met you and talked with you. I cannot quite express what this means to my life. This makes me think how big the world is, and gives me a kind of hope. Please when you go back to your village, tell the people about the soldiers you met at Ta Krabey. And tell them about the peace you found here. I will never forget this day for the rest of my life."

He stopped, looking embarrassed, but his comrades burst into applause, and I leaped to my feet, pressed my hands to my heart and said, "*Agung! Agung! Agung!*" Then I asked Mr. Kim to say that I would definitely tell all my fellow villagers about the kind soldiers I had met at Ta Krabey and the inspiring peace I had found there. And that I too would never forget this day.

Mr. Kim dropped me at my hotel in Siem Reap at 5:00 P.M., and we parted with assurances that we would see each other again. I had thought I would visit Angkor Wat one last time, but instead, I decided to have dinner at the hotel and spend the night in my room. I had a day's worth of flying ahead, but even more important, I wanted to end my stay in the place where Cambodia had come alive for me, in Banteay Chhmar. So I sat in my room scrolling through memories of the days just past, until one scene stopped me.

On the second morning of my stay in Banteay Chhmar, I awoke before dawn to explore the main ruin where Sarun had taken me the day before. I made my way by flashlight along puddle-pocked paths to the eastern entrance and admired the bas-reliefs of warriors and dancers again. Then, just as day was breaking, I followed a footpath to the right that led past the collapsed wall and into the heart of the temple.

Alone in the ruins, I lost all sense of time. I picked my way over mossy rocks, extricated myself from clinging vines, slowly stepped up and over stairs and crumbling walls, butt-slid down precarious inclines, then turned to find a beautiful carved maiden encased in a tiny niche, an intricate carving of a Buddha under a bodhi tree, an ornamented head here, a shield-bearing torso there, a half dozen bodhisattvas buried among grasses and leaves.

I moved deeper and deeper into the ruin, sloshing through puddles, slashing through vines, clambering over toppled stones, avoiding millipedes, swatting at mosquitoes, parting branches, and plucking persistent stickers. At one point I stopped for a swig of water, and when I slapped at the whining mosquitoes that danced on my neck and hands, I slipped and slid over some tumbled pieces of rock, grabbed at branches to stop my fall, and landed just in front of a bas-relief of warriors, maidens, and fish alive in stone.

Sweat poured into my eyes, and as I mopped the stream with a sopping bandanna, I saw a stony face—lips, nose, eyes—at the top of a tower of tilting stone. I fumbled with my camera, and rain started to fall, first a pitter-patter on the forest canopy and then an insistent downpour that penetrated the branches and leaves.

I stood in the downpour and felt electrified, closer to the wild heart of life than I had been in a long time. I was sweaty, dirty, dripping, exhausted, utterly alone in the wild and connecting with things so far beyond me I could barely comprehend them.

Part of me was transported back to this same stony spot eight centuries before, gazing in wonder at that tower face in pristine splendor, wrapped in the awe this kingly complex compelled. And part of me was exploring the woods behind my childhood home in Connecticut, wondering at the stone walls I found there and the thrilling sense of communion with older histories and hands that they bestowed.

I thought of puzzles: the puzzle of the GHF archaeologists attempting to restore the ruins piece by piece; the puzzle of this enchanting, elusive country—its glorious ancient past and agonized recent past, the promise and peril of its present; and the puzzle of my own ruins, from the woods of Connecticut to the wilds of Cambodia.

Why was I here? Why had I chosen this path?

Now, in the jungle gloom of my Siem Reap hotel room, a glimmer of understanding grew. This is what I do, this was as close to the wild core of me as I could ever hope to get: I follow the compass of my heart, venturing off the map, making connections, asking questions, going deeper, trying to penetrate the essence of a place, so that I can understand it better and bring back precious pieces to share. Piecing together the puzzle of Cambodia was a way to piece together the puzzle of me.

I thought of the soldier at the Peace Temple, of the speech he had made and how he had waved and waved as we had driven away. I thought of Mr. Kim, Sarun, Sopheng, the towers of Banteay Torp and Ta Prohm, the Pol Pot Baray, the unforgettable face in the jungle, my stilt house home. Here I was, a temporary traveler on a spinning globe, alone yet connected to every single one of these: a piece in a puzzle of a journey whose design I would probably never know, but whose path had restored my sense of the whole, in the ruins of Banteay Chhmar.

Epilogue: Travel Writing and the Meaning of Life

This essay was inspired by a memorial service for a great friend and fellow writer, editor, and adventurer named Lynn Ferrin, who passed away in 2011 at the age of seventy-three. I had known Lynn for almost three decades, and the death of someone so close to me personally and professionally, the first death of such a close friend and colleague, spurred me to think about her legacy, and my legacy, and the point of what we do with our days. It gave everything a new clarity and perspective. Viewed in this context, the questions we should be asking suddenly seemed very clear: Why not dedicate ourselves to the highest goals? If we truly honor the planet and ourselves, is there any other choice?

⁓

IN THE FALL OF 2011, I attended a memorial service for Lynn Ferrin, a great friend and a great writer, editor, and adventurer who passed away at the age of seventy-three.

The service began with a procession of friends reading excerpts from Lynn's own travel articles. Three of the pieces read were stories that she had written for me, for a quarterly travel magazine that I edited for many years called *Great Escapes*. All three of these pieces—one about exploring Morocco on an equestrian tour from Meknes to Fes, one about searching for tortoises on a grueling expedition to the rim of Alcedo Volcano on the

Galápagos island of Isabela, and one about riding by horseback across the plains of Inner Mongolia—were magnificent; they were not only beautifully evoked descriptions of particular travel experiences, they were also meditations on the meaning of those experiences and by extension, on the larger meaning of life.

In the years since then, the lesson that service reaffirmed has resonated within me: Every piece of travel writing should be about the meaning of life. It doesn't have to be the central theme of the piece—it *shouldn't* be the central theme of the piece—but it should be a filament of the story. To my mind, this is the subject that great travel writing—like great travel itself—is ultimately all about: What is the condition of our journey, what is the point, what do we learn from each trip, what pieces of the vast puzzle do we bring back with us, what notes and hints and intimations about the broader picture of it all.

If, as a writer, you approach travel writing thinking this way, you can see how just about any story—whether a piece on the best taco stands in Taxco or an exploration of off-the-beaten-track Bhutan—can be about the meaning of life. It's up to you, the writer: If you give yourself permission to think that big, to put your subject in that context, you create a richer, deeper, more meaningful experience for your reader. Your piece is about the best taco places in Taxco—and about the place of tacos in the larger worlds of Mexico, and eating, and humanity; about the role of craftsmanship in food preparation; about the importance of passion and adherence to high standards in any craft; about the value of the passionate enjoyment of a simple meal. All of these are filaments that tie us to a much larger story—the purpose of our lives, the meaning underlying our journeys every day, at home and away. These are filaments that only we as writers can spin, and to do so, we have to prod ourselves, and give ourselves permission, to spin them.

The greatest travel writers I know bring this larger sense to their writing, as did Lynn. She infused her pieces with the wonder that was at the core of her life's journey, with the big-heartedness, big-mindedness, and sense of limitlessness that graced her days. She dared to bring these gifts to her writing, to reach far and dream big in her stories, to write about the meaning of life. And because she did so, she touched all of us in big, and deep, ways.

This is what we all need to do as travel writers. We need to dream big, think big, fling out filaments that tie our travels to a wider perspective. Our work matters only as much as we make it matter, and we need to write pieces that matter. We need to honor ourselves and our readers in this way. We need to honor the act of writing and the act of connecting—connecting with the world when we travel, and connecting with our readers when we write. In the same way that we look for the interlocking pieces of the whole, we also need to be those pieces—we need to interlock, article to article, reader to reader, becoming a part of the vast puzzle we seek to understand and replicate.

Now, as I think back on all the writers and writings that have enriched my life, I understand the truth that has paved and inspired—and still paves and inspires—my way: If we can make great travel writing, we can extend our world and our life beyond the limits of our temporary stay; if we put the words together right, we can transcend, connecting the precious pieces of our puzzle—curiosity, passion, dream, adventure, wonder, gratitude, love—into wanderlust without end.

Acknowledgments

Putting this book together has made me realize how blessed I have been throughout my life to have the care, support, guidance, and inspiration of a seemingly endless succession of wonderful people. It's impossible to acknowledge everyone who has assisted and encouraged me along the way, but I do want to mention some people who have had an especially profound influence on my life and on this book.

As a teenager in suburban Connecticut, I found an exemplary role model in the Reverend Charlie Luckey, pastor at the Middlebury Congregational Church, who infused the world around him with the love he preached. During this same period, an English teacher named William Nicholson at the Taft School first fired my passion for literature. In college at Princeton, I was lucky to connect with a vivacious community of friends and teachers who widened and deepened my love of literature, learning, and life. I took my first steps on the professional path I would eventually follow under the guidance of the legendary and loveable John McPhee. I was a student in his first Literature of Fact workshop, and it taught me that great nonfiction belonged on the same pedestal as the fiction and poetry I had learned for years to revere—and planted the seed that would blossom into my career.

I'm indebted to Georgia Hesse, the renowned former Travel Editor of the *San Francisco Examiner*, who effected a quantum leap in my life as a travel writer by choosing me to work in her stead when she took a one-year leave of absence from the newspaper. I ended up working at the *Examiner* for fifteen fruitful years, and I'm grateful to my colleagues and to my readers there, who nurtured my fledgling efforts to spread my writing and editing wings, and to Will Hearst and the management team, who provided the resources and autonomy for me to publish the travel section of my dreams. I'm also grateful to the folks at Salon, who, in the heady early days of the Internet, invited and enabled me to create Wanderlust, a website purely devoted to great travel writing. And I'm profoundly grateful to Tony and Maureen Wheeler, co-founders of Lonely Planet and great global friends since the mid-1980s, who offered me the job of a lifetime as Global Travel Editor at LP from 2001 to 2007.

I'm thankful to Keith Bellows, former Editor in Chief of *National Geographic Traveler*, who contacted me as soon as he heard I was leaving Lonely Planet and asked me to write a column for the magazine. Working with the dedicated and insightful editors at *Traveler* has been and continues to be a great gift. And I'm grateful to Jim Sano, Jean-Paul Tennant, and all the passionate staff at the San Francisco adventure travel company Geographic Expeditions, with whom I have been happily consulting, writing, editing, and now tour leading since 2007.

I also want to thank Elaine Petrocelli and Bill Petrocelli, owners of a place that is sacred to me, Book Passage bookstore in Corte Madera, California. More than two decades ago, Elaine approached me with the "crazy idea" of starting a multi-day conference for travel writers in Marin. Twenty-four years later, it has evolved into the celebrated Book Passage Travel Writers & Photographers Conference, and it's one of my proudest co-creations. I cannot imagine my world without Book Passage, and Elaine and Bill, and Karen West and Kathryn Petrocelli, who have become cherished friends and conference collaborators.

Acknowledgments

My life as a writer and editor has been immeasurably enriched by more friendships than I can possibly acknowledge here; so many big-minded, big-hearted, big-talented writers and editors have become intertwined parts of my journey. I do want to mention four writers who have integrally enriched my professional and personal life for decades: Jan Morris, Simon Winchester, Tim Cahill, and Pico Iyer all began to write for me when my career was just starting, and they have helped me grow as a writer, editor, and person throughout. They are truly treasured friends. Equally treasured is the magnificent Isabel Allende, a lusty saint who makes the world a better place with her personality and her prose, and the talented actor-turned-travel-writer Andrew McCarthy, whose generosity of spirit is both humbling and ennobling.

When I landed in the Bay Area—specifically, under the pear trees on the terrace at the Caffe Strada in Berkeley—thirty-five years ago, I immediately knew I had found my home. For me, the Bay Area is the best place in the world, and I feel deeply blessed by the enlightened, impassioned, and embracing travel/writing community here. The richness of this community is manifest every month at the Weekday Wanderlust reading series that I have been privileged to co-create and co-host with the effervescent duo of Kimberley Lovato and Lavinia Spalding, two former students who have become beloved partners in travel lit exaltation (and champagne celebration). And two people who have played profoundly important roles in my life here almost from the beginning are Jeff Greenwald and Larry Habegger. Jeff has woven through my world as my children have grown and my career has morphed and has been a steadfast soulmate through all my incarnations. Larry has been a sympathetic, savvy, sustaining colleague, confidant, and counselor for more than three decades; I cannot adequately express how exhilarated and honored I feel to have this book published as part of his and James O'Reilly's laudable Travelers' Tales series, and how thankful I am for their profound and wholehearted support.

A number of people helped me in the preparation of this book. I want to thank the great editors who first published these pieces—Sara Cuneo, Horace Sutton, Barbara Coats, Susan Shipman, Joan Tapper, Kaitlin Quistgaard, Keith Bellows, Norie Quintos, Amy Alipio, Leslie Magraw, Julia Cosgrove, Derk Richardson, Elizabeth Harryman, Grant Martin, Jim Benning, Allison Busacca, and Ellie Cobb. I also want to thank Kim Fortson, who helped me begin to collect all the material for the book, and Marguerite Richards, who read the entire manuscript and offered valuable suggestions.

I especially want to offer a huge thanks to Candace Rose Rardon. Candace persistently prodded me to pursue this book, efficiently organized all the story candidates to make the task as easy as possible, and then helped me to select and sort the final stories. She also created the enchanting, wanderlust-incarnating cover illustrations as well as the transporting maps and icons that enrich the inside pages. She has been an integral inspiration and support throughout the process of putting this collection together, and without her energy, enthusiasm, and expertise, this book would still be a glimmering dream.

My life's journey began, of course, with my mom and dad, and my deepest gratitude and love go to them. They took me on my first trip abroad, to London and Paris when I was a junior in college, and they supported every step of my wandering way, from college to international adventures after college, to graduate school and post-grad explorations overseas. When I returned to the U.S. to start my career, they assuaged my doubts, encouraged my yearnings, and cheered me on my professional forays. Their unbounded love and support gave me the freedom and the courage to follow my dreams, and their lessons and love interlace everything I do to this day.

And finally, I feel inexpressibly blessed to share a life-path with three joyous, brilliant, sensitive, compassionate, and wanderlust-filled fellow travelers: my wife, Kuniko, and my children, Jenny and Jeremy. From far-flung family expeditions abroad to everyday adventures in our Piedmont home, through trial and triumph, setback and celebration, our journey together has been a source of endless wonder and delight; as they have from the beginning, they grace my days, every one, with the grandest magic, and meaning, and love.

Story Credits

Prologue

"Every Journey Is a Pilgrimage" originally appeared in *Yoga Journal*, April 2004. Copyright © 2004 by Don George.

Part One: Pilgrimages

"Climbing Kilimanjaro" originally appeared in *Mademoiselle*, November 1977. Copyright © 1977 by Don George.

"A Night with the Ghosts of Greece" originally appeared in *Signature*, May 1981. Copyright © 1981 by Don George.

"Ryoanji Reflections" originally appeared in the *San Francisco Examiner*, October 25, 1987. Reprinted courtesy of The Bancroft Library, University of California, Berkeley.

"Connections: A Moment at Notre-Dame" originally appeared in the *San Francisco Examiner*, October 2, 1988. Reprinted courtesy of The Bancroft Library, University of California, Berkeley.

"Conquering Half Dome" first appeared in Salon, at www.Salon.com, on July 31, 1999. An online version remains in the Salon archives. Reprinted with permission.

"Impression: Sunrise at Uluru" originally appeared on lonelyplanet.com, May 29, 2001. Reproduced with permission from the Lonely Planet website www.lonelyplanet.com. Copyright © 2001 Lonely Planet.

"Castaway in the Galápagos" originally appeared in *Islands*, January/February 2004. Copyright © 2004 by Don George.

"Machu Picchu Magic" originally appeared on Gadling.com, September 15, 2010. Copyright © 2010 by Don George.

"A Pilgrim at Stinson Beach" originally appeared on Gadling.com, July 25, 2011. Copyright © 2011 by Don George.

Part Two: Encounters

"Making Roof Tiles in Peru" originally appeared on GeoEx.com, September 24, 2012. Copyright © 2012 by Don George.

"Living-History Lessons in Berlin" originally appeared on NationalGeographic. com, August 5, 2014. Copyright © 2014 by National Geographic Society. Reproduced with permission.

Part Three: Illuminations

"At the Musée d'Orsay" originally appeared in the *San Francisco Examiner*, September 18, 1988. Reprinted courtesy of The Bancroft Library, University of California, Berkeley.

"California Epiphany" originally appeared in the *San Francisco Examiner*, October 16, 1988. Reprinted courtesy of The Bancroft Library, University of California, Berkeley.

"Japanese Wedding" originally appeared in the *San Francisco Examiner*, October 21, 1990. Reprinted courtesy of The Bancroft Library, University of California, Berkeley.

"Prambanan in the Moonlight" originally appeared in the *San Francisco Examiner*, April 4, 1993. Reprinted courtesy of The Bancroft Library, University of California, Berkeley.

"In the Pythion of Time" originally appeared in the *San Francisco Examiner*, June 27, 1993. Reprinted courtesy of The Bancroft Library, University of California, Berkeley.

"Finding Salvation in the South Seas" originally appeared in *Islands*, December 2005. Copyright © 2005 by Don George.

"The Intricate Weave" originally appeared on GeoEx.com, December 1, 2008. Copyright © 2008 by Don George.

"Unexpected Offerings on a Return to Bali" originally appeared on Gadling. com, November 22, 2012. Copyright © 2012 by Don George.

"Spin the Globe: El Salvador" originally appeared in *AFAR*, August 2013. Copyright © 2013 by Don George.

"French Connections in Saint-Paul-de-Vence" originally appeared in *Northern New England Journey*, August 2013. Copyright © 2013 by Don George.

Epilogue

About the Author

National Geographic has called Don George "a legendary travel writer and editor," and he has been lauded as the most influential travel writer and editor of his generation. Don has been exploring new frontiers as an author, editor, and adventurer for almost four decades, and is also an acclaimed teacher, speaker, and tour leader. He has visited more than ninety countries on six continents, has published hundreds of articles in dozens of magazines and newspapers around the world, and regularly speaks and teaches at conferences, campuses, and companies from San Francisco to Singapore to London.

Don's first job was as Travel Writer and then Travel Editor for the *San Francisco Examiner*. After fifteen years at the paper, he founded and edited Salon's groundbreaking Wanderlust travel site, then became Global Travel Editor for Lonely Planet. Don is currently Editor at Large and Columnist for *National Geographic Traveler*, Special Features Editor for BBC Travel, and editor of GeoEx's travel blog, Wanderlust: Literary Journeys for the Discerning Traveler.

Don literally wrote the book on travel writing, *Lonely Planet's Guide to Travel Writing*, the bestselling travel writing guide in the world. He has also edited ten award-winning literary travel anthologies, including *An Innocent Abroad*, *Better Than Fiction*, and *The Kindness of Strangers*. Don has received dozens of awards for his writing and editing, including ten Lowell Thomas Awards from the Society of American Travel Writers. He is a highly sought-after keynote speaker and workshop leader, and is interviewed frequently as a travel expert. He also consults nationally and internationally on travel and social media, and hosts a popular national series of onstage conversations with prominent travel writers.

Don is co-founder and host of the award-winning San Francisco-based reading series Weekday Wanderlust, and is co-founder and chairman of the celebrated Book Passage Travel Writers & Photographers Conference.

Don grew up in Connecticut, and lived in Paris, Athens, and Tokyo before settling in the San Francisco Bay Area with his wife; they have two children. He is a graduate of Princeton University and the Hollins College graduate program in creative writing. His website is www.don-george.com.